TRANSVESTISM
A Handbook with Case Studies for Psychologists, Psychiatrists and Counsellors

TRANSVESTISM

*A Handbook with Case Studies for
Psychologists, Psychiatrists and Counsellors*

by

HARRY BRIERLEY

PERGAMON PRESS

OXFORD · NEW YORK · TORONTO · SYDNEY · PARIS · FRANKFURT

U.K.	Pergamon Press Ltd., Headington Hill Hall, Oxford OX3 0BW, England
U.S.A.	Pergamon Press Inc., Maxwell House, Fairview Park, Elmsford, New York 10523, U.S.A.
CANADA	Pergamon of Canada, Suite 104, 150 Consumers Road, Willowdale, Ontario M2 J1P9, Canada
AUSTRALIA	Pergamon Press (Aust.) Pty. Ltd., P.O. Box 544, Potts Point, NSW 2011, Australia
FRANCE	Pergamon Press SARL, 24 rue des Ecoles, 75240 Paris, Cedex 05, France
FEDERAL REPUBLIC OF GERMANY	Pergamon Press GmbH, 6242 Kronberg-Taunus, Pferdstrasse 1, Federal Republic of Germany

First edition 1979

British Library Cataloguing in Publication Data

Brierley, Harry
Transvestism.
I. Title
616.8'583   HQ77   78-41288

ISBN 0-08-022268-4 (Hardcover)
ISBN 0-08-024686-9 (Flexicover)

*Printed in Great Britain by William Clowes & Sons Limited
Beccles and London*

Contents

Acknowledgements

Much of this book could not and should not have been written without the help given to me by transvestite clients, the Beaumont Society, and the Beaumont Trust. I am most indebted to Kate, Margaret, Penny, Rosemary, Sheila and Shirley, for permission to quote them and to Vicki and Jacqueline for their help and comments.

I appreciate the kindness of Isaac Marks and John Bancroft in allowing me to use diagrams from their published works.

As always, my great gratitude goes to my wife, Lillian, for her constant forbearance, help, and understanding.

Introduction

I agree with Dr. Benjamin that a transvestite "has every right to be accepted as a woman" (or man). This is part of personal freedom in a democracy. I also agree that society should be "treated" by way of public education so that it may develop a better understanding of the problems involved. I think, however, that to do justice to the transvestites we must also educate the patients themselves.

Emil A. Gutheil (1954) in the
American Journal of Psychotherapy

In the last 20 years there has been a startling and rapid change in social attitudes towards so-called sexual problems. Pressure groups representing male homosexuals, lesbians, transsexuals and transvestites have sprung into public attention and are attracting large numbers of adherents.

Their claims amount to a call for freedom to live in the style they choose within the limits that they do not cause harm or interfere with the rights of others. However, the very occurrence of these groups has complicated the understanding of them. Their precise delineation becomes abominably difficult since sexual taboos continue to preserve an enormous secret reservoir whilst at the same time individuals emerge who are apparently well content to accept their life styles. It has, indeed, been suggested that assertive groups representing minorities have brought together people who would not otherwise have identified themselves with these groups. They may well have found a solution to more nebulous personality difficulties in their acceptance of such identities. We cannot, therefore, say with the confidence which was previously felt what the limits of, say, the homosexual group are. If we are honest the established understanding of what was medically regarded as homosexual probably only related to a relative minority of those who now call themselves "gay".

If this is the case with the homosexual group which has by now found much security in numbers, the problem is much more acute in groups with other problems. The transsexuals who were regarded as "very rare" 20 years ago are now well recognised medically. In this country alone units including those in Charing Cross, Manchester, and Newcastle-upon-Tyne have specialised in the care of transsexuals. Literature on the subject is copious. Popular autobiographical accounts of transsexual experiences, if unreliable, have nevertheless softened public attitudes to sex-change cases. The legal status of transsexuals has gone a long way towards resolution, although not always as the transsexual would prefer. The transsexual group defines itself by the step from the secret world to the cold light of a demand for surgery. As late as 1959 one writer remarked that only one female transsexual was known but in 1978 the condition can only be described as "relatively common".

It may be that the most crucial development of understanding in this area is the fact that transsexualism is far less commonly regarded by psychiatrists as a "sexual perversion". The most appropriate term seems to be a "gender dysphoria" — a term which might be literally translated as a state of discomfort associated with the masculine or feminine role appropriate to the physical sex of the individual. However, closely allied to the transsexual is the transvestite. Indeed the two shade together with some writers regarding the transsexual simply as the more severe form of transvestism. Whether the two differ only in degree neither the individuals themselves nor medical authorities readily agree. The distinction which is made is that of the transvestite's sexual motivation as opposed to the purely gender needs of the transsexual. Unfortunately this distinction is based on assumptions about the phenomenology of the two conditions when what is known of transvestism is conflicting and uncertain.

✗   This state of affairs has a number of origins. The most important cause seems to be the fact that the nature of transvestism means that transvestites rarely seek medical help. Transvestite needs being apparently somewhat periodic, they can be confined by the shelter of closed doors. Transvestites are also found to claim that their transvestite experiences are both innocent and enjoyable, thus they are a source of happiness and relaxation rather than discontent. Transvestites seeking therapy almost invariably are under some sort of duress, from the law or family perhaps, in the context of their own reluctance as patients. They see their problems as being wholly resolved by a simple change in the attitudes of others and on the whole resent interference with their transvestite activities. Thus the transvestites presenting themselves for clinical investigation are likely to be the more emotionally disturbed and sexually deviant. The unknown pool of adequately adjusted transvestites can validly argue that their ways are "wholly pleasurable" and need cause no one distress. It is, therefore, illogical for them to seek treatment.

A further problem lies in the traditional assumption of such states as primarily sexual disorders, an assumption which is based on very nebulous evidence. Autobiographical studies by transvestites protest their largely a-sexual nature but they seem disregarded in favour of uncertain clinical beliefs. Almost invariably, studies of transvestism play permutations with rather bizarre case studies written up by zealous therapists arriving at confused and shadowy generalisations.

An attempt is made here to identify the transvestite group looking at the cases seen in clinical practice and also outside. The author has been given very generous help by the Beaumont Trust, an independent charity promoting the welfare of transvestites. Assistance has also been provided by the Beaumont
✗ Society with its membership of some 500 transvestites. Whilst this society does not advertise its existence it is associated with transvestite societies all over the world. In America there is an

organisation called "Phi Pi Epsilon". Transvestite societies in
New Zealand and Australia are both called "The Seahorse Club"
(because of the seahorse's capacity to assume male and female
roles!) and there are also organisations in South Africa, France,
Belgium and Scandinavia.

There is a wider question which arises from the study of
transvestism which challenges the traditional concentration on
the apparently sexual aspects of these groups. It may well be
more profitable and nearer the truth to look for an understanding of the transvestite, transsexual, homosexual, and others, as
whole people characterised by the array of their talents and deficiencies rather than by the nature of their sexuality alone.
After all the bulk of the behaviour involved in living the life of
a transvestite or a homosexual is not erotic behaviour and has
nothing to do directly with sexual preference. It is a matter of
the uncomplicated acceptance of a way of life. As soon as ever
it is realised that many of the problems we call sexual are
approachable in this way then the "lie" of the problems of
social and therapeutic help and understanding alters drastically.

This introduction is prefaced by a quotation from a paper by
the New York psychoanalyst Gutheil whose work with transvestites was highly regarded. It is in the spirit of Gutheil's
remarks that this book is written, particularly as far as they
concern education.

CHAPTER 1

The Transvestite

It is barely 25 years since Kallman (1952) undertook a classic study of the genetics of homosexuality. His work took him into unsavoury places to seek out people in fear of prosecution and he might well be forgiven for forming a concept of homosexuality which he may have found quite repellent. Research into transvestism also deals with people under threat of prosecution and might also lead us into a false and unnecessarily unwholesome concept of the transvestite. The error of seeking and finding the worst is to be avoided and we may be best guided by beginning with a thumb-nail sketch of a real person who has neither fallen foul of the law nor been socially disgraced and has not found it necessary to seek medical help at any time.

Pauline Franks appears to be a woman in her late thirties. She is decidedly overweight, her hands are too large and her legs are less well rounded than one would expect. Her mode of dress is not outstanding and bears the stamp of the mail-order house. Her make up is carefully and skilfully applied but the eyelashes are long and flutter remorselessly. In the High Street she would attract no attention, she would "pass" but she drinks "pints" and her voice has the resonant tone of the North Country docker which "her brother" is. Pauline is a transvestite.

Pauline would say that she experiences transvestism as the bringing together of herself and only in the role of a woman does she feel whole and at ease. Her "brother" makes no pretence of being feminine, knows that he is not female and when not "dressed" betrays no femininity in manner nor for that matter effeminacy. He is a happily married man but a previous marriage to a wife who could not tolerate his transvestite urges ended in divorce. His present wife accepts his transvestism but does not participate in it. The experience of being "en femme" is not apparently sexual in a physical sense, he finds a predominant feeling of calmness and relaxation rather than sexual excitement. He never dresses to aid sexual experiences and mostly he seeks to pass unobtrusively, accepted by others as a woman. He is deliriously happy when the shop assistant addresses him as "madam". He feels that he would like to experience childbirth as a woman does but is repelled by the thoughts of sexual relations with a man which he would feel were homosexual. His marriage is highly important to him, and his wife, like wives of other transvestites, finds him a conforming, domesticated person who can be more companionable and understanding than if he had the more usual male indifference to feminine affairs and duties.

Although cross-dressing is a secretive matter in Western civilisation, there is no doubt about its occurrence almost from the beginnings of human history. It is also apparent that attitudes of severe condemnation of cross-dressing have been usual. The Bible does not mince matters for in the Book of Deuteronomy we read: "The woman shall not wear that which pertaineth unto a man, neither shall a man put on a woman's garment: for all that do so are abomination unto the Lord thy God." However, the offence would appear relatively small even in Old Testament Jewish Law. In comparison in the previous chapter death by stoning is prescribed for "a stubborn and rebellious son". It is also odd that women seem to have been absolved from this law long, long ago.

In a curious way cross-dressing seemed to obsess Christian civilisation. Priests to this day wear garments which have a more striking similarity to female wear than male dress. Bishops adorn themselves in bright colours, jewelled rings, and other ornaments not belonging to normal male attire. The expression "to put a boy into skirts" was a common expression for sending a youth into the priesthood, not training for a drag act.

Even in the framing of laws related to hermaphrodite animals the severe opposition of the Christian Church is seen. As late as the fifteenth century a trial was held in Basel at which a cock was indicted for laying an egg. The cock's defence was that the act was involuntary. Moreover, being an animal the cock would not have made a compact with the devil. However, the court ruled that although the cock itself was innocent, the act was that of a sorcerer masquerading as the cock and the sorcerer should be punished. Accordingly the cock and its supposed egg were solemnly burned at the stake.

The apparent hysteria at Basel over the cock's egg arose from the belief in the mythical cockatrice. Today a cockatrice is a rather bizarre piece of cookery but the animal itself was far from delectable. It was believed to be hatched by a toad or snake from the egg of a cock — the ultimate of hermaphrodite wickedness. Its fore quarters were those of a cock and the hind part was a serpent — in effect a serpent defying Genesis by travelling half-erect rather than creeping on its belly. Its qualities were truly diabolical. It was lethal to all living things other than a cock and a weasel. Indeed if the weasel had eaten rue it had a power to destroy the cockatrice. The cockatrice's breath was hot and poisonous and burned up all the vegetation around it; it is not surprising to find that it made its home in the desert. Emitting such noxious fumes it seems unnecessary for the beast to have a poisonous bite but such it had. There was no antidote for the poison which would turn a man's blood yellow, itself killing all who touched the body. Not even the vultures would pick the carcass of the cockatrice's victim. Even more lethal than just this, the cockatrice could kill by its hiss or by the beams emitted from its eyes. It seems quite possible that epidemics could be attributed to the malign presence of the cockatrice although Galen dared to doubt their existence. There was, however, biblical authority for the cockatrice. And all this was a consequence of the confusion over the sex of a cock, a clear demonstration of a deep-rooted fear of transgressing the gender line.

Nevertheless, almost all the great writers of Greece and

Rome seem to have made references to changes of sex or cross-dressing. St Augustine referred to women changing into men with some surprise but no apparent alarm. Herodotus describes the "Skythian illness". The Skyths, who lived on the shores of the Black Sea, had amongst them apparently normal men who would wear the clothes of females, affect their manners, and do the work of women. Herodotus explained this curse of the Skyths as being a divine punishment. The Skyths had outraged Aphrodite by plundering her temple in Askalos. Hippocrates had another explanation more consistent with an organic school of medicine. He felt that the effeminacy of the Skyths arose from the physical injuries sustained in too much horse riding — an explanation of transvestism still current into the nineteenth century.

In mythology cross-dressing is common. Jupiter himself appears impersonating Diana in Boucher's painting "Jove surprises Callisto" (Wallace Collection). Not only did he cross-dress he also changed from a bearded giant into a soft attractive female. Hercules, also a somewhat archetypal male, served Omphale, Queen of Lydia, as a woman and spun wool with her handmaidens — whilst Omphale wore his lion skin! Adonis, a modern symbol of masculinity, was bridegroom to Aphrodite but also served Apollo as a girl. The priests of Adonis were self-castrated and wore female attire. Achilles too was sent as a child to live as a girl with the daughter of Lycomedes King of Scyros. In this guise he assumed "Pyrrha" as a "femme name".

Sardanapolus, the last King of the Assyrian Empire of Nineveh, was believed to enjoy appearing as a woman about 600 B.C. Roman emperors also cross-dressed. Caligula and Heliogabalus did so whilst Nero was positively preoccupied by intersex and cross-sex matters. He had a team of hermaphrodite mares, used to dress himself as a courtesan, and brought into his household a young transvestite with some likeness to his wife.

Benvenuto Cellini recalls how he dressed as a woman so effectively that various gallants made improper suggestions to him and he escaped only by confessing that he was pregnant. His detailed description of his clothing and his belief in his feminine appearance have some striking similarity to contemporary transvestite writings amongst which one also finds the story about needing to confess to pregnancy also. Samuel Pepys described a "very merrie" party at his home when all the males dressed as women and women as males.

Karl von Weber, the composer, wrote of his friend Emil August, Duke of Saxe Gotha and Altenburg, that there was about him "despite his great stature, something soft, almost feminine, whence comes his fondness for feminine adornment." Emil August was a great grandfather of Edward VII of Great Britain and whilst his obsession was unpopular he liked to see himself as a considerable feminine beauty. The Governor of New York between 1702–9 was the cousin of Queen Anne, Edward Hyde, Lord Cornbury. He spent much of his time as a woman parading publicly in his finery.

Later in the eighteenth century the Chevalier de Freminville, a French sea captain, exhibited a curious change of gender. He fell in love with a girl in the West Indies but had to leave her suddenly under secret orders. When he returned he found that the girl was dead. He was so grief stricken that he left the sea and for 23 years until his death he wore a white gauze dress with a green silk sash and green slippers — the attire his beloved had worn when he last saw her.

The two most celebrated cross-dressing males were also Frenchmen, L'Abbé Choisy and Le Chevalier Déon Beaumont. The term "Eonism" is derived from the name of the latter and he was a considerable public figure both in France and in this country. Unfortunately various biographies clearly embellish his story with improbable detail. Apparently he was born in 1728 so small and pretty that his mother brought him up as a girl. He delighted in dressing as a girl and in his youth was always flattered as a girl even by people who knew of his male identity. He eventually became an officer of Dragoons in the French Army and an expert duelist. He acquitted himself well as a soldier. His cross-dressing skill was employed by the French Government when the Russian Government was unwilling to receive a French ambassador. Déon was sent as a woman to become a lady in waiting in the Russian Court.

He was a great success in court but the ruse was finally exposed and he returned to his commission in the Army. The incident raised a political storm which was resolved by the French insisting that Déon really was female after all. He was forced to declare himself female and doctors produced evidence to support this. He undertook to live as a woman for the rest of his life under suitable threats — a common transvestite fantasy. An alternative story was based on a court scandal but eventually he was exiled to London where he made a curious career as a female swordsman, teaching and giving public exhibitions. His identity was the subject of much social chit-chat, foolery, and wagers. However, as age overtook him his female role became increasingly pathetic and against his wishes. He died at 83 years in 1810 and was then officially declared male after all.

Déon Beaumont's story is substantially dependent on a biography compiled by Gaillardet (1972) shortly after Beaumont's death and apparently with access to secret government papers. Gaillardet made great play on Beaumont's heterosexuality, involving mesdames Pompadour and du Barry as well as Empress Elizabeth of Russia. He is said to have been the father of Queen Sophie Charlotte's son, later George IV, hence the revelation of his male sex precipitated George III's final madness. On the other hand, affairs with Louis XV and Beaumarchais are reported as evidence of his feminity. However, little in the whole story carries much of the stamp of truth. Gaillardet incorporated a great measure of pure fiction and in the end admitted to this; other sections were based on forgeries and the most shaky foundations. The French Revolution took place of course between the Russian incident and Gaillardet's examination of the secret government documents. It would appear that even Beaumont's grave, supposedly in St. Pancras', lay in the path of the Midland Railway and does not now exist. Doubtless Charles Geneviéve Louis Auguste André Timothée Déon de Beaumont existed and spent part of his life living as a woman but further information about his life is quite unreliable. Curiously quotations supposedly from his diaries do not seem to have much of the strong character of transvestite writings.

The memoires of Francois Timoleon de Choisy, born in 1644, are a different matter. He was reared as a girl and was the son of the chancellor to the Duke of Orleans. Choisy was a public figure to the extent that female fashions were modelled on him. In his early days he attempted to go on the stage but at the age of 32 he inherited the abbey of St Seine in Burgundy. As a priest he travelled widely usually wearing female garments under his violet abbé's robes. At one period he not only kept a mistress but went through a marriage ceremony, as a girl, with a girl dressed as a man. Choisy's memoires have a more characteristic quality. The following quotation reflects at least four of the common features of transvestite writings, the ecstasy of transvestism, a preoccupation with details of dress, some special importance attached to the physical constriction of female garments, and the female figure compelling him to adopt a female role.

> I had a bodice embroidered with natural flowers on a silver ground and a skirt of the same material with a long train. The skirt was fastened up on both sides with yellow and silver ribbons. . . . My mother made me wear bodices that were extremely tight. . . . It is beauty which creates love and beauty is generally the woman's portion; when it happens that men have, or believe they have, attractions for which they may be loved, they try to increase them by putting on women's attire. They then feel the inexpressible pleasure of being loved. I have had that pleasant experience many a time. I have felt a pleasure so great that it is beyond all comparison.

Other French aristocrats, including the brother of Louis IV and L'Abbé d'Entragues, were also transvestites and well documented. It is curious that cross-dressing should appear so frequently in the French aristocracy in comparison to other nationalities. It has been suggested that cross-dressing in males is most common when male dress is drab. This explanation is a tempting suggestion to account for the outcrop of drag shows which emerged during the last two world wars but it can hardly explain cross-dressing in the French aristocrat of the eighteenth century.

To assume that all those just mentioned were necessarily transvestite simply because they wore the clothes of the opposite sex is an unjustified generalisation. Leaving aside the issue of cross-dressing for some "legitimate" reason such as a policeman impersonating a female to arrest an attacker of women, various categories of cross-dressing have been described. There are five principal groups.

Theatrical female impersonators are the most public of these. In Western civilisation a number of strands of female impersonation on the stage are dominated by religious morality. The need arose from the Judeo-Christian exclusion of women from an active role in religious ritual. Religious drama either excluded female figures entirely or had such parts portrayed by boys. In the first instance, perhaps only the Virgin Mary appeared in a non-speaking tableau. Then with the development of the mystery plays active female parts were included and still played by boys. Secularisation of the mystery plays gave rise to the mummers' plays and these not only called for actresses but socially they were influenced by a broad social rejection of the idea of a female actress. A new character developed in the mummers plays who was an aggressive, rumbustious woman. She rapidly acquired a comic quality and is easily recognised as the beginning of an almost unbroken line of panto dames lasting almost 800 years.

The secular theatre and strolling players were also socially constrained to use male actresses, females would have been received with disgust. Even early in the seventeenth century audiences greeted female actresses with derision and hostility. Apart from the religious moral aspect, the medieval theatre was, with some justification, regarded as no place for a woman. It was essentially bawdy, somewhat insanitary and a notable place for contracting disease. In this context boys were apprenticed to experienced actors and trained as female impersonators with great care and expertise. These male actresses were accepted by audiences as the normal convention of the theatre of the day and not in the context of something rather odd and funny as with the dame parts or present-day drag acts. Indeed it could well have been more provocative for a female to have played the woman's part.

Even in Elizabethan theatre female parts were quite sophisticated. Not only did Shakespeare write parts like Juliet and Desdemona to be successfully played by male actresses but he also wrote a number of parts like Rosalind, Viola, and Portia in which the male actress would be dressed as a man. Why Shakespeare did this so frequently is hard to understand for it would have called for immense skill for a man to play the part of a woman whilst dressed in male clothes.

With the Restoration the theatre was drastically reorganised, not only in its physical structure but in the introduction of female actresses who could be accepted in the improved atmosphere. Companies employing male actresses and others with female actresses shared the stage. Indeed some companies employed both male and female actresses side by side. The first female portrayal was probably Desdemona in 1660 and it is not surprising that the male actress's days were numbered from then on.

Although the drag acts and dame parts persisted and perhaps are as popular now as at any time, there is a clear and important distinction between these parts and the female impersonation of the Elizabethan theatre. The dame part and the drag act depend very heavily on the success with which the audience is kept aware that the female on the stage is in fact male. The actor continuously makes innuendoes, voice changes, and gestures to betray his real identity and if he did not do this successfully his act would have no point. This was not true of the Elizabethan male actress who had no need to exploit the audience's knowledge of his true sex.

It is not entirely true that only drag acts survive, there is the occasional successful impersonator. About 15 years ago a female ventriloquist, Bobby Kimber, retired after a fairly successful career on the stage and on television. She was in fact a male who adopted the impersonation in order to make the act more unusual and hence commercial. The impersonation was complete and successful so that managers, audiences, agents, and TV viewers were deceived by the somewhat chubby but otherwise unremarkable female figure. When the deception was eventually exposed there was a degree of public disapproval even in theatrical circles.

One thread of female impersonation has survived and continued since medieval days. Drama has long been found an acceptable educational activity and boys' schools — again associated with church foundations — found female impersonation necessary. In the sixteenth century troupes of boys were employed in a semi-professional way to present somewhat scurrilous plays outside the reach of the law. Even today very many of the most important names amongst male actors have played female parts during adolescence.

Homosexual cross-dressers form a very large group in which the motivation for female impersonation is by no means simple. It is a popular assumption that effeminacy is a common characteristic of all homosexuals and it is a small step to the assumption that this effeminacy is identical with femininity. The reverse argument then follows that cross-dressing and the assumption of femininity is a phenomenon of homosexuality in the male. This is a fallacy in that effeminacy in this sense has little to do with femininity and in any case is by no means a general feature of homosexuality. Lisping speech, mincing walk and theatrical gestures attributed to the male homosexual are no more a characteristic of a woman than of a heterosexual male.

The homosexual and the transvestite are differently motivated in cross-dressing. The homosexual is in no doubt about his gender or for that matter his physical sex. The male homosexual recognises himself as a homosexual man and neither wants to think of himself as a woman nor to be thought of as feminine. Homosexual relations are same-sex relations, as the term implies, and neither partner seeks to fully identify himself with a partner in a heterosexual relationship.

Thus cross-dressing for the homosexual does not have the object of seeking acceptance as being of the opposite sex. There seem to be two main types. The first is essentially caricature and the second has political implications, although these groups are not distinct. "Gay" clubs have their drag-queen contests and homosexuals to some degree patronise drag balls. The whole cross-dressing has something of a party atmosphere with a quality of burlesque, more poking fun at the image of the opposite sex than attempting to assume that image. The political motivation, relatively common in the present day, attempts to demonstrate the homosexual's right not to adopt the social conventions of his own sex. Thus in adopting some parts of female dress the homosexual male is defying society and its wish to impose on him a masculine and essentially heterosexual way of life. Most homosexuals in this group whilst wearing clothes of the opposite sex would only incompletely cross-dress since they would also wish to appear manifestly not of the opposite sex. To masquerade as a female would make no point for the male homosexual; to appear as clearly male dressed in female clothes protests a right to be what he wants to be. The two uses of cross-dressing overlap in circumstances where homosexuals make public appearances as at drag balls and take the opportunity to make the public point that they are homosexual.

Fetishistic cross-dressers are a section of the fetishist group as a whole. Fetishism is the experience of erotic sexual arousal associated with objects which are not normally of sexual significance. Some degree of fetishism is extremely common in the sense that female garments and some male garments assume a sexually evocative quality. The numbers of advertisements for female "glamour wear" and male "exciting figure-moulding wear" in the Sunday papers bear out this contention. However, fetishism may be of a degree where heterosexual competence may be wholly dependent on a fetishistic object. A male may prove impotent unless his wife wears a plastic mac or he himself wears high-heeled shoes or some other item of female clothing.

In this way fetishists are more concerned with the direct facilitation of erotic experiences in intercourse or masturbation and would only wear fetishistic garments to that end. Moreover, these garments are likely to be unusual. A firm catering for fetishists advertises high-heeled shoes with 18 inch heels! The garments also tend to be specific items rather than full dress as would be worn by transvestites.

Fetishism may produce serious legal difficulties if the practice demands that the articles are stolen. This is not so uncommon since the fetishistic value of female clothes may be enhanced by the knowledge that they have already been worn by a female. This, of course, leads to stealing from washing lines rather than legitimately buying the fetishistic garments. The transvestite would be unlikely to steal clothing because the rightful possession of female things would be an important component of his fantasies.

Exhibitionistic cross-dressing produces the most serious involvement of cross-dressing in sexual crime. Whilst this group is rare and infrequently distinguished in the literature it undoubtedly represents cross-dressing with a motivation distinct from the other groups. The nature of the behaviour is closely related to that of the exposeur who exhibits his genitalia to a female with the intent to cause offence or in some cases as a sexual invitation. In this group of cross-dressing persons the man will appear at least partly dressed in feminine garments showing himself to a female stranger apparently to provoke fear. Again the partial cross-dressing is not for the purpose of passing as a female but apparently intended to convey some hostile sexual gesture to the victim. Such cases of rather severe sexual disorder usually show other forms of sexual misbehaviour as well as that involving cross-dressing.

Transsexual cross-dressing with the transvestite are the two remaining groups of cross-dressers. Transsexualism as a term has been in general psychiatric use for about 15 years, precision in the use of the terms is almost confined to the specialist Gender Identity Units. In very many ways transsexualists and transvestites are similar, both wish to acquire the appearance, manners and mode of dress of the opposite sex. The most fundamental difference lies in the depth of conviction about the individual's femininity. The male transsexual will express the belief that his basically feminine personality is trapped in a male body and that his make-up is in conflict with his physical sex. He presents himself as having a lifelong striving for life as a woman, shedding all trace of masculinity.

The transsexual is frequently described as rather feminine in manner, with low sexual drive. He seeks not only the outward identity of a female but frequently the opportunity to marry as a woman and in some cases to have children by adoption. In early life the transsexualist will claim to have preferred girls as playmates and to have chosen girlish games. Cross-dressing might have begun very early in life whilst, on the other hand, some protest such a strong feeling that they dislike cross-dressing until they feel they can no longer regard themselves as males and are at least under consideration for gender re-assignment. Usually though cross-dressing is not accompanied by fetishistic sexual excitement but by a feeling of happiness, well-being, and frequently relaxation.

Whilst transsexuals are described as intellectually fairly bright (Ball, 1960), their achievement is said to be less good. They have vocational problems in that they find masculine employment amongst groups of men very stressful. In contrast homosexuals appear to welcome belonging to groups of the same sex.

The transsexual claims to be revolted by or at least indifferent to his sexual organs and desperately wishes their removal. In addition he seeks hormone therapy to develop breasts and suppress the remnants of his male sexuality. He also hopes such treatment will change his emotions, his voice, and so on. Some transsexuals even insist that hormones have changed their height. He obtains electrolysis to remove facial hair and in some cases self-castration is attempted. In fact the transsexual has an almost delusional belief in himself as feminine but how far this is a self-induced conviction as a means to obtaining medical help is hard to say. Many transsexuals do not conform to the pattern described above. Roberta Cowell was a racing driver, played rugby football, was married and had children. Jan Morris was an Everest mountaineer and also married with children. April Ashley was a merchant seaman albeit an unhappy one. Della Aleksander (Jacobson, 1974) says that she did not consider herself transsexual before hormone therapy. The best-known transsexuals would seem the least typical perhaps. The distinction between the transsexual and transvestite is far less clear than is frequently assumed. It is always an error to believe that most individuals are incapable of obscuring and distorting the truth to attain a required objective (Stoller *et al.*, 1960). One report is of a very detailed study of a transsexual and the problems of his sex reassignment over a number of years. He was described as having almost all the psychological and physical characteristics normally attributed to transsexuals. He had a lack of facial hair and had well-developed breasts. Psychological, sociological, psychiatric, and even endocrinological studies were made in detail. After the completion of the report the patient revealed that much of his account was false and his lack of secondary masculine features was due to the fact that he had been taking hormones prescribed for his mother, since the age of 12. Such extreme deception must be rare but the intent amongst transsexuals and some mistaken transvestites to pursue surgery demands a great personal committal to a belief in evidence of femininity from childhood. Fact and fantasy become inextricably combined in these fantasies and the patient himself is unable to disentangle the truth, let alone the doctor. The two syndromes are very likely, then, to be artificially distinguished by reported features founded on fantasy as well as fact.

Transvestite cross-dressing cannot be regarded as entirely distinct from any of the above groups. In some cases the overlap may be considerable. Transvestites and transsexuals are both in some association with homosexuals because within homosexual society they can find a role and support they do not find within heterosexual society. Although it is probably rare, both transvestites and transsexuals find homosexual relationships supported by female fantasies a practical compromise. The

question of whether or not a male transsexual fantasy of a
relationship with a heterosexual male constitutes homosexuality,
as Feldman and MacCulloch (1971) assume, is a complex problem. It involves the intriguing point that such a relationship is
impossible since the heterosexual male would hardly share the
transsexual's belief in his femininity and, therefore, could only
regard the relationship as homosexual.
The dividing lines between fetishism, transsexualism, and
transvestism are much in dispute. Some writers appear to feel
that the discernible fetishistic element in transvestism is so important and the transsexual group is so large that the transvestite group is either very small or simply does not exist. This
argument depends on the extent to which fetishism can be
regarded as abnormal on the one hand, and the needs for a
female role too compelling on the other. A separate transvestite
group would only be meaningful if there was a substantial body
of people who were neither sexually aroused by cross-dressing
in a fetishistic way, nor had the compelling need for femininity
which demanded a complete eradication of masculinity on the
other. Too little is known about fetishism, certainly most
people respond at a sexual level to articles of clothing even if
only in a way which is purely pleasurable and acceptable. Similarly we know relatively little about people presenting themselves as transsexual who do not obtain surgery, in other words
we do not really know how compelling the need really is. The
distinction of the transvestite group is thus largely a matter of
individual clinical opinion.

Stoller (1968) defined transvestism in this way:

> Let us define adult male transvestism as completely
> pleasurable. . . . He has learned a woman's role so well
> that he can or wishes to successfully pass undetected
> in society as a woman, when he does so the activity
> alternates with living most of his life in a man's role.
> While his transvestism started in childhood or adolescence
> with sexual excitement precipitously provoked by a
> single garment there is a gradual emergence over the

years of a non-erotic desire to sense himself intermittently
as a woman. . . .

The concept here is of a condition in which there is a relatively stable feminine gender persona, in the context of desire
to preserve male heterosexuality, and which we primarily
observe in cross-dressing. This is what we regard as transvestism
for the present purpose.

Stoller is not consistent in that this definition does not
appear to fit in with his categorisation of cross-dressers (Stoller,
1971). In this latter paper he emphasises very much more
strongly the erotic element in transvestism. Nevertheless in the
passage quoted above Stoller describes accurately what is meant
by transvestism here.

It might be fairly said that this view is most nearly in accord
with most common current thinking but there is abundant confusion in the literature. Ellis regarded transvestism as "really a
modification of normal heterosexuality". Stekel regarded it as
"a mask for homosexuality" and the first edition of the current
standard psychiatric textbook by Mayer-Gross, Slater, and Roth
(1954) described it as "a form of fetishism in the homosexually
inclined". However, such is the developing state of understanding
of transvestism that the third and most recent edition of the
latter work expresses a view of the problem very close to
Stoller's.

This view of transvestism is in accord with Walinder's view
(1967) that the term transvestism should be reserved for a
primary desire or need to dress in the clothes of the opposite
sex. That is to say, it should not be a secondary feature of some
other state such as homosexuality or fetishism. Roth and Ball
(1964) called the condition of secondary cross-dressing
"symptomatic transvestism". In this case there is no doubt that
transvestism is closer to transsexualism than is generally
appreciated and the most important factor which relates the
two states is the gender dysphoria or lack of ease in the sex-
appropriate role, rather than an erotic sexual component. As
Walinder says, "One of the most important characteristics of

both transvestism and transsexualism . . . is that they have nothing to do with sexual satisfaction." He cites Benjamin (1954), Hamburger *et al.* (1953) and Roth and Ball (1964) in support. Moreover, both Benjamin and Roth and Ball argue that transvestism and transsexualism overlap. Hampson (1964) also takes this view. It does seem though that the idea of two static conditions "overlapping" is unreal. It is more likely that the two shade into each other rather as if they were levels of adjustment to a common problem and differed mostly in degree. Also it seems that at times the adjustment pattern has to change from an intermittent transvestite need to a more permanent and hence more transsexual-like one.

Randell (1959 and 1975) is one authority who is seemingly unconvinced about this concept of transvestism. Whilst he unequivocally accepts that such a group exists he is inclined to relegate it to a phenomenon of some rarity. Many writers of less expertise in the field than Stoller, Benjamin, Hamburger, Roth and Ball, Hampson, and Randell adhere to a concept of transvestism as very much a branch of fetishism. This will be particularly obviously when a review of therapeutic attempts is made. It could be that motivation to treat is higher in the case of sexual disorders. Also objective criteria are easier to establish so that the fetishistic, secondary, or symptomatic transvestite becomes the most usual candidate for therapy.

Krafft-Ebing (1924) appears to have first presented clinical studies of two transvestites under the name "metamorphosis sexualis paranoia", but the general opinion is that the cases he described were psychotically ill and cross-dressing was a symptom of the illness rather than true transvestism. Hirschfeld (1910) presented seventeen cases of cross-dressers and attempted a classification of them which had the particularly interesting contribution of distinguishing heterosexual transvestism from homosexuality. It was in fact Hirschfeld who coined the term "transvestism". Havelock Ellis (1928) used the term "sexo-aesthetic inversion" but not surprisingly later substituted the term "eonism" derived from Déon Beaumont's name. However, it is important to realise that until fairly recently transsexualism at least and probably other problems were included within the concept of transvestism, e.g. as known by Hirschfeld and Havelock Ellis. Unfortunately although somewhat pragmatic distinctions have now been made between transvestism and transsexualism, no great progress has been made towards understanding the relationship between the two. As Stoller (1968) suggests, transvestism might develop from fetishistic experiences and it is not impossible that transsexualism in turn emerges from transvestism. It is not unlikely that, as Roth (1975) indicates, transvestism may be simply a level of adjustment in a developing transexual personality. Finally the two states could have radically different etiologies.

CHAPTER 2

Transvestism as Illness, Perversion, or Choice

The incidence of transvestism is quite unknown. It is probably true that in normal practice a general medical practitioner will be consulted by no more than one or two in his career. Few psychiatrists will have under their care more than one known transvestite at any time and hence there is a considerable lack of studies of groups of transvestite patients. Lukianowicz's (1959) most important study of transvestism reports four transvestite patients found in a population of half a million in 3 years. Many writers have regarded transvestism as very rare indeed. Hamburger (Lukianowicz, 1959) found five cases in the whole of Denmark and described it as "an exceedingly rare condition". Curiously Denmark is one of the countries with a flourishing transvestite society. At the opposite extreme Ellis (1928) regarded transvestism as quite common, not unlike homosexuality in occurrence. The reason for the difficulty is obvious. Transvestism is very much a hidden phenomenon. Most transvestites achieve a reasonable level of adjustment and do not conceive themselves as in need of medical help. It can be contained within limits which do not offend against the law and it is largely a secretive affair perhaps involving a wife but rarely anyone else.

One cannot ignore the significance of the self-help societies for transvestites in many countries. In Great Britain the Beaumont Society established around 1969 has 400 or 500 members and currently advises about as many new transvestite enquirers each year. The Beaumont Trust is a charitable society providing counselling for transvestites. Neither of these organisations are concerned with homosexuals although transsexuals are sometimes included in the absence of a viable transsexual society. A society allied to the Beaumont Society operates in France and the Low Countries, another in Scandinavia. The largest society is the American "Phi Pi Epsilon" (Full Personality Expression) and in Australia and New Zealand there are societies known as the Seahorse Clubs (Buhrich, 1976). A transvestite society also exists in South Africa. One can, therefore, reject confidently the assertion that this is other than a fairly common problem and Ellis's comparison with the incidence of homosexuality seems not irrational.

The picture of the transvestite found in the literature is changing rapidly and there is little point in considering too deeply reports dating back many years. As with a number of other allied personality problems the majority of transvestites do not seek or require medical help. Cases appearing as patients are likely to be those a-typical cases where transvestism and a psychiatric disturbance coexist. Perhaps the coexisting conditions are independent but this is very difficult to determine in patient groups. As the data about transvestites are considered points will become obvious where patient studies and the conclusions drawn from clinical groups differ sharply from non-clinical studies.

The vast majority of clinical papers concern either very small numbers of transvestites or individual case studies. The most comprehensive study is that of Lukianowicz based on the treatment of four patients. Ball's (1960) unpublished thesis, primarily concerned with transsexualism, studies six transvestite patients in detail, Taylor and McLachlan's (1962, 1963a, 1963b, 1964) research was on ten cases of transvestism in prison for various offences. Morgernstern *et al.* (1965) made an outstanding study of nineteen cases of transvestite patients, and their conclusions point to very important considerations. Using psychological tests they attempted to predict the response of transvestites to treatment. They described transvestites as "among the more highly intelligent of the population,

introverted, highly suggestible and anxious". Furthermore, they
found a small negative correlation between neuroticism and
feminine identification, that is to say the more feminine the
individual the less neurotic he is likely to be. In other words,
the evidence was rather opposed to either the belief that transvestism is a form of neurotic reaction, or that transvestism gives
rise to neurotic symptoms. The lack of a relationship between
neuroticism and transvestism as shown by this research indicates
that clinical studies are more likely to illustrate unrelated neurotic features rather than true, representative transvestite ones.

Two other studies of the personalities of transvestites support
this sort of finding. These were made by Bentler and his co-
workers (1970a, 1970b) but unlike previous studies cases were
taken from the general non-clinical population. In the first
study 180 transvestites who subscribed to an American
magazine *Transvestia* and seventy-six control subjects were
tested with a test of nineteen scales assessing psychiatric disturbance. These scales assessed such features as depression,
neurotic disorganisation, socially deviant attitudes, sadism,
familial discord, and so on. Even using discriminant function
analysis, a powerful statistical method for discriminating between groups, no differences were found between transvestites
and normal controls. That is to say, the transvestites did not
show neurotic, psychotic or personality disorders with any
greater frequency than normal men.

The second study by Bentler concerned twenty-five transvestites from Los Angeles who again were drawn from the
general population and not from psychiatric clinics. These men
were tested with the Holtzman Ink Blot Test. In comparison
with a group of non-transvestite men considerable differences
were found but as the transvestite group were so much above
average general intelligence a new control group was selected
from a student population. In this case the differences became
much less marked. The transvestites were shown to be intellectually capable and imaginative, they were somewhat rigid personalities, showed some thought illogicality, anxiety and most
marked of all a preoccupation with body features. The authors

thought that there was evidence of a "vaguely specifiable" latent thought disturbance but this seems not to have been particularly significant and again there was no evidence of clear-cut psychiatric disturbance.

Evidence consistent with this view was presented by Brierley (1975) in the form of a comparison of the personality profiles of patient groups of fifteen transvestites and forty-four homosexuals. For comparison groups of male and female hospital staff were also tested. All four groups were given the Cattell 16PF questionnaire and significant differences appeared between them. Differences between homosexual patient, homosexual prisoner, and general population group data on this test have already been shown (Cattell *et al.*, 1970) to be largely the same factor of general anxiety and guilt feelings which appear in most psychiatric patient profiles.

Figure 1 shows the 16PF profile for a group of twenty-two transvestites, most of whom were patients on account of their cross-dressing.

The general transvestite profile again showed the features of high guilt feelings as previously found for homosexual groups and again apparent in this study. The transvestite group, however, did not show high tension or emotional instability and the homosexual group did. In comparison with the male and female controls the transvestites were more serious minded. They were also more conscientious than either the controls or the homosexuals. Transvestites differed from the females in being less assertive and more inhibited. They did not show a lack of self-sufficiency and control which sharply differentiated the homosexuals from the male control group.

These groups are different in that it may fairly be said that most homosexuals seeking treatment feel under greater pressure socially than transvestites are. The homosexual group feels less able to disguise its problems and often feels that it is socially and vocationally threatened. The transvestite group is usually seeking help over a more personal problem which is covert and less likely to be a threat beyond the level of personal relations. The transvestite group rarely feels that others know its secrets

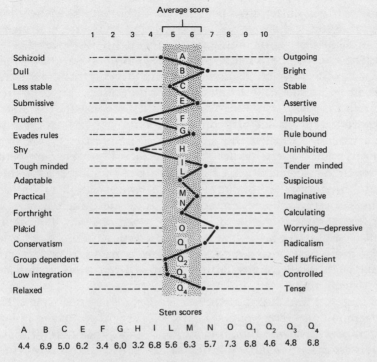

Fig. 1. Cattell 16PF profile. Twenty-two transvestites

as homosexuals frequently suspect. Such differences may well underlie personality profiles in patient groups which suggest that homosexuals have more serious problems and are more sharply differentiated from non-patient groups. The transvestites are more characterised by their obsessional traits and feelings of guilt than in any other way.

The position then seems to be that not only do non-clinical groups of transvestites fail to show the pathological features reported in clinical studies, usually of individual cases, but the transvestite in the normal population appears to be normally free of psychiatric pathology.

This might be seen as one side of the coin and it is interesting to evaluate the other side. The evidence does not show the transvestite to suffer gross psychiatric pathology, how then does the transvestite himself see his condition, does he conceive it as an illness or perhaps as just a way of life? Brierley (1974) presented evidence on this question. The investigation attempted to show how far transvestites and psychiatrists saw transvestism in terms of the same concept of illness or disability. Repertory grid technique was used. This consisted of asking subjects to rank a set of people (elements) on various qualities (constructs). The elements included a transvestite, a father, a neurotic and so on, whilst "ill", "peaceful", "peculiar", etc., were the constructs. In this way each research subject's rankings could be formed into correlations between all pairs of constructs. In turn these were analysed into the principal pairs of construct dimensions on which the positions of all elements could be plotted. As it is possible to combine a group of grids from individuals into a single grid from a group of people, grid plots were derived representing groups of ten transvestites and ten psychiatrists.

Figures 2 and 3 put simply have two main dimensions. The horizontal one (component I) we can regard as "tranquillity" and the vertical one (component II) we can regard as "illness". Twelve sorts of people (elements) are shown plotted on these dimensions. The nearer they are to the bottom of the figure the more "ill" the group appears to see them and the more to the left of the figure the more "tranquil". Conversely, elements towards the top of the figure are not construed as ill and those to the right are construed as disturbed. Thus, for instance, the transsexualist is found well into the bottom right quadrant and is construed by psychiatric registrars as both ill and disturbed.

It was expected that the psychiatrists would tend to rate transsexuals, transvestites and homosexuals as people with illnesses and disabilities. The plot shown in Fig. 2 demonstrated that this was indeed so and that transvestism and transsexualism were regarded as more extreme than say the behaviour of sexual criminals, etc. Figure 3 shows that the transvestite group also rated elements along a clear illness disability dimension very

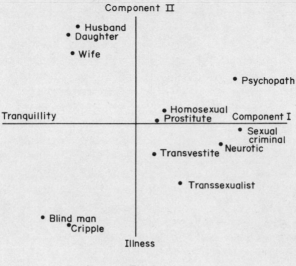

Fig. 2

similar to the one used by the psychiatrists except that they did not see themselves as ill or disabled. Indeed they placed themselves amongst the ordinary "normal" people. —

The same technique was applied to a group composed of social workers and psychologists whose conceptual system could be expected to be less medical in form and this group was, in fact, found not to use an illness–disability dimension. They substituted some concept of peculiarity in the sense of being hard to understand and odd, and again they regarded the transvestites as extreme on this dimension. Thus it seems that whilst transvestites see themselves as essentially fairly ordinary people professional workers tend to regard them as ill, hard to understand, and peculiar in the extreme. This is a situation which does not seem to auger well for therapy and counselling, of course, and reflects a great disparity between how the transvestite and professional workers conceptualise this sort of behaviour.

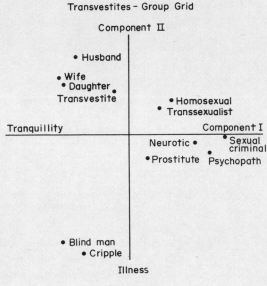

Fig. 3

The survey of any group like transvestites is not only hampered by difficulty in defining the group itself but in finding any meaningful and representative sample. It is reasonable to accept a group of law-breakers as representing the more serious criminal population but a similar group of people who transgressed laws on, say, homosexuality would most certainly not be representative of homosexuals. No more can a group of imprisoned transvestites such as that studied by Taylor and McLachlan (1962, 1963a, 1963b) be representative of transvestites. Less obviously perhaps people seeking psychiatric help tend to show the common characteristics of psychiatric patient populations more strongly than any specific qualities. This has certainly been found true of generalisations from homosexual patient groups. In other words, patient groups tend to show patient characteristics first and foremost.

Transvestism may present an unusually difficult problem because of the large proportion of transvestites who choose never to reveal their transvestism and retain their transvestite feelings and habits behind closed doors. Social disapproval makes this desirable whilst the very nature of transvestism makes it possible. Even transvestite societies are unlikely to be representative, even if they are likely to be more so than patient groups. Apart from the recruitment policies of such groups there are implications in membership of a particular rather hearty conviviality which is anathema to the transvestite. The most detailed study of American transvestites was carried out by Prince and Bentler (1972), based on another sample. Postal enquiries were made of 1300 presumed transvestites who subscribed to a magazine called *Transvestia*. Five hundred and four replies were obtained, approximately 40%, which is a relatively good return for a postal survey although by no means convincingly representative.

Transvestia is not a pornographic magazine but deals mostly with advice to transvestites together with accounts of social activities organised by transvestites, etc. It is explicitly not aimed towards homosexuals and would contain little of interest to fetishists or other groups. However, whilst the readers of *Transvestia* are likely to be almost entirely transvestite, by no means all transvestites would wish to read chit-chat about the subject or seek the advice it offers. The philosophy of *Transvestia* is, rather like that of the homosexual press, that transvestism is an acceptable way of life providing the individual does not feel alone or ashamed. Legal risks can be minimised and the social outlets which societies provide may relieve some pressure from the transvestite. Such a message has an optimistic quality but may well not please transvestites with chronic social difficulties, who find social gatherings too expensive, or who are far from being convinced about the acceptability of the transvestite way of life.

Such limitations of different sample studies must always be borne in mind but despite the limitations of the Prince and Bentler survey, they present a large body of information which is valuable if regarded with caution.

Table 1 shows their data on the physical characteristics and

TABLE 1. *Personal characteristics of 504 transvestites*

Median height	Between 5 ft 8 in. and 6 ft
Age	20-29 30-39 40-49
	20% 34% 28%
Education	University degree 37%
	Higher degree 13%
Income	Under 5000 5000-10,000 Over 10,000$
	16% 56% 25%
Marital status	64% married; 22% single; 14% sep, wid, div.;
	74% parents

personal features of transvestites. Clearly these males are physically unremarkable. They are not of short or slight, feminine build as one might expect. In age distribution a substantial part are in their middle years.

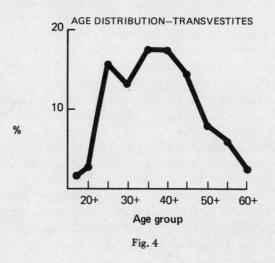

Fig. 4

This is borne out by the recruitment figures provided by the Beaumont Society which have a median age of 36 and 32% are over 40 years (Fig. 4). Indeed members aged over 80 years are recorded. Table 1 shows that 37% of Prince's transvestites were of at least degree standard in education, thus the generally good level of intelligence in transvestites again is reported. This is also reflected in the income levels. Moreover, this group of transvestites were found to be socially upward moving in that their social and occupational levels were superior to their fathers'. One must conclude that the group are not only able but achieving — rather the reverse picture to that found by Ball (1960) for a transsexualist group.

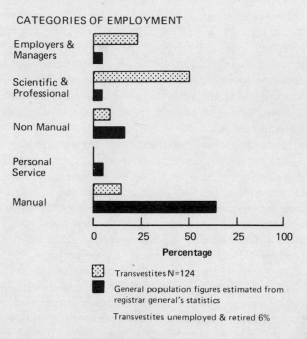

Fig. 5.

Not only is it rather surprising that transvestites seem successful in their male roles but one also finds the nature of their employment to be strikingly masculine. Figure 5 shows the distribution of occupations in the British sample (Brierley, 1974). The professions are grossly over-represented and there is a comparative absence of the personal-service occupations which might be regarded as in some sense feminine, e.g. cooks, hairdressers, shop assistants. The most interesting figure is that 25% of this group are either scientists or professional engineers. According to Sexton (1970) these occupations ought to be associated with strong masculine identification. Some degree of selection must be suspected but there is in fact no evidence that the sample could have been unrepresentative in terms of occupations.

The inference seems to be that there is a bi-polarity in the gender role-taking of the transvestite. In the masculine role he takes on a masculine vocation and is successful, yet nurtures a capacity to slip into a feminine role. This seems very different from the picture of the transsexual who shows no evidence of this bi-polarity, e.g. in occupations (Hoopes *et al.*, 1968). The concept of the transvestite as having a bi-polarity of gender identity is quite important and is enhanced by a study of the names chosen by transvestites.

In the feminine role transvestites tend to adopt extremely feminine images which are hard to quantify. As masculine males one might anticipate transvestites to choose to masquerade as somewhat masculine females, but much the most frequent is the totally inappropriate highly feminine role. One aspect which can be quantified to some extent is the feminine name chosen, as almost all transvestites seem to adopt a female name for themselves even if it is only used in the privacy of their own thoughts. A study of transvestite names was reported in Brierley (1974). The preference appeared to be for names like Susan and Caroline as opposed to the general population preference for Elizabeth or Margaret. Indeed the difference of name distribution amongst Beaumont Society transvestites and that of a female patient group was statistically significant.

It is, of course, not possible to match the transvestite and general populations really closely for want of knowledge of the members of a semi-secret society. Name counts seem likely to vary with social class, age group and location at least, but Table 2 presents a comparison of all names found more often than a rate of 15 per 1000 in populations taken either from the Beaumont Society, a general hospital sample, or a sample from the

Newcastle-upon-Tyne electoral roll. By this standard twenty-four names are included. Twelve of these names appear because of their frequency in the transvestite list, a further ten because of their frequency amongst the names of hospital patients, and another two from the electoral-roll list.

TABLE 2. *A comparison of the names chosen by trans-vestites with those of women in the general population. Frequency per thousand calculated from random sample*

Name	Transvestites	Hospital patients	Electoral roll
Susan	52	15	11
Angela	40	8	2
Carole	33	23	8
Anne	35	66	60
Barbara	26	7	9
Helen	26	11	24
Sandra	18	2	4
Linda	18	15	11
Janet	18	8	2
Julia	16	0	0
Jean	16	15	11
Rosemary	16	2	0
Joan	14	16	15
Mary	14	59	77
Jane	14	7	30
Catherine	14	27	23
Margaret	2	63	86
Elizabeth	7	61	67
Dorothy	5	21	26
Isobell	2	16	38
Ethel	0	16	6
Florence	2	30	13
Sarah	0	16	30
Joyce	0	8	17
Number in random sample	423	400	532

It is quite clear that the distribution of names in the general population groups are very similar and the transvestite name distribution is very different. Only the name Anne appears in all groups as popular but it is interesting that the transvestites tend to use this name to feminise others, e.g. Jo Ann, Sally Anne. Apart from Anne none of the transvestite group names appears popular by this standard in the other groups, where names like Margaret, Mary, and Elizabeth are common.

The difference in nature of names like Susan and Elizabeth seems clear but hard to define. Brierley (1974) asked a group of women to rate the popular transvestite names and the popular general population names and found that the transvestite names were rated significantly more feminine than the general population names. In addition the femininity rating of the names was significantly correlated with their frequency of use by transvestites.

"Folk lore" says that transvestites tend to feminise their own names, e.g. Robert to Roberta, John to Jan. In Table 2 there is no indication of this and the majority of the popular transvestite names seem incapable of derivation from male names. It has also been popular belief that transvestites tended to choose names ending in "a" whilst homosexuals using female names choose diminutives ending in "e", like Julie. Curiously this rather unlikely belief seems to be supported by the table since five of the twelve popular transvestite names end in "a" and not one of the general population names. It might be that the suffix "a" tends to be associated with nouns of feminine gender and hence gives names a more feminine sound. Certainly male names ending in "a" are most uncommon.

However, there is little doubt that the transvestite choice of name aims to promote an image of extreme femininity — more royal than the queen! And this in the context of male roles which are strongly masculine and successful, illustrating the transvestite's tendency to form a combination of gender role extremes — perhaps well described as a bi-polarity of gender.

Stoller (1968) has commented that he has never seen a successful transvestite marriage and one would expect perhaps that transvestism is an insuperable marital difficulty. It seems from Table 1 that 78% of the American sample had married, 12% said they had married more than once. The authors could not be certain what percentage of divorces had taken place but it was between 19 and 29%, and 36% of divorces recorded were related to transvestism. It is perhaps more interesting that 64%

of divorces did not cite transvestism as a cause. Only 20% of wives were in fact unaware of their husbands' transvestism and it would seem to indicate that in divorce a curiously high number of wives did not regard their husbands' transvestism as a major cause of marital breakdown when they might well have done so.

Seventy-eight per cent of transvestites were currently married or had been married. In a sample with a minimum age below 20 years this figure is unlikely to be much different from the normal population. Much the same results are seen in Fig. 6 which shows the percentage of single men in the Beaumont Society. Fewer men up to the age of 30 are married than in the

%UNMARRIED BY AGE

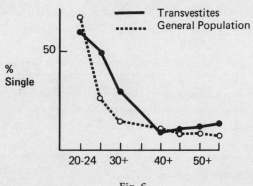

Fig. 6.

general population but this might be attributed to the high percentage of professional men who would in any event tend to marry later in life. Beyond the age of 30 there is no difference between the transvestites and the general population for the proportion married. In this British sample 9.1% declared themselves as divorced. Divorce rates are hard to compare with general population statistics since the age range of the transvestite group is so wide and divorce has become so much more common in recent years. However, currently the Registrar

General's Statistics show the annual number of divorces to be about one-tenth the number of marriages. On this basis the figure of divorced transvestites in Britain is likely to be close again to the general population figure.

Another interesting feature of Prince's figures is that whereas 78% had been married 74% were parents. The heterosexual competence does not seem in doubt in this sample but, of course, the pattern of their sexual behaviour may be abnormal nevertheless.

Pearce (1963) also provides data on the marital status of transvestites. Amongst his group of twenty-six transvestite patients eighteen had married, two of whom were divorced and a further four separated. Eight were single and four were apparently homosexual. Of the eighteen married transvestites fifteen had children, one to seven was the range of numbers of children per family. This means that the eighteen families had an average of 1.7 children.

TABLE 3. *Sexual characteristics of 504 transvestites*

Sexual orientation	Exclusively heterosexual		89%
	Bisexual		9%
	Exclusively homosexual		1%
Homosexual experience	28%		
Sexual interest in the opposite sex	Below av. 14%	Average 62%	Above av. 24%
Taking female hormones	5%		
Considering surgery	14%		

Table 3 summarises the declared sexual orientation in Prince's group. The strong denial of homosexuality is quite clear. One would expect in the general population a figure of about 5% being exclusively homosexual and about 37% declaring previous homosexual experiences. It is, of course, fruitless to argue that such figures might either reflect frank lying or unconscious denial of homosexuality. Both this survey and other writers have emphasised the infrequency of homosexuality amongst transvestites at least in terms of their known sexual behaviour.

As we have commented, the relationship between transvestism and transsexualism is complicated and uncertain. However, Table 3 would show that amongst these heterosexual transvestites only a relatively small proportion are likely to be preoccupied with sex reassignment. Only 14% are even considering surgery and only 5% are taking hormones. Newman and Stoller (1974) have also shown that female hormones administered to transvestites with strong transsexual desires reduce the transsexuality. On the other hand, Stoller asserts that the hormones increase the sex change desires in the transsexual. Hence we might assume that some of the 5% taking hormones might do so to reduce their transsexual desires rather than to enhance them.

In Table 4 the transvestites' attitudes to their problems are presented. The most significant fact illustrated is the low percentage of transvestites who wish to end their transvestism. Seventy-two per cent even wish to develop their transvestite skills, and their cross-gender desires. Seventy-eight per cent

TABLE 4. *Feelings about transvestism of 504 transvestites*

Future plans	Hoping to try to stop		1%
	Continue as things are		22%
	Trying to develop female self		72%
Negative feelings to cross-dressing	Previously destroyed wardrobe		69%
	Some guilt after dressing		22%
	No current guilt feelings		32%
Some sadomasochistic interests			15%
Transvestism entirely secret			50%
Reactions of persons other than wives to being told about his transvestism	accepting 56%	neutral 35%	antagonistic 9%
Attitudes of men and women to transvestism	Men accepting 23%	Women accepting 77%	
Valuing transvestite experience highly			41%
Feel a different personality when dressed			78%

feel that in changing clothes they change personality. They report this as a subtle effect which is described as "coming". The transvestite tends to cross-dress not so much because of a strong current urge to do so when he feels overwhelmed by some feminine-like impulse but more in a search of feminine feelings. Indeed the immediate motive for cross-dressing may be vague perhaps even at the level of a simple habit or regular ritual. He does not experience a full immediate change in personality as he dresses, as the fetishistic cross-dresser might feel heightened sexual arousal, but is rather slowly overcome by what he senses as femininity. This may take an hour or more during which time he feels he is acting a part until "she comes" and femininity feels instinctive.

Amongst twenty-six cases, eighteen of which were culled from Maudsley Hospital records, Pearce (1963) found twenty patients who experienced cross-dressing as relaxing rather than sexually exciting, although five said they were occasionally sexually excited. For the six remaining cases cross-dressing was essentially sexually erotic. It is rather illustrative of the difficulty of obtaining representative groups of such patients as transvestites that Pearce found that in his own experimental group six out of eight masturbated when in women's clothing, whilst in the cases found in the hospital records only three out of eighteen did so.

It is a finding common to most writers that transvestite patients are usually inadequately motivated towards treatment. On the other hand, it is common for transvestites to purge themselves periodically, destroying their wardrobe of female possessions and attempting to reassert a wholly male existence. These attempts seem invariably short lived and there is no simple explanation of why they should occur. They usually seem to be spontaneous but sometimes more a result of the transvestite's inability to achieve the effect he seeks rather than any repugnance at his transvestism itself. With painful efforts such as plucking his entire beard from his face with tweezers, he strives for a female appearance always to be continually frustrated by the unremitting masculinity of the image in the glass.

Masochism appears to play a part in transvestism. Fantasies of being in very passive roles are common, being in some way bullied into a female role, perhaps as a servant girl. There also seems to be some preoccupation with the constricting garments worn by women, corsetry, high-heeled shoes, and "tights". This masochistic element is hard to evaluate since whilst it might be masochistic for a male to wear corsets and high-heeled shoes, a woman normally does so. Thus the 15% reporting masochistic impulses seems an under-estimate viewed as male behaviour but perhaps not if some transvestite masochism is simply part of effecting the female disguise. It is even less easy to assess how far the sense of being dominated or constricted is sexually arousing and how far the actual constricting garments are simply fetishes. It is possible, of course, that there may be masochistically motivated cross-dressing in which the female role is important not because of the gender identity implications but because of the masochistic elements of an adopted female role. A parallel would be the masochist who dresses as a schoolboy as part of the ritual of being caned, the caning has sexual significance and the individual has no simple desire to be a schoolboy apart from it. A masochistically motivated cross-dresser seems unlikely to show the complex striving for public acceptance as a female however.

TABLE 5. *Pattern of transvestism of 504 transvestites*

Number going out dressed in public	Total between 18–34%	
	On public transport	11%
	Restaurants	13%
	Public meetings	13%
	Trying on female garments	10%
	Buying cosmetics	13%
	Drag parties	12%
Seen at close range by people who would know him		18%
Definitely not going out dressed		40%

Half of Prince's group had always kept their transvestism secret. One supposes that as the questionnaire was inducing them to break secrecy to some degree this might underestimate the fraction of secret transvestites. It is a special feature of transvestism that the practice is so private in many cases. Even in the case of the transvestite appearing in public it is important that he feels undetected as a female. Even if accepted as a man dressed as a woman the transvestite would usually find little special pleasure in the situation. Some transvestites would seem to value the fantasy of ultimate disclosure as if finally putting the deception to the test. This may suggest that the objective is not the transsexualist's wish for complete femaleness but a half-way man–woman role or as some would have it a woman with a penis. However that may be, transvestism is largely practised in private and a very large fraction of transvestites remains completely hidden.

Transvestites do not evaluate the attitudes of others very realistically. If they stray out in public dressed as women they lay themselves open to prosecution but are disproportionately fearful. They anxiously inspect every person they meet for a sign that they have been "read", whereas of course the vast majority barely give them any attention at all. A small number of transvestites make themselves widely known and as Prince and Bentler find only a small percentage of people are definitely antagonistic to them. Men find the problem harder to accept than women do and it frequently mystifies the transvestite that his wife can go a long way to treating his transvestism in a very matter of fact fashion. Of course, acceptance in this sense is a different matter to acceptance in all situations. The most relevant antagonism is found amongst women who feel threatened by a transvestite who they believe is in a state of abberrant sexual arousal. A man who would not necessarily accept a transvestite's behaviour would rarely lay a complaint but a woman meeting an obvious transvestite, say, in a lonely place at night would feel in danger and more likely to complain to the law.

As Table 5 shows only about one-third of transvestites ever appear in public dressed as women. Forty per cent definitely avoid doing so. From the number going out as indicated here many simply attend public "drag balls" or go to restaurants where they know they are acceptable. Such functions and meeting-places exist in almost all British cities. So it seems that perhaps only 25% of transvestites at most ever appear in normal public places or run material risk of prosecution.

Nothing has so far been said about the masculinity or femininity of the transvestite other than their "assumed" roles. We have commented on an apparent bi-polarity of roles and we might well ask if the transvestite is fundamentally a very masculine personality who adopts, imitates or simply acts a feminine role at a conscious level, or if he is a person with a more stable trait of femininity. Certainly transsexuals present themselves as essentially and fundamentally feminine, despite specific evidence of very masculine roles in the male existence of some specific cases. Moreover, there is a certain antagonism between some transsexuals and transvestites in which the former scorn the latter as being essentially masculine and not possessing a true conviction of femininity.

The differences in the personality profiles of transvestites and normal males and females has already been mentioned. Curiously masculinity-femininity as a personality variable has proved rather elusive and although a number of tests have been designed few are thought even moderately satisfactory. This may be because what is masculine and what is feminine is so largely culturally determined. The most comprehensive test to have been used is the Attitude-Interest Test of Terman and Miles (1936) which simply purports to be a masculinity-femininity measure. Views on the tests are usually rather like those expressed by Bancroft (1974) which might be summarised as inferring that the test is superficial and goes little further than assessing the obvious. However, a strong feature of the test is that the person completing the test is unlikely to be aware that it is other than a conventional general personality inventory and even if he did suspect its true purpose it would not be easy to "fake" a desired result.

Brierley (1975) presented the results of Terman–Miles Tests on general population males and females, homosexuals and transvestites. An analysis of the results of the tests, the Cattell 16PF test, and clinical data suggested that the Terman–Miles did produce a valid measure of masculinity–femininity and it differentiated the groups as in Table 6. It is seen that transvestites produce the most feminine scores (negative), and male homosexuals show weak masculine scores. Only the transvestite and general female scores were not significantly different.

TABLE 6. *Significance of Differences between means on Terman–Miles test*

	Transvestite	Homosexual	Female	Male
Mean score	−29	+17	−23	+65
Transvestite		.001	N.S.	.001
Homosexual			.001	.001
Female				.001

The test is composed of seven sub-tests; two of these did not seem effective in differentiating any groups. On the other five tests the pattern was not simple. For example, test 4, which is composed of questions about emotions, e.g. things which are felt disgusting, fear-provoking, etc., seem to produce a false feminine response from transvestites (Table 7). They seem to

TABLE 7. *Statistical significance of differences between groups on Terman–Miles sub-tests*

	Male — Female	Male — homosexual	Male — transvestite	Female — homosexual	Female — transvestite	Transvestite — homosexual
Sub-test						
1	.003			.02		
2	.01			.03		
3	.02	.04				
4			.03		.02	
5	.001	.01	.001	.001		.002
6						
7						

depict emotional reactions which are stronger than females' who were themselves not different from the male group. On this test transvestites were more "feminine" than either general population males or females. Then again test 3 is a form of general-knowledge test based on information apparently biased to one sex or the other, e.g. about the size of a brick or the weaning of babies. On this test homosexuals were significantly more "feminine" in knowledge than the general population males but not so the transvestites. The test which most strongly differentiated all groups was test 5 which records preferred activities, e.g. vocational, recreational, travel, etc., on which the transvestites had feminine scores. Further evidence suggested fetishists had conventional male scores.

The overall result would seem to be that the attitudes and interests of transvestites on the whole are closer to those of females than males but in an inconsistent way. In one area at least male homosexuals may have more feminine attributes than transvestites, but whilst this test evidence is interesting it does not take the investigation of stable personality traits of femininity in transvestites very much further without a good deal of additional support.

It would be surprising indeed if studies of transvestism did not throw up facile reasons for the development of the condition. This is especially so where single cases have been studied. On the one hand simple explanatory hypotheses usually prove too elusive to put to precise test and on the other such data as have become available are discouraging. Other states such as homosexuality are also plagued by a multiplicity of fairly unfounded explanations.

Table 8 presents data from the Prince and Bentler study which are appropriate to a cursory examination of various ideas about the causation of transvestism.

Broken homes are, of course, a general index of a disturbed background. Here however the vast majority of homes is intact although of course this does not mean that they are necessarily good homes. The belief that the transvestite child is identifying with a weak or defective father image is equally not supported

TABLE 8. *Early history of transvestites*

Home background	Intact homes	82%		
	Divorced parents	18%		
Father's image	Normal masculine image		72%	
	Defective because of absence		14%	
	Defective because of drinking or cruelty		5%	
Dominant parent	Father	Mother	Undecided	
	51%	45%	4%	
Childhood memory	Treated as a boy		83%	
	Treated as a girl		4%	
	Made to wear dresses as punishment		4%	
	Had curls longer than others		6%	
Beginnings of cross dressing	Under 5 yrs	5-10 yrs	10-18 yrs	Over 18 yrs
	14%	40%	37%	8%

in most cases. The transvestites report that 72% of fathers presented to them as normal masculine models. Absence of fathers and sundry deficiencies were quoted in 28% of cases which does not seem to be an unduly high figure, especially when the divorce rate is considered.

Maternal dominance is also often involved as an explanation. Here slightly more fathers than mothers are reported as dominant family figures. As with all Prince and Bentler's data no control group figures are available and the only conclusion is that maternal dominance is by no means a universal cause of transvestism. Indeed it seems more likely that in answer to a questionnaire item it is not easy to decide which parent is dominant in a normal home so that the results simply indicate the lack of an overwhelming experience of maternal dominance.

Three common hypotheses relate to child training, the treatment of the boy child as a girl; the use of "pinafore punishment" i.e. punishing and ridiculing the boy by making him wear girl's clothes; and keeping the boy in dresses, with girlish hair etc. for an unduly long time. Again Table 8 shows that the vast majority of transvestites were treated normally as boys. The small percentages treated as girls, subject to pinafore punishment, and kept in curls, would certainly require comparison with a carefully selected control group before being accepted as meaningful.

Thus the coarse data provide no support for the popular hypotheses but they do not expose the more subtle family factors which could be involved. A child might be fully recognized as a boy but chided frequently that he is "soft" and by implication girlish. He may not be brought up wearing curls and frocks for an unduly long period and yet be dressed and admired by mother as a girl would be. Data like those provided by Prince and Bentler have little hope of disentangling causes of human problems like transvestism and it will require a great deal of detailed persistent research to find positive answers to the problem of causation.

Table 8 also gives the distribution of ages at which cross-dressing began in this group. This is interesting particularly in the wide distribution and the fact that the age of onset was found to be totally unassociated with other factors. Importantly it appeared that strong transsexual desires were not necessarily associated with early onset, this is quite contrary to the accounts of transsexuals themselves and the beliefs of most writers on transsexualism.

This then is the transvestite. A person who, to quote Money (1974), has two names, two wardrobes and two personalities. On the one hand in everyday life others see him as masculine, successful and intelligent; heterosexually he seems reasonably well adjusted; but his transvestism brings a marked change in personality. Transvestism has little or no sexually erotic component although many transvestites have grown through strong fetishistic feelings and are still somewhat fetishistic. The transvestite does not want to be a woman in reality, he wants a foot in both camps, as if he wants to preserve the facility to change role where he wishes to escape from the pressures of masculinity — and this is a facility he values highly.

CHAPTER 3

Sex, Gender Identity, and Gender Role

Freud broke through the conventions of the Victorian age with an elucidation of the role of sexual needs in human development. Once it was accepted that sex drive was indeed a key to understanding human problems the Freudian model grew broader and broader until all striving became perceived as sexually derived. Thus psychodynamic theories appeared entirely based on the principle that all human behaviour was primarily sexual.

As working hypotheses, models of human development of this kind seem more or less satisfactory providing that a degree of flexibility is involved in the concept of sex. The man in the street thinks of sex as a biological process directly involving erotic experiences clearly acknowledged as the precursor of orgasm and related to reproduction. Hence to assert, as Fenichel (1930) does, that the waste-pipe in the bath is thought of as a castrating, devouring mouth; or that in skipping the child is rehearsing a role in intercourse (Sonnenberg, 1955), is likely to be greeted by derisive laughter. That both the psychoanalyst and the man in the street may be correct at the same time is probably due to different concepts of the term sex.

A consideration of homosexuality makes this even clearer. Homosexuality has not yet been satisfactorily defined. Some writers like Money (1970) define the homosexual as a person who has a potential for same sex copulation and one would assume that this would satisfy many professional and lay people. However, there is no doubt that there are far more points of difference between the exclusively homosexual and the exclusively heterosexual than a pattern of copulatory behaviour alone. Differences in personality (Cattell *et al.*, 1970), aptitudes (Wilmott, 1975), and interests (Terman and Miles, 1936) have been demonstrated. Only by using a concept of sex much broader than the simple biological sex can the heterosexual be made to differ from the homosexual in sex alone. Homosexuality is not adequately defined by biological sexual behaviour, but includes a vast array of human qualities and inter-personal affinities which are not frankly sexual in the layman's sense of the word.

The concept of "latent homosexuality" is used, as is the case in some explanations of transvestism (Gutheil, 1954). It seems unlikely that the psychoanalyst means that the person he regards as latent homosexual is simply a person who might copulate with someone of the same sex. It is more probable that he is referring to a broad pattern of development and human relations which may well have very little to do with same sex copulation. Alternatively, the individual's behaviour in some ways represents a defence against his homosexuality which again may have little to do with same sex copulation it seems.

Freud fully appreciated all this and certainly recognised that homosexuality was not solely a matter of biological sexuality. In his paper in 1905, "Three Essays on the Theory of Sexuality", he differentiates "organic sex" from "mental sex".

It is odd that we tend to assume that all homosexual characteristics are biologically sexual whilst rejecting the hypothesis that all heterosexual characteristics are equally sexual. The implication is that homosexuals only meet to seek erotic experiences, thus the attitude to the homosexual's erotic behaviour determines the attitude towards the homosexual as a whole. Likewise, the transsexual and the transvestite are often only understood as persons motivated by erotic sexual experiences because they appear to choose a perverse female role and "female" is one of the sexes. The homosexual, transvestite and transsexual thus become "sexual perverts" whereas in many, if not most cases, perverse biological sexuality is irrelevant or at least incidental. Psychoanalytic explanations and social preconceptions of Western civilisation possess a common defect — not surprisingly. Both are firmly rooted in a differential evaluation of masculine sexuality. Thus it is central to psychoanalytical thought that the penis is to be envied and the female must recognise her genital inferiority. The alternative that the male might recognise the superiority of the womb and the subordinate function of the penis escapes mention, but it is equally rational if even not more realistic. One might expect psychoanalysts to have more than usual difficulty in explaining transsexualism and transvestism in which womb-envy and the inferiority of the penis might appear obvious. Of course, the unilaterality of psychoanalysis is without adequate factual justification.

Let us attempt to clarify the picture. It seems that from conception the boy child is endowed with an undisputable biological sex. He is conceived as male and in all probability will be born with the bodily characteristics of a male and at maturity he will take a male role in the sexual procreative act. From the birth of consciousness he will learn to feel a sense of masculinity which appears to be radically different from the sense of femininity held by the girl. In this sense he will develop as he grows the personal habits of play, posture, speech, dress, and so on, which are more or less appropriate to a man. If he doesn't he will be called a "sissy" and, if possible, licked into shape by parents and society. He will later learn the social behaviour expected of a person of his biological sex, how to make his presence felt with others, the way in which a man behaves in social groups and so on.

At one extreme one can argue that this pattern of development is irrevocably determined from conception. If conceived male then the distinct pattern of male personal and social behaviour must develop. At the other extreme it can be argued that beyond the sex at birth the pattern of sex-linked behaviour is entirely learnt and independent of the biological sex. As always the answer must lie between and, as Freud indicated, physical and mental sex are likely to be somewhat independent.

The most cogent argument for independence comes from the

work of John Money and the Hampsons (1957) on hermaphrodite children and from that of Robert Stoller (1968). Stoller, a psychoanalyst, has been primarily concerned with clinical case studies and usually in the field of transsexualism and allied problems. Hermaphrodites, as studied by Money and the Hampsons, are very rare conditions in which physical sex is in doubt at birth. For example, adrenogenital syndrome is a condition where the adrenals secrete abnormal amounts of androgens (male hormones) so as to produce masculinisation. Not only does the female acquire a deepened voice, but external sex organs which appear to be small male organs. Turner's and Klinefelter's syndromes are inter-sex states resulting from abnormalities in the chromosome complement of the body cells.

Not infrequently it is difficult to determine definitely the sex of the hermaphrodite child at birth. Even then the parents of the child might themselves be unconvinced by medical advice. So that a child might well be reared in the opposite-sex pattern. Of course, with time, the true biological sex may become clearer and efforts made to change the "sex" of the child. In studying such problems the first difficulty lay, perhaps surprisingly, in designating "true biological sex" since even the physical correlates of sex are not always in harmony. In Money's work the following indicators of biological sex were considered:

1. Appearance of genitalia — the presence of a recognisable penis, etc.
2. Presence of internal reproductive structures — in particular the existence of the uterus.
3. Hormones and secondary sexual characteristics — in particular features like breasts and hair distribution.
4. Gonads — presence of ovaries, testes.
5. Chromosomes — types of chromosome structure can be identified typical of male, female or inter-sex states.

It is characteristic of the usually unexpected complexity of the subject that any of these factors may indicate a sex identity different to the remainder. Money studied groups of hermaphrodites where there was conflict between one of these factors and the sex in which the child was reared. He attempted to ascertain whether the patient accepted the sex role in which he was reared or the role of the discrepant biological sex indicator. The results are summarised in Table 9.

TABLE 9. *Summary of Money's findings concerning discrepancies between rearing pattern, biological sex, and accepted role*

Factor discrepant with rearing pattern	No. of cases	No. accepting role in accord with rearing
Genetalia	25	23
Hormones	27	23
Internal organs	25	22
Gonads	20	17
Chromosomes	20	20

Money had, therefore, made 131 comparisons and only thirteen had led to the finding that the patient did not accept the sex role assigned, albeit in conflict with the biological factor. It should be noted that although there were 131 factors discrepant with the rearing role some of these occurred in the same patient, only 113 of whom were involved.

However, the suggestion seems much in favour of an overriding rearing factor in the acquisition of a sense of masculinity or femininity. Unfortunately, it is a far cry from the study of extremely rare conditions, especially where many cases are also mentally sub-normal, to general theory of the learning of sex-linked roles. It is far from a simple matter to determine whether or not one role or the other is accepted. No more simple, one would think, than determining what role the transvestite accepts.

More tenuous are the further observations of Money (1955a) on the effects of changing rearing pattern from male to female. This occurred where as the child grew older the true biological sex became more clear and opposed to the originally ascribed sex. The parents might then endeavour to change the child's upbringing from, say, boy to girl. Money found that up to about 3 years of age this was not difficult and the child could adopt the new sex assignment and grow up accordingly.

Suppose, for instance, that a hermaphrodite girl was wrongly believed to be male at birth and reared as a boy. If at, say, 18 months the error became clear the parents could change the rearing style and treat her as a girl. In these circumstances the child might accept she was a girl and not a boy and grow up feeling herself to be feminine and a woman. If, however, the change in rearing style was delayed until after about 3 years of age the child would not accept the new role. She would retain the feeling that she was a boy, that she was masculine, although she might accept the conventions of dress and manners appropriate to her new status as a girl. It would be tempting to take this as a transvestite or transsexual model, of course.

Thus it seems that there was indeed some independence of biological sex and a sense of being masculine or feminine. Simply being male or female did not dictate the acquisition of a sense of masculinity or femininity. It is this latter sense which Money and Stoller refer to as "gender core identity".

There seems to be very considerable difficulty in grasping the sex-gender division conceived by Money, the Hampsons, and by Stoller. For example, Kohlberg (1967), summarising Money's work, seems to completely misinterpret the point.

> A firm gender identity as "male" is possible even though the individual neither thinks himself, nor is, "masculine" by cultural standards. . . . When we meet a male at a party we categorise him as male regardless of the masculinity or femininity of his behaviour and appearance and so, does he himself. We take this fact of "gender identity" for granted in adults.

> The Money and Hampson data suggest to us (that) Gender Identity, i.e. cognitive self-categorisation as "boy" or "girl", is the critical and basic organiser of sex role attitude.

One is bound to feel that Kohlberg's assumptions about categorisation of maleness and masculinity are confused, but his reinterpretation of Money's work is quite out of step with the original. Money clearly recognises Gender Identity as a matter of sense of masculinity or femininity and not unawareness of being biologically male or female.

A number of writers choose not to adopt Money's differentiation between sex and gender. Purely etymologically there is no reason why they should, but that is not the question. The crucial point is to what extent we regard sex defined as a physical, biological phenomenon fixed at birth, as defining and determining gender which is a more global and partially culturally determined thing. In this sense we only categorise a man at a party as male if we assume he possesses a penis or has no breasts and so on. It is, however, more likely that we would be preoccupied by his masculinity which as Kohlberg implies is not highly related to his sex. Indeed, the man himself knows whether he is physically male or female and it is in no sense a problem area, unless he suffers from a biological intersex defect. What is an important area as a source of associated anxieties and interpersonal difficulties is his masculinity. To push gender in this sense aside or infer that it is simply organised by biological sex is unhelpful and misleading especially in the consideration of areas like transsexualism, transvestism, or homosexuality.

Bancroft (1972) describes an interesting three-factor model illustrating the interrelationship between sex and gender (Fig. 7). He sees the three factors of sexual object choice, method of relating, and gender identity as functioning in a homeostatic relationship. Each factor is associated with intellectual, emotional, and behavioural components, or the ways the individual thinks, feels or behaves. The whole system operates to achieve and maintain an equilibrium and possibly to oppose external constraints disturbing its stability.

Clearly the system is in an unstable state in transvestism, if only because of the bi-polarity of gender mentioned in Chapter 2. The sexual object is heterosexual, the means of relating to the object choice is heterosexual but there is a division in gender identity, one component of which is in conflict with the

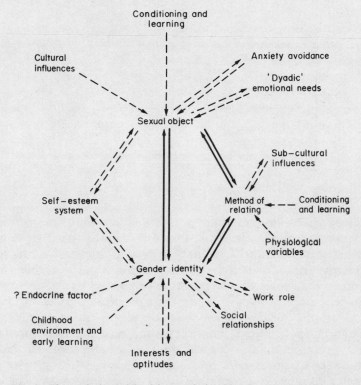

Fig. 7. Theoretical model of inter-relationship between sexual object choice, method of relating to object or partner, and gender identity.

sexual object and means of relating. It is quite possible, as Bancroft suggests, that the resolution of the disequilibrium is a move to a transsexual pattern. Alternatively it may be a divided system in which the feminine gender identity is maintained in stability with fantasy sexual objects and methods of relating. That is the male heterosexual with parallel feminine gender identity, relating in fantasy with a male sexual object. The fantasy component could well not be at a consciously sexual level of course.

It is Money's view that gender core identity becomes irrevocably fixed within the first 3 years of life, see Fig. 8. Following

Gender Role Learning Model

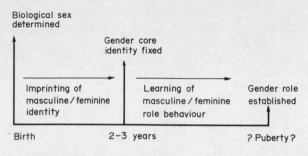

Fig. 8.

this point further learning of sex-linked behaviour is devoted to learning of gender role. This does not involve the deep conviction of the individual's identity as psychologically a man or a woman, but consists of learning more superficial behaviour patterns. One feels that the picture ought to be completed with a stage of learning of gender relationships, that is the inter-personal and social skills appropriate to gender. These appear to become fixed perhaps in adolescence and become important in the consideration of transsexualism and homosexuality.

Because of the resistance to modification of the gender core identity Money proposed that its acquisition was by a process of imprinting and that the first 3 years was a so-called critical period. Imprinting is a form of learning readily observed in the animal kingdom first described by Konrad Lorenz. For example, Lorenz found that if when goslings were hatched he and not the mother goose was sitting by the nest the goslings would regard him as the mother. They would subsequently reject the true mother. Indeed, the behaviour of the goslings was quite complex and not apparently learned in any simple way by association or conditioning. They even showed a tendency to maintain their distance from Lorenz such that the top of his head subtended a constant angle to the horizon. That is, if he stood up the goslings would stay at a greater distance than if he sat down. Moreover, simply established though this learned pattern was it seemed almost impossible to break it down and reinstate the goose as mother.

The similarity here is superficially obvious, that the child becomes imprinted on the parent by whose side he or she is reared and as in the imprinting process this is very hard to revoke.

The critical-period hypothesis is that imprinting and some other forms of learning occur most efficiently at specific periods in life. Thus, imprinting on the mother does not occur in the gosling after the first few days of life. Apart from learning by imprinting, skills such as reading seemed to be acquired most quickly in childhood. The acquisition of literacy in adolescence and adulthood seems far more difficult and laborious a process than it is for the child. That is, the critical period for literacy is past.

Convenient though such a learning paradigm might appear it has grave objections. Imprinting as seen in animals has not been found in humans whose learning processes seem much more complex. Then again there is no way in which one can explain how the male child should become imprinted on father so frequently when, male or female, the human children spend almost all their time with the mother in the early years of life. Similarly, it is hard to verify the critical-period hypothesis particularly in the absence of much more data than can be obtained from the relatively small number of hermaphrodite children who have been subject to an attempt to change their gender. The more parsimonious hypothesis that the longer the child is reared in one gender pattern the harder it is to alter, appears sufficient and a limit appears to be about the first 3 years of life. There are other objections to conceiving gender learning as simple imprinting which are bound up with the explanation of transvestism, transsexualism, and homosexuality.

These three states can be regarded as "gender dysphorias", in the sense that they manifest some degree of rejection of the more common gender roles associated with their biological sex.

According to Money (1970) homosexuality can be explained

in terms of a failure to learn a "negative valence" for opposite-gender identity. That is, the male homosexual fails to learn a strong enough rejection of a female role. Thus he is free to adopt a female role in sexual relations. Such an explanation is quite deficient. It does not explain the homosexual's rejection of the more usual gender role, nor does it go any further than attempting to explain homosexual copulation. It is quite inadequate to define homosexuality only in terms of copulatory patterns. It is a very limited understanding of homosexuality which is restricted to sexual activity only. Homosexuality has to do with the whole gamut of emotions, intellect, personal and social behaviour as well as sexual preferences. Equally, Money is preoccupied with the sexual ambitions of the transsexual. He argues that as the transsexual has learned a poor negative valence for the opposite sex and is thus able to take on a full female role; he is, as it were, the ultimate homosexual. One might be forgiven for saying this is phenomenology gone mad. One cannot disregard the subjective evaluations of gender roles in this way. As Bancroft (1972) points out, "as far as gender identity is concerned, it is how the individual sees himself rather than how others see him that is most important". Neither does this viewpoint permit any explanation of the active role in homosexual acts, nor does it explain why the homosexual seeks sexual relations with other homosexuals rather than heterosexuals of the same sex. In this context one has to bear in mind the evidence that homosexuals do not consistently adopt passive or active roles, but change the role according to circumstances. Hooker (1965) found that 80% of a group of male homosexuals she studied would take either role. Money's hypothesis certainly does not explain why the homosexual perceives his relationship as essentially neither masculine nor feminine. As put by Bancroft (1972), "the homosexual, if he is to achieve stability, usually needs to produce a special type of gender identity — 'I am a homosexual' ". On the other hand, the transsexual sees a wholly heterosexual relationship as a "biological" woman with a heterosexual man and would usually resist sexual relationships with a homosexual male.

However, the major obstacle is the concept of the negative valence. Whilst it is doubtful if imprinting occurs in humans there is certainly no evidence of imprinting a negative or imprinting behaviour to be avoided. It seems rather like arguing that Lorenz's goslings learned not to follow the goose they did not see. Additionally, Money's argument that failure in the male to learn to reject a female role allows him to adopt that role seems to make a nonsense of the gender-role learning theory as a whole. It would seem to infer that any innate capacity for both masculine and feminine gender identities and gender roles becomes limited to single gender preferences by learning to reject the gender associated with the opposite sex. This seems very unlikely and very difficult to explain by imprinting.

It seems that the imprinting and critical-period hypotheses have confused the gender learning theory. There is no reason why gender learning should not be simple associative learning which involves both reinforcement of gender identity and role-taking congruent with sex and some elements of punishment of incongruent behaviour. In some cases the learning process goes awry as where the child finds the congruent role punished. How does the boy acquire the congruent gender role and "grow up big and strong like daddy" when daddy is an alcoholic psychopath who treats him with unreasonable cruelty? Especially what happens to gender if mother is equally fearful of daddy and is the provider of all happiness, comfort, and security? Needless to say, as pointed out previously, there is no simple consistent pattern of the boy fearing father and loving mother to account for the gender dysphoria of the transvestite. This model is infinitely idealised. Not only does the child learn from models other than mother and father, it seems unlikely that gender models are just individuals. The child manifestly is not just an imprinted copy of father or mother in terms of gender. To the extent to which gender is learnt it is learnt from the gender behaviour of father and mother as they both exhibit masculine and feminine behaviour patterns. It is learnt from toys, television, uncles, aunts, teachers and a thousand and one other sources all including some combination of behaviours congruent with both sexes. In other words, a gender role and identity is not a black and white, male or female matter, it is some balance of self-concept and behavioural patterns which align the individual with male or female groups. Freud (1933) was fully aware that the gender model was not just a person, but a complex role occupied by many persons. He described the first love object as the mother's figure "together with figures of nurses and other attendants that merge into hers". Amongst those providing the maternal model Freud would thus, in modern society especially, see some aspect of the father too.

It is not at all surprising that some people live in an intermediate area or even that the gender needs of some are opposed to their biological sex. Learning to accept or reject sex-linked roles is likely to produce a considerable array of different gender patterns. Figure 9 shows a possible outline of the origins

Deviations in Gender Valuation in Identity and Role Learning

	Gender identity		Gender role	
Feminine	Homosexual	—	Homosexual	—
	Transsexualist	+	Transsexualist	+
	Transvestite	(normal)	Transvestite	+
Masculine	Homosexual	—	Homosexual	—
	Transsexualist	—	Transsexualist	—
	Transvestite	(normal)	Transvestite	+

Developmental stage

Fig. 9.

of gender patterns of homosexuals, transsexuals, and transvestites. A system of this kind is no more than a speculative model based on very weak research evidence. However, suggestions about how such phenomena might be inter-related in terms of learned patterns of behaviour are scarce. The figure suggests that the homosexual derives an excess of negative valances towards both genders which leaves him in a state of non-committed gender identity and role. Thus he does not perceive himself as masculine or fully feminine, but only in the qualified way, e.g. homosexual masculine. The transsexual has strong over-evaluation of femininity or positive values for femininity from an early age. He also has a negative valence or rejection of masculinity and thus grows up with a committed gender identity or a sense of being really feminine or psychologically a woman. His gender role is equally feminine and his negative valences to the male role produce the feelings of hate and distaste for masculine patterns of behaviour. The transvestite might be seen as a phenomenon of unusual learning patterns related only to the gender-role period and after. Thus he learns normal sex–congruent gender identity and the sense of being masculine, but an over-evaluation of gender roles both masculine and feminine. Such a learning pattern might well explain what has already been noted (Chapter 2) as some bipolarity of gender role taking in transvestites. In the male role they tend to be both successful and strongly masculine and in the female role seek to be hyperfeminine.

This gender-learning model is sometimes wrongly conceived thus suggesting that biological sex and gender are quite independent, indeed Moncy's early papers gave this impression, although it seems unlikely that this was intentional. Of course, there is a strong and direct line of influence from the hard fact of having a clear biological sex to acquiring the gender pattern prescribed by society. The question is how far this is determined purely by inheritance and biological events rather than learned.

In many ways to the transvestite, transsexual, and homosexual a biological explanation seems more acceptable than a psychological one and to the scientist it appears more capable of convincing proof and a more persuasive concept. There is a variety of biological argument. Even in the last 20 years or so techniques in investigating cell structure have developed to the point that some find optimism about biological explanations. In the gender dysphorias this is centred on the discoveries of what might be regarded as chromosome errors.

In 1949 Barr and Bertram distinguished normal male and

female cells by the presence of what became known as a Barr body in the nucleus of the female cell. It then was found that Barr bodies also appeared in the body cells of some apparently male subjects such as the cases of Klinefelter's syndrome.

In the normal nucleus there are twenty-three pairs of chromosomes, one pair apparently determining the sex of the individual. In the male this pair includes a chromosome type X and a chromosome type Y. The latter type Y chromosome is absent in the normal female, the sex complex being XX. It was once believed that the number of X chromosomes determined the femaleness of the embryo, since only one was present in the male and two in the female. The Y chromosome seemed effectively inert. However, the chromosome studies of subjects with abnormal chromosome patterns shows it is the Y chromosome which dictates maleness. The Y chromosome is regarded as dominant over the presence of the X chromosome producing a normal male, but only incompletely dominant in, say, an XXY complex. In these cases the sex is male in that the individual possesses a small penis and testicles, but is sterile. He may develop small breasts and the pubertal growth of body hair is weak. Most cases of the male Klinefelter's syndrome show an extra X chromosome in this way, i.e. have an abnormal sex chromosome complex XXY.

It is reported that some cases of Klinefelter's syndrome are transvestite, but other sex-related problems occur, such as homosexuality and fetishism. The body build tends to be unusual, frequently such men are tall with a rather slight frame but acquire a rather flabby figure in adult life. The diagnosis of Klinefelter's syndrome is not solely based on the chromosome abnormality and cases with XXXY and XXYY chromosome complexes are also found for example. Turner's syndrome is associated with the absence in the female of a second X chromosome, hence it has been called the X_0 variant and the cells do not show a Barr body. There are also XX cases with Barr bodies where an abnormality of one X chromosome is detectable and there are more complex patterns with "Turner-like" features. If sex was entirely determined by this chromosome complex one supposes the X_0 variant might equally be regarded as the absence of a Y chromosome in the male. However, as there is no Y chromosome the subject possesses female genitalia, but does not develop secondary sexual features — breasts, secondary hair, and so on. She tends to be physically stunted, but in childhood plays as a girl, develops maternal fantasies and matures as a female, if sterile. Here the absence of homosexuality and any malelike features is noted.

XYY chromosome complexes are found in about one in 350 males and at present seem to be much the most common chromosome error. XYY males, as yet, seem unexceptional although relatively high numbers appear to have been found amongst criminals, leading to the hypothesis that the extra Y male chromosome might be associated with criminality and some types of violence. However, this is speculation based on a detailed examination of criminals without adequate control studies of normal populations.

Rather like the XYY case the female XXX (triple X syndrome or super-female) is, as yet, unremarkable. She is physically and psychologically normal, but with perhaps some cases of mental retardation.

Armstrong and Marshall (1964) have described cases of "true hermaphrodism" in which both ovaries and testes appear. Usually, they are genetic XX females. The case described by Armstrong in 1955 lived as a female, but was masculine in appearance with a male hair distribution and masculinised genitalia and no breasts. There are many other variants of an intersexed type, but their etiology is unclear and their consideration does not contribute to the present argument. Mention might be made, however, of conditions like hypospadias in which the urethral orifice is located as in the female in an otherwise normal male.

In their relevance to transvestism the difficulties about such studies is that they tend to begin with the investigation of abnormal populations, e.g. the lack of pubertal development of Klinefelter's syndrome, violent crime or for that matter transvestism itself. The finding of chromosome errors in such groups is always interesting, but in the absence of equivalent studies of normal populations it is not possible to conclude that gender dysphorias are necessarily derived from chromosome errors. Some chromosome errors such as the triple X syndrome seem not to be of very great importance. In any event it is a far cry from a condition such as transvestism to the presence of a chromosome error on grounds such as an increased frequency of transvestism in Klinefelter's cases, even if this was true. Other sex and gender abnormalities also appear in this syndrome and this should not be surprising in sterile males with unusual body build.

Where, however, the research is centred not on the chromosomal abnormality but on the sex and gender problems of homosexuality, transvestism, and transsexualism one conclusion is quite clear. As yet, it has been impossible to implicate chromosomal abnormalities with the appearance of such states. There is no difference between transvestites, homosexuals, or other males in terms of the presence or absence of Barr bodies. There are no discrepancies in chromosome numbers despite the rare Klinefelter problems.

Inheritance is, of course, attributed to genes carried by the chromosomes and not to the chromosomes themselves. As yet, no techniques are available to make a physical study of gene structure in any way which might throw light on the acquisition of gender. Even if and when such methods become available the task will be one of incredible complexity and fallibility.

An examination of cell structure is only a part of the verification of genetic hypotheses. Indeed the more traditional methods of investigation of families produce more interesting data. Again because of the unavailability of samples of transvestites the argument has to rest heavily on the similarity of the homosexual problem. Many investigations have been carried out of homosexual twin pairs, the birth order of homosexuals amongst their sibs, and so on.

In the general population it is found that males have 106 brothers for each 100 sisters. Darke (1948) found homosexuals to have a brother/sister ratio like that of the general population.

Kallman (1952) found 125 brothers for each 100 sisters and in a survey of over 1000 homosexuals Lang (1940) found 121 brothers. Lang also examined the ratios within age groups and for homosexuals over 25 the ratio was 128:100.

This finding does not necessarily mean that there is some abnormality of inheritance pattern. It could just as easily be interpreted as showing that homosexuality might simply be more likely to occur in boys reared without the influence of sisters. Koch (1956) matched groups of 5- and 6-year-old boys and girls and assessed the extent to which the boys were sissyish and the girls tomboyish on the basis of a behaviour inventory. Boys with a slightly older sister tended to be more sissyish, but, regardless of the sex of an older sib, there was a complex relationship between sissyness and the age gap between the child and the sib. No similar relationships were found for tomboyishness of girls.

A suggestive finding of a similar kind was made by Slater (1958). He found that male exhibitionists had relatively too many female sibs — a ratio of 109 brothers to 144 sisters.

Martensen-Larsen (1957) also found that homosexuals had more male sibs than males in the general population had. He analysed the sibling order of homosexuals showing that they came more frequently than expected from the younger third of the family. Slater (1958, 1962) found a similar pattern with homosexuals tending to be born later than their siblings and to be children of older mothers. In Martensen-Larsen's work the families not only of the homosexuals themselves, but also of the parents showed abnormal sex ratios of siblings. There was a preponderance of brothers in the families of both fathers and grandfathers, but on the other hand the mothers and grandmothers had a preponderance of sisters. Lesbians in contrast showed a preponderance of sisters amongst their sibs and came from upper or lower thirds of the sibships rather than from the middle third.

Of course, again such data are ambiguous. The effects may well be those of inheritance or the rearing environment. It could well be said that the homosexual coming from a male-loaded family is more likely to be estranged from and socially inadequate with the opposite sex but such explanations seem facile. Certainly it appears that problems of the gender dysphoria type appear in families where the pattern of sib relationships is different to a small degree from the general population.

Twin studies are more persuasive as evidence of inheritance. Kallman (1952) indeed found virtually 100% concordance for homosexuality in like twins. That is, if one twin was homosexual, the other was almost certain to be. By comparison only 42% of the brothers of homosexuals in unlike twin pairs were homosexual in any sense. Of these 42% only 11.5% showed strong enough homosexual inclinations to be rated exclusively homosexual for 3 or more years between 16 and 35 years of age. In the general male population Kinsey's results would lead us to expect very similar percentages of homosexuality to those shown by the unlike twin brothers of homosexuals.

Clear cut as Kallman's study appears to be there are a number of serious deficiencies in the evidence. Most particularly like twins tend to be reared according to a special rearing pattern. Parents make something of a ritual of presenting them with similar toys, dressing them alike and attributing similar characteristics to them. Unlike twins tend to be treated more as normal brothers without the same parental preoccupation with their similarity. For this reason alone one has to question whether the different concordance rates arise from hereditary factors or the rearing pattern. One could only examine this by observing twins reared apart from birth but these cases are very rare. One published case (Davison *et al.*, 1971) shows a pair of like twins one of whom is heterosexual and one homosexual. These twins were reared separately in the first month or so of life and subsequently treated rather differently because the mother regarded the homosexual twin as "rather sickly". There are also the unusual problems of ascertaining and defining homosexuality. Kallman's American study of 1952 necessarily involved many subjects convicted of homosexual offences and something can be gathered about his case material from the fact that he found the investigation rather distasteful.

Kallman's evidence is frequently overstated without regard to his own cautionary introduction:

> We are ready to concede at this point that an investigation of the sexual habits and self-protective devices of an ostracised class of people and their family relations is not a promising field of exploration for research workers who are in any way concerned about their conventional peace of mind. Psychiatrically it has been interesting to confirm, however, that the problems and attitudes of a sexually aberrant group look less wholesome in the twilight of gloomy hiding places than they do from the perspective of an ornamental desk or a comfortable therapeutic couch.

One must not only consider the limitations of the evidence which Kallman recognises, but also the implication that such an "unwholesome" sample would be barely likely to be representative. Kallman has also been criticised in general for too great a dedication towards the demonstration of the effects of genetic factors rather than unbiased dedication to genetic hypotheses but that fault largely lies with his interpreters.

An even more crucial problem in twin studies is the difficulty of determining whether they are monozygotic (like) or dizygotic (unlike). For example, in a number of studies involving genetic disorders like mongolism or Turner's syndrome it has been found that twins who were identical by all the usual criteria, like blood type and fingerprints, had chromosomal differences. It appears that as time goes by we constantly find more ways in which twins thought to be identical prove to differ. It is quite reasonable to feel now that twins cannot confidently be regarded as fully identical in genetic studies until an adequate technique of gene study is found.

So then, genetic and inheritance studies of transvestism and allied gender problems hint, perhaps strongly, at some features by which these groups might differ from other males. It is easier to believe perhaps that these are differences based on inheritance and not on rearing, but the evidence is a long way from watertight.

The concept that the Y chromosome is the active determinant of maleness carries with it an important implication. Despite the teaching of the book of Genesis that God first created man, there is every indication that man was created from woman. That is, the basic sex is more correctly regarded as female. As the human embryo develops both sexes show rudimentary sex organs which are identical. If a male child is to ensue some additional factor must be involved, otherwise a female child will result. If the foetus is castrated in the uterus at this early stage it will, whether male or female in genetic terms, become a child with female external sex organs. This effect has been produced in animals surgically and also by the use of hormones antagonistic to the production of male hormones known as anti-androgens. When an anti-androgen such as cyproterone acetate is injected into a pregnant mother and is passed to the foetus the cells of the foetus become insensitive to the hormone androgen. The result is that the cells in the male foetus, which depend on their sensitivity to androgen to develop masculine structures, function only as if they were female cells, so that the genetic male will be born with the external appearance of a female. There would be a relatively normal vagina, but no uterus or fallopian tubes. The development of the internal organs is not dependent on the presence of androgen. At puberty such an offspring would have active testes which would produce some masculinisation. This could be controlled by administering anti-androgen and oestrogens (female hormones). Under these circumstances the genetic but feminised male would behave as a female.

Experiments of this sort are, of course, carried out on rats but a human analogue is found in the testicular feminisation or androgen insensitivity syndrome. This condition is hereditary and it is not known what the source of this androgen insensitivity is. The child appears a normal female at birth but at adolescence either lumps in the groin which are, in fact, the unexpected sterile testicles or the failure of the "girl" to menstruate brings the cases to light. The vagina may need some surgical attention to permit intercourse. The body cells remain insensitive to androgen at puberty and as the testes in the male also produce oestrogens the overall effect is feminising. The "girls" are often tall with strongly feminine appearance and their psychosexual orientation is emphatically female with strong maternal feelings. As Money (1970) points out the androgen insensitivity syndrome presents a peculiar conundrum for the moral theorists. Such cases frequently marry as women and have sexual relationships although they cannot bear children as they are genetically male. What then is the nature of the relationship, homosexual or heterosexual? There is also a legal problem as in transsexual marriages (such as in the case of April Ashley). A marriage between two males does not constitute a legal marriage in English law. It would seem that in marriage for the androgen insensitivity-syndrome case the sex of the individual is a matter only of the external sex organs and the wish to use the existing organs in the normal heterosexual manner. In the transsexual this manner of defining the sex of the individual does not seem acceptable, perhaps because the organs have been artificially created by surgery. The dividing line is both thin and rather perverse, however.

To some degree the adrenogenital syndrome is the female counterpart of the androgen insensitivity syndrome.

If the pregnant female is injected with male sex hormones a masculinised genetically female offspring may be born.

The effect occurs in humans in congenital adrenal hyperplasia and the adreno-genital syndrome. Here the genetic female's adrenal cortex functions abnormally causing secretion of an excess of male hormones. The former condition seems to be inherited. The result is that the foetus develops a penis, but the gonads are female ovaries and testicles are absent. The uterus has no external orifice but opens into the urethra, i.e. there is no vagina. A similar effect can be found in some female babies of mothers who have been treated with hormones to prevent miscarriage.

These babies tend to be regarded as boys from birth and

reared as boys. Minor surgery to prevent menstruation and the use of male hormones to enhance masculinity at puberty are used. The outcome is an individual with a male appearance and male psychosexual disposition.

Not only is there now evidence of the influence of hormones on the physical body structures, but also on the brain in animals. The hypothalamus is part of the brain structure which plays an important part in regulating the periodicity of sexual function in the female. The part played by hormones in the development of this hypothalamic mechanism is illustrated by the administration of radioactive androgen. Experiments on rats show that the androgen finds its way into the cells of the hypothalamus. In the female this will cause a masculinisation of the hypothalamus which will not then acquire the female pattern of a sexual cycle. Periodic ovulation will not occur. Other cortical effects are involved and the sexual behaviour of the female will be abnormal and disorganised. Similarly, a genetically male foetus castrated at an early stage in its development will give rise to an animal in which the pituitary gland can be shown to function in female cycles. When treated with hormones either male or female they exhibit female sexual responses.

In the case of the female the administration of androgens can be timed after the differentiation of the sex organs so that a physically normal female exhibiting male sexual behaviour is produced. However, this evidence is not directly applicable to humans as androgens do not so clearly disturb the hypothalamic mechanisms and the menstrual cycle. The hypothesis that hormone-induced brain changes might be the cause of gender dysphoria is tempting but pure speculation. Perhaps the best evidence comes from cases such as adrenogenital syndrome where the evidence of physical masculinisation is corrected soon after birth by surgery and the administration of hormones. Here the patient should not be directly materially influenced postnatally by the pre-natal physical or hormonal defects. Ehrhardt *et al.* (1967, 1968), however, examined such cases and reported that they are nevertheless rather tomboyish. Both in the eyes of mothers and playmates they tended to choose boys' sports and games. They preferred boys' toys rather than dolls and did not appear to rehearse motherhood or play as most girls do. Subsequently, they seem to choose to have careers and they prefer the functional styles of dress rather than feminine or pretty ones. This did not mean that they showed homosexual erotic interest, just that they were not much interested in the opposite sex. The nearest male analogue is the boy with an abnormal penis who may be "surgically corrected as a female". Those who are reared as males will request reassignment as females according to Money.

It could be that hormonal influence on the brain could account for such findings, but the evidence is very slim indeed. Whilst "surgical correction" might be carried out it will not completely obscure the birth abnormality. Continuing medical care alone places anxieties and stress on parents who are likely to communicate to the child their doubt that he or she will not achieve a normal adult sexual role. In this event it is not surprising that the corrected adreno-genital girl does not rehearse her fantasies of motherhood. One must also bear in mind that verbal reports tend to be uncertain in such investigations frequently reflecting the expectations of the observers rather than reality. Nevertheless, judgement has to be reserved on chromosomal genetic and hormonal factors as the crucial determinants of gender.

We have shown that there is no distinct pattern of environmental, physical, or psychological factors to explain the causation of gender problems in the transvestite. It may be that the genetic explanation is the most thoroughly pursued and certainly the standard of scientific endeavour is higher in some respects in the genetic studies than in those of post-natal learning of gender. Optimism for a genetic explanation of the problem of transvestism is always high. Kallman, Slater, and many workers expected studies of cell structure to resolve the etiology of homosexuality, but they certainly have not done so nor have they promised a great deal in the study of transvestism. Some consensus is reached, albeit an uncomfortable one, in the conclusion (cf. Diamond, 1965) that there may be a pre-natal disposition to incongruous gender; it may lie in cell structure or in the brain influenced by abnormal intra-uterine environment. It does not mean a gender role already determined completely at birth which will come about in some inevitable instinctive way, but rather an amenability to respond in an unusual fashion if the pattern of rearing and environmental pressures conspire in a particular way. It could also involve a third possibility that the intrauterine events modify the ˌpost-natal environment to some degree. For example, through anxious and irritable mothers in early life. Certainly the gender learning theory has much to commend it.

CHAPTER 4

The Learning of Gender

Even if theories of gender learning are based on somewhat unsatisfactory evidence there can be no doubt that learning plays
a material part in the formation of adult gender roles. This
must surely be so unless some complex genetic inheritance of
culture patterns is hypothesised, since much of what we regard
as the gender role varies widely from culture to culture.

Margaret Mead's (1950) studies of the New Guinea tribes,
the Arapesh, Mundugumor, and Tehambuli are the most clear
statements of culture differences in the gender roles of the
sexes. The Arapesh minimise the gender differences, no
temperamental differences between males and females are
recognised. No concept of the male as the dominant sexual initiator and the female as subordinate is found. Sexual intercourse, at least as regards reproduction, is regarded frankly as
work, not pleasure. Both parents are said "to bear a child",
not just the mother and men as well as women are commonly
felt to show the ravages of having children. The men indeed go
to bed while the child is born. In the Mundugumor Mead found
that both sexes behaved rather like the males of Western civilisation. Both were assertive, hostile, and independent and had
similar personalities. Both detested the whole business of pregnancy and child-rearing. The Tehambuli, on the other hand,
differentiated the gender roles quite sharply, but in quite the
reverse way to Western civilisation. Women were assertive and
practical whilst the men were gossips, prone to show their
feelings and be weak and isolated. The men wore ornaments,
did the shopping, and danced while the women shaved their

heads and did not adorn themselves. The boys were teased, pampered, and neglected whilst the girls were more alert and enterprising.

Henry's (1964) observation on the life of a tribe in the highlands of Brazil records the equal sexual aggressiveness of the men and women. The term used for intercourse may have either a masculine or a feminine object, a fact which might be compared with vulgar English which only admits a female object. Amongst the Zuni Indians it is the male not the woman who affects anxiety about the wedding night. Davenport (1965) writes of a Pacific people where the men dress decoratively with flowers in their hair and they are chaperoned lest they are seduced by the women.

Socially, human societies tend to allocate activities unequally to the sexes. Barry *et al.* (1957) surveys reports on 110 different cultures. Eighty-two per cent of the cultures press girls into nurturant roles and 87% press boys into achievement roles. Murdock (1937) surveys no fewer than 224 societies for some forty-six activities. He reports, for instance, lumbering as exclusively a female activity in six and cooking as exclusively masculine in five. In many societies where women take on roles involving heavy work as in agriculture even child birth barely interferes; the Bamenda women (Kaberry, 1932) work on the farm with only about 3 weeks' rest at the time of childbirth. Alor women take about 10 days and Yahgan women take something between 15 minutes and a day. The Tubatulabel women and the Japanese Iainu women as well as the women of a Saharan tribe believe that hard physical work is an essential during pregnancy.

In many societies including the Eskimo and the Mbuti pygmies, the woman is regarded as the fighter. The women of Dahomey were recruited by their king into the army in large numbers. In 1845 they were described as fighting with knives and muskets just as the men did. In more recent times women have fought on equal terms with men in resistance forces.

At the same time there are many examples of cross-gender roles rather like the transvestite and transsexual roles or possibly homosexual ones. Among the Konaig people some males were regarded as women and when they were of age were said to be endowed with magic powers, becoming wives to important members of their community. The Shamans of the Chukchee in Siberia lived as women and married. They sometimes had heterosexual relations and they were socially respected. The Lango and Tanala had males called sarombavy who lived as women, but this group had apparently homosexual relationships, Linton (1936) interpreting this phenomenon as a refuge for impotent men.

"Berdache" is perhaps the best known transvestite behaviour described by the anthropologists. Seward (1946) describes "berdache" as a state voluntarily accepted by the plains Indians. The berdaches continued to support themselves by hunting, but they were quite often able to excel the women in their own activities. They appeared to be heterosexual though they did not often have heterosexual marriages. Some had homosexual marriages. Socially, the berdache was accepted at least more readily than the unsuccessful warriors of the tribe. In the homosexual marriages the mild disapproval was directed against the "husband", but this was largely because he was felt to be unduly concerned about having someone to support him and look after his house.

The Blackfoot Indians of North America had women who adopted male roles, although the culture was quite male dominated. They indulged in male activities and were sexually aggressive. They dominated their husbands and their sexual attitudes were unconventional in the Blackfoot culture.

The Mohave Indians allowed members of the tribe of prominent families, both men and women, to adopt a permanent gender reversal. The males, termed *alyha*, lived wholly as women and took male husbands. They assumed a female role in sexual relations. They would fake menstruation by cutting their thighs and fake pregnancies by padding themselves with rags and going through all the rituals of giving birth to stillborn infants. The women transvestites, *hwame*, lived as men and married as men. If a wife became pregnant they claimed fatherhood. They joined in male company and boasted of the sexual qualities of their wives. Devereaux (1937) reports that unlike the true men they were industrious and for this reason some women preferred them as husbands.

Female transvestism, but not male, is reported by Laubscher (1937) amongst the Bantu who ascribed the phenomenon to witchcraft. The Iatmul of New Guinea seemed to have a periodic transvestite ritual where women dressed as men in great grandeur whilst the men dressed as women in the worst available female clothes. Both paraded, the men to the derision of their fellows. Bateson (1936) reports that the outcome for both is a sense of relaxation and tension release reminiscent of the reports of transvestites in Western culture.

Even within Western civilisation countries differ in a way which is readily detectable in their rearing patterns as applied to children of both sexes. Devereux *et al.* (1963) gave a group questionnaire to matched groups of American and German boys and girls. They showed that German fathers were more active in discipline and affection, but American mothers were more expressive of disapproval and pressure to achievement in their children. Boys in both countries were more often disciplined by a deprivation of privileges than girls and in the American sample attention from the same-sex parent was stronger than in Germany.

If then gender is dependent upon the culture and is learned it is interesting to look more closely at the processes of acquiring gender which must presumably conspire to teach incongruous gender to the transvestite.

There is no question that from the earliest moments of life gender differentiation begins. Male babies are placed in cots with blue blankets, females in cots with pink ones. Mothers, aunts, dads, and uncles coo at the child "Who is a lovely little girl?", "Who is a smart little chap?". The process is, of course, more complex than a series of conventions which follow the declaration of the child's sex. Johnson (1963) describes males as characteristically instrumental and expressive in their personalities whilst females have only expressive components.

Maternal behaviour with a boy is also found to differ from that with a girl. Moss (1970) showed that at 3 weeks mothers held male babies almost half an hour longer in each 8-hour period than girls. After 3 months the difference was still 14 minutes. To some extent this is a direct response to a difference in "irritability" between the sexes. Lipsitt and Levy (1959) showed that male and female children differ in their sensitivity to electric shock even in the first 4 days of life. Weller and Bell (1965) measured the skin conductance of new-born infants and again found boys and girls to differ. The 2½-year-old premature children examined by Wortis *et al.* (1964) showed that premature birth was more likely to result in deviant behaviour in boys than it was in girls. Even at the age of 12 Sontag (1947) showed, using psychophysiological measures, that girls were more reactive to stress, but relaxed more readily and recovered more quickly. Gatewood and Weiss (1930) showed that similar sex differences were found in white and negro infants up to 11 days old. Even in the animal kingdom Devore and Jay (1963) reported sex differences in baboons and langurs in early life, females being less active and more passive.

Male babies sleep less and they cry more. This behaviour has been attributed to the fact that birth can be more traumatic in the case of male babies. The explanation is not just as simple as this suggests since examining the behaviour of mothers shows that even when male and female babies are behaving in the same way the mother tends to stimulate the boy more. She tends to imitate the girl's noises and actions thus strongly reinforcing parts of the female child's behaviour within her own repertoire.

As the boy grows older mother begins just to tolerate rather than soothe him. She expects him to fight and assert himself and does not wish to impede this. "He has got to stand up for himself", she tells herself. She treats the boy as more autonomous, able to demand what he wants whilst the girl is much more an extension of herself, expected to share in the things she does and have emotions and needs in harmony with her own.

Hartley (1966) has drawn attention to the four processes of

gender differentiation in young children. The first is manipula-
tion. The mother dresses the girl in detail, spends large periods
of time on her hair and examines her at length, telling her how
pretty and feminine she is. The second process is canalisation.
The baby's play pattern is constricted into different channels
by the use of toys which the parents prescribe. As the child
accepts and plays with the toys the parents show pleasure and
join in the play. Of course the toys frequently represent objects
in later life which retain the early pleasurable quality of the
toys. These may be teas sets, motor cars, cuddly dolls, or build-
ing bricks. Thirdly, Hartley noted the use of sex-typed verbal
appellations. The child is repeatedly told he is a boy, that he
must grow up to be a big, strong man or to stand tall like his
Daddy, whilst the girl is told she is a pretty lady or a bonnie
wee lassie. The fourth category is that of activity exposure. The
parents expect the child to take part in activities of different
kinds according to its sex. Girls help to lay tables, to dust or
cook whilst the boys knock nails in wood, tidy the garden, or
clean the car. In this way it will be obvious that even at the age
of, say, 5 years the patterns imposed on the boy will be one of
activities external to the home and those of the girl internal to
the home. All this clearly goes on without the parents being
fully aware of what they are about. Even when they are conscious of discriminating they tend to see this as the simple
reaction to the child's interest and not something they are
themselves imposing on the child.

As the child grows older the parents become more conscious
of attempting to impose gender standards. Toys become increasingly sharply differentiated; a skipping rope or a child's tea set
for the girl; an "Action Man set" or a football for the boy.
Should the child choose inappropriate toys the parents will
react adversely. In many ways the child's role in play and the
toys he or she chooses are the clearest early indices of gender
differentiation. Hartup and Moore (1963) presented groups of
boys and girls between the ages of 3 and 8 years with attractive
toys of a type appropriate to the sex opposite to the child and
unattractive neutral toys. Both boys and girls tended to choose

the neutral toys and reject the opposite-sex toys, but the older the boy the stronger was the tendency to avoid the opposite-sex-type toy. A further interesting factor was that the presence of the researcher seemed to reinforce in boys the rejection of the inappropriate toy. Within this range age did not seem to alter the girls' preferences nor did they seem to be affected by the researcher's presence.

By the age of 4 children have a clear perception of their gender identity, seeing themselves in the fixed role of being either a boy or a girl. At this age children will be able to choose toys which society regards as appropriate to their sex. This being so, parents not only observe their children's play patterns, but feed him with what they see as appropriate toys, sometimes in the form of emotionally loaded rituals such as birthdays or visits from Father Christmas.

The boy's gender differentiation, especially at play, is more difficult than the girl's. To a small degree the girl simply needs to play with much of the real world at her fingertips at home. She can make cakes from real dough, but the boy can't shoot real bullets — he has to put up with shouting "Bang, bang". She can wash dolls' clothes in the sink, but he cannot paint the front door of the house. In addition, though, the girl is not subject to the constraints put on the boy. She can play football, saw wood, and play with an aeroplane and at worst she is laughingly called a tomboy. The boy who chooses to play with a pretty doll, tries to knit, or even avoid dirt is sternly told he is being a "sissy". He is instructed to go and play with other boys or subjected to ridicule. One such child, the son of a bank manager, was punished for his lack of masculinity by dressing him in his sister's clothing, standing him in a baby's cot, and ridiculing him for hours on end! He later came to attention as an adult transvestite. On the basis of interviews with 8- and 11-year-old boys, Hartley (1959) felt that rigid anti-women views seemed to be associated with a pressure not to be "sissies" even though the boys were expected to obey mother. Apart from the children who had developed a well-balanced and flexible role, some were over-striving with rigidity about their gender roles although not always showing hostility towards women. Others showed a tendency to give up the struggle towards masculine identification.

However, a large part of gender acquisition comes from the child's identification with his parents. The child seems to want to belong to the family group and most easily identifies with the parent of the same sex as himself. The origin of this might simply be in social learning, and society undoubtedly rewards this pattern of imitation and identification. On the other hand, the process may be cognitive and because the child knows he is a boy he elects to do what other boys do and the rewards this offers are, of course, gratifying to him. There is a third possibility presented by psychoanalysis which seems to relate gender learning to the development of sexual rather than gender consciousness. The fundamental hypotheses laid down by Freud are very complex, but in addition many analysts since Freud have adapted and varied his principles to such a point that it is barely possible to summarise the psychoanalytic viewpoint. Freud spoke of the process of identification in which "one ego becomes like another . . . as it were, takes it into itself". However, he contrasted this with "object choice" so that in identification the boy wants to be like his father, and when he makes him the object of his choice he wants to have and possess his father. In identification the ego becomes modified to be a model of his father, but not necessarily so when father is his object choice. In psychoanalytic terms the difference is less great than it might seem to the uninitiated because of the basic hypothesis that both may be sexually motivated processes. The ego is said by Freud to be strongly influenced by the sexual object. For example, if the object choice is lost the individual may compensate for the loss by identifying with the object and in effect incorporating it within the ego as in identification.

Freud describes the establishment of identification with parental function in which the oedipal complex is a vital stage.

The oedipal complex is essentially that situation occurring in approximately the 3- to 5-year range in which the boy loving his mother is in rivalry with his father. The source of his anxiety is seen to arise from the fear of castration. The boy recognises that in possessing a penis he is different to a girl and prizes his penis. He, therefore, fears father particularly as he may be castrated by him. Freud hypothesised that the oedipal situation was relevant to the girl also. The girl, like the boy, at first takes mother as her love object, but on her way to normal object choice she must take father as her love object. In other words, she has to pass from a masculine to a feminine role. Freud suggested that the basis of this was the strength of the girl's sexual attraction to the mother until she "falls victim to penis envy". She recognises that she does not have the penis the boy has and not only does she strongly desire one she believes it is mother who has castrated her. In her wish for a penis she turns to father, particularly since, as Freud asserts, an equivalence exists between having a penis and having a baby. That is, if father will not give her a penis she at least expects him to give her a baby. This desire places her in the oedipal situation as a rival with mother, a situation which tends to persist until later in life in the girl.

In resolving his oedipal conflicts the boy represses his love for mother and identifies with father. Out of the resolution of the male oedipal situation comes the severe super ego. Incidentally, the oedipal situation for the girl itself becomes a haven and does not necessarily demand resolution. Consequently, the super-ego formation suffers and thus the feminine character does not develop a culturally important super-ego strength and the independence of the male — according to Freud. Sears *et al.* (1957) indeed showed that amongst kindergarten children there were differences which could be seen as related to super-ego development. However, it was the girls who were found to have more highly developed consciences. In whatever way the oedipal complex is overcome it means the loss of a strong sexual bond with the parent. The loss of this "object-cathexis" means that there will be a compensatory incorporation into the ego and identification with the parents. The oedipal complex might not be fully resolved and hence the identification may be incomplete. Freud adds an important general point that one must remember that the child values parents differently at different periods in life. In early life they may be splendid figures, but in the general course of development they lose prestige. He suggests the development of the super ego is determined largely by identification with the early perception of parents as "splendid figures".

The most crucial problem for the psychoanalytic account of the development of masculine and feminine identities lies in its conflict with the evidence which is virtually irrefutable that gender identity is irreversibly fixed earlier in life than it is possible to date the oedipal situation in the psychoanalytic model. Rabban (1950), for instance, finds that boys and girls above the age of three are already differentiated in their preferences for being boys or girls or playing mother or father. However, it is probably true to say that gender-learning theory and psychoanalytic theory are really only partial insights into different aspects of the same problem. Money is simply speaking of the child's recognition of the fact that he is boy or girl becoming irreversible before the age of 3 years. The process of filling out the gender role details — effectively as unspecified in gender-learning theory as in psychoanalysis — goes on into adolescence at least and both orientations recognise this. The evidence, say, that the preference for same sex roles or opposite sex sexual relationships being irreversible at the age of three is certainly not sound. Indeed Ramsey (1943) has produced evidence that it is still very much in the balance at age 9. Freud recognised clearly some strong measure of identification at an early age which he seemed to regard as cognitive. He clearly sees in the girl a need to identify with the mother in playing with dolls and assuming a mother role in the pre-phallic phase which is quite different to the later sexual love of mother as an object choice in the oedipal situation.

Bancroft (1972) makes the point that as the evidence suggests that the gender identity factor is established long before the sexual object preference, the sex-object choice might be innately determined only through its homeostatic relationship with gender identity. Put in another way, once gender identity is formed in a way subject to innate factors, the subsequent sex object choice will be constrained by needs for equilibrium with the gender identity and the appropriate means of relating will be acquired.

Paul Kline (1972) has made a detailed review of objective studies of psychoanalytic theory. Looking at the evidence he marshals concerning the oedipal situation there seems to be a strong evidence of sex-related differences at this age of the type consistent with Freud's description of the oedipal situation. It is true that work like that of Conn (1940) has shown that less than half of 5-year-old children are aware of genital differences between boys and girls, but the questions posed by such investigations may be too black and white. It is quite possible that oedipal fears may be more cogent if based on some vague uncertainty about genitalia rather than clear-cut conscious differences. In any event many studies of pre-school children have shown quite intense interest in genitalia and that the genitals are a source of pleasurable sensation. It is likely that some element of sex differences in genitals is communicated between pre-school children in almost all cases whether or not it is a clear knowledge of the anatomical differences.

However, there is a multiplicity of extrapolations from basic psychoanalytic theory, e.g. hypothesising that the oedipal situation is of much earlier origin, but the evidence to support these lacks objectivity in the present state of knowledge. The strength of Freud's work seems to lie in the many valuable insights which appear to make sense in the context of new findings. Examples have already been given of Freud's differentiation between physical sex and mental sex and his recognition of the complexity of parental figures. It is also perhaps startling to note that he did not think it possible to explain problems like homosexuality solely in terms of physical sex and clearly he seems to foreshadow the sex/gender dichotomy elaborated by Money and Stoller.

Despite his heavy emphasis on infantile sexuality in the development of personality, Freud did not seem to place sexual differentiation at the beginning of the chain. As with the girl playing with her dolls identifying with mother at a cognitive level, differentiation at a sexual level appeared at a later stage in development. It is, of course, not easy to distinguish behaviour arising from sexual development and the process of identification. Pre-adolescents between 11 and 13 were showed by Erickson (1951) to differ in the use of space in play. Boys used height, motion and its arrest and channelisation, whilst girls were concerned with static confined spaces. The findings were attributed to psychosexual factors but seem equally attributable to simple same-sex identification. There is certainly ample evidence of identification at a cognitive level with parental figures. Gray and Klaus (1956) got American college adults to complete the Study of Values test for themselves and how they thought their mothers and fathers would. The actual parents also completed the tests. Children showed greater similarity to the like-sex parent both as tested and as perceived by the child. Women tended to be more like their mothers than sons were like their fathers. Of course, this is complicated by the important emotional values in the relationships. Meltzer (1943) concludes that for both boys and girls, mothers evoke more pleasant feelings than fathers but the predominant hostility amongst girls is towards mother and in boys towards father.

Caution must always be taken in preferring or dismissing the psychoanalytic model and perhaps the importance of psychoanalysis is like that of the Bible, not its absolute truth but its contribution to truth. We must also think of gender learning in terms of the child as a functioning part of the family. Many researchers have shown that the power structure within the family is highly important. Kagan and Lemkin (1960) observed that whilst children of both sexes choose the same sex parent as a model to emulate, girls in particular also wish to see father as the wiser and stronger parent. Both sexes tend to evaluate more highly the parent who manifests the greater influence and resource control. This is not at all surprising. One would not expect the child to align himself with the weakest sector of the family. Thus in a mother-dominant home boys will tend to form stronger bonds with mother than in father dominant homes. This is not solely a matter of punishment severity although this is a relevant factor. Gordon and Smith (1965) carried out an experiment with the doll play of nursery children and 6- to 7-year-olds. They found that maternal strictness was associated with aggression in girls but with non-aggression in sons. The effect of physical punishment was to increase the girl's aggression and reduce the boy's aggression. Again the perception of parental figures as disciplinarians differs with the sex of the child. Henry (1957) concludes that girls are more likely than boys to see mother as the family disciplinarian. However, father may be aggressive and even violent to mother and children, but if he does not have the control of family destinies the child will not form a close identification with him. On the other hand, he may be punitive to the level that the child fears his discipline and yet he will be the child's model if he also exercises control over the family.

In an important study Bandura *et al.* (1963) observed the imitative behaviour of children in simulated family situations where, for example, one parental figure acted as resource controller whilst the other was either ignored or a major rival for rewards. The Freudian oedipal situation would appear to be similar to the rivalry situation, with the child imitating or identifying with the rival, but the tendency to imitate the resource controller was much stronger. Boys showed a preference for the imitation of male-resource controllers but girls were ready to accept cross-sex roles. Bandura comments:

> Failure to develop sex appropriate behaviour has received considerable attention in the clinical literature and has customarily been assumed to be established and maintained by psychosexual threat and anxiety reducing mechanisms. Our findings strongly suggest, however, that external social learning variables, such as the distribution of rewarding power within a family constellation, may be highly influential in the formation of inverted sex-role behaviour.

It is only fair to point out, however, that the imitative

behaviour in Bandura's experiment was more a matter of whether the child chose, for instance, to say "licket-sticket" or "wetosmacko" rather than imitate behaviour socially identifiable as masculine or feminine. Bandura says that when

> children are exposed to multiple models they may select one or more as the primary source of behaviour but rarely reproduce all the elements of a single model's repertoire. . . . Children are not simply junior-size replicas of one or the other model — rather they exhibit a relatively novel pattern of behaviour representing an amalgam of elements from both models . . . within the same family even same sex siblings may exhibit quite different response patterns, owing to their having selected for imitation different elements of their parents' response repertoires.

According to Grinder and Judith (1965) boys are more likely to see father as controller and girls to see mother as controller, and according to Mussen and Rutherford (1963) highly masculine boys saw their fathers as more punitive and nurturant than less masculine boys. By recording discussions of child rearing Hetherington (1965) selected father-dominant and mother-dominant families. Children of these families in the 4- to 11-year range were tested for gender-role preference. Girls developed role preferences later than boys. Children were found to resemble the dominant parent particularly when mothers were dominant, and boys from mother-dominant homes were more feminine. Evidence in terms of permissiveness rather than control is found in Patterson *et al.* (1964) who found that whilst mothers were more successful in conditioning sons and fathers more effective with daughters, in permissive homes the same-sex parent was more effective than in highly disciplined homes.

Amongst the tokens of power material things are very strong. Father who "goes out to get pennies" is perceived as stronger than mother who actually spends the earnings. It has already been pointed out that children coming later in the birth order might have greater gender-identity problems. This could well be related to the fact that older children, especially when they contribute to the family income, confuse the power structure of the family.

We know that girls persist longer in identifying with father in Western culture than boys do with mother. However, the behaviour of parents is unequal as Ruth Tasch (1952) found in a study of the role of fathers in the family. Fathers tended to participate more in the daily care of girls and the motor development of boys. After about 6 years of age boys were much more involved in rough-and-tumble play with fathers than were girls. This greater ambiguity in the gender identity of girls again appears in evidence presented by Hall and Domhoff (1963) about the content of dreams. It was found that men dream more often about men than women do. Women dream equally often of men and women. In much of Western civilisation at the present time the structure of families seems to be altering considerably and it would be interesting if the age of the "working mum" changes the patterns of identification with parents. Some evidence already exists that female children of working mothers (Nye and Hoffman, 1963) differ from those of other families but not in a way which suggests stronger maternal identification. Again in families where the gender roles are much blurred by father's involvement in day-to-day chores there is as yet no evidence of problems in gender differentiation amongst children. Such a situation might appear to exist in the Israeli kibbutz and Rabin (1958) found that boys reared by kibbutz nurses had weaker father identification and oedipal conflicts of lower intensity. However, the results seem reducible to the simple statement that the less seen of the parents the weaker will be the emotional attachments.

In this sense one might see the identification process as a search for security and a flight from anxiety, the child finding the safest corner of the family. Just the same motivation may lie behind identification based on warm affectionate relationships. Of course, Bowlby has written a great deal about the importance of good emotional relationships with mothers but others including Andry have found strong evidence that

paternal emotional relationships are also relevant and important. Indeed Andry argues that for male delinquency they may
be more important. Andry (1957) paired remand-home recidi-
vists who did not come from broken homes with non-delinquents
of similar socio-economic status, age and I.Q. He found that
there was more evidence of paternal rejection than maternal
deprivation amongst delinquents and the children tended to
feel rejected by their father and not to identify with them.

The concept of "compensating masculinity" is also of some
importance in the study of delinquency. Certainly in delinquent
groups one can see evidence of aggressive and assertive
behaviour which seems to express an overwhelming need to
assume intensely masculine roles. The significance of this com-
pensation for gender anxieties or as part of the process of competition for a place in the hierarchy of the delinquent group
need not concern us more. However, it is a phenomenon which
illustrates the social importance of the gender role and in view
of Andry's findings might be predominantly related to unsatisfactory paternal relationships. Certainly the impression of
workers concerned with delinquents is that many unduly identify with mother rather than father. Parkes (1969), in a study
of approved-school absconding, found absconders saw their
fathers as authoritarian figures and felt rejected by them.
Hence unlike the non-absconders they had difficulty in identifying with housemasters functioning in *loco parentis*.

Cultures have elaborate mechanisms for disseminating stereotypes and perhaps nowhere can this be more easily observed
than in the story books for children. Nursery rhymes themselves
are relatively vicious propagators of particular genderal stereotypes.

> What are little girls made of?
> Sugar and spice and all that's nice,
> That's what little girls are made of.
> What are little boys made of?
> Snaps and snails and puppy dogs tails,
> That's what little boys are made of.

Elementary readers in schools are strongly biased towards specific gender patterns. "When Richard and Mr Sparks were out in the farm yard with the horses, Dora helped Mrs Sparks in the big farm kitchen" (*Royal Road Readers*). On the whole the activities of girls are more realistically described since they are largely a matter of play dictated by experience common to both boys and girls, of what mother does in the home. A reader describing play modelled on father's behaviour could be vague and meaningless since there is little common knowledge of what all fathers do at work, in the pub, or with their mates. We have a good idea what Dora and Mrs Sparks might be doing in the kitchen but can hardly imagine what Richard and Mr Sparks might be doing with a horse in the farm yard!

Hartley and Klein (1959) asked children and teachers to sort 133 typical adult activities. Children and adults sex typed roughly the same number of activities but boys disagreed with girls in sex-typing of domestic activities. The children of working mothers sex-typed fewer items and when asked what they would enjoy doing middle-class girls tended to reject activities for class reasons.

Patricia Sexton's (1970) book *The Feminised Male* deals with the educational problem of the demasculinising influence of education. Her thesis is rather that technology represents the quintessence of masculinity and the tradition of the woman teacher has an undesirable effect on the masculinity of male children, by adding an additional strong female model to the child's environment with no compensating male figures.

In school games there seems to be important gender differences between children in their response to the educational environment. For example, McClelland (1953) found that boys responded more than girls to simple academic competition. On the other hand, girls responded more than boys to social competition. In school games assumptions are made about the value of games as a training for life which, although probably invalid, emphasise aggression, gregariousness and physical violence in the male, and tenderness and passivity in the female. Tennis, gymnastics, and badminton for the girl; boxing, rugby, and soccer for the boys. The professed greater risks of injury to girls are largely mythological of course. Public schools foster military training for boys but rarely if ever for girls.

The educational assumption which is apparent is that boys are fundamentally more aggressive than girls. As a very broad generalisation this may be true but both boys and girls vary very widely in this respect. Levin and Sears (1956) observed aggression in play and compared this in interviews with parents. They found that boys who strongly identified with father were the most aggressive but girls who had severely punishing mothers were also characteristically aggressive. Hall (1964), in a psychoanalytic study, found that aggression was not a common content of men's dreams, they were more often concerned with simple misfortune. However, aggression was more frequently a factor in women's dreams but they were usually victims of the aggression. The difficulties which are experienced by non-aggressive boys in conflict with school régimes based on assumptions about the aggressiveness of males, are common themes in literature as well as real life. There is very little, in fact, to lead us to think that in this respect we are beginning to treat the non-aggressive boy more kindly.

The move into adult life brings with it even stronger pressure to conform to the gender stereotype. A study of college men's and women's day dreams led Lagrone (1963) to the conclusion that women had greater needs for affiliation in the context of marriage and family whilst men sought mostly new experience, and money and possessions were the most important daydream content.

Assumptions are made about chosen occupations. A girl would find little help from school if she wished to become a marine engineer. The time-table would not be organised to give her the appropriate "A" levels in the sixth form. Professional and trade-union pressures would make her career rather unpredictable and socially she would be regarded as odd and "mannish" in a derisive way. There are far fewer "women-only" careers to worry the boy. Certainly if he wished to become a midwife the professional institution would have actively pre-

vented him doing so until very recently, quite regardless of his
skill, vocational suitability, the ready acceptance of him by
patients or for that matter the established role of male gynaeco-
logists. The inference is that "it would not be nice". The boy
would find obstacles to a career in dress design or ladies hair-
dressing but these would be by social implications of being
"sissy" or "queer". Vocational-guidance workers would attempt
to entice him to more "manly" work. Potential girl friends
would wonder if he was "all right". On the whole society tends
to formalise rules against women invading masculine preserves
protesting concern for their welfare. At the same time it
excludes men from feminine preserves by ridicule and threats
of social expulsion. This is the case in transvestism. The woman
is permitted by the rules of fashion to the wearing of suits,
slacks, and clothes identical to the man's, indeed many articles
of female attire have their origins in male dress. Male fashion
rarely, if ever, adopts traditional female garments. If men wear
skirts and make up they become subject to social scorn to the
level that they are generally accepted as "being likely to cause a
breach of the peace". Even the kilt, conventional male wear
for centuries, remains a subject of embarrassment and music-
hall fun.

Oakley (1972) comments that adolescence represents a
critical period at which learned gender roles must be translated
into activity. The boy must behave like a boy and the girl like
a girl, putting into practice socially what has been learnt in
childhood. It goes without saying that the maturing of the inter-
sex relationships is very strongly governed by the motions of
acting out gender roles. The desirable male requires a large
repertoire of masculine postures from aggression in social relationships, authority amongst other boys, athletic prowess
as well as a capacity for exhibiting the appropriate masculine
courtship techniques. The girl desirably must demonstrate
dependence, availability, and the socially prescribed adornments
of make-up and dress.

The male is under far greater pressure in his role to maintain
a high level of aspiration and to achieve a financial success.

Aberle and Naegele (1952), studying American middle-class fathers, found the boys were expected to go to business or professions through university. Fathers were concerned if their sons lacked responsibility, initiative, academic achievement, athletic prowess, if they were over-conforming, excitable, fearful, or if they showed homosexual traits. Girls were expected to marry, be pretty, be sweet and affectionate. The fathers had more clear cut ideas about what was required of a boy than of a girl. Bennett and Cohen (1959) asked 1300 people aged 15 to 64 to select adjectives which described them best. The results indicated women felt more socially benevolent and moral, with greater personal satisfaction but more inadequacy and vulnerability. Men on the other hand felt greater achievement needs and capacities but were more ruthless and saw the world as more hostile. The women showed higher covert hostility than the men.

Education plays a part in this and the success of the masculine role is partly judged by the badges of examination success. To allot the seal of being academically "brilliant" to a male child is unequivocally high priase but slightly ambiguous in qualifying a feminine role, being capable of a slightly adverse implication. Middle-class parents strive hard to push their male children educationally, whilst educating the girls is not all that important to them. The gender rearing pattern varies with social level. In families with lower socio-economic status Bronfenbrenner (1960) found mothers more influential than fathers. Mothers were more domineering and materialistic. Responsibility in boys was associated with father's authority and affection from mother, whilst in girls it was associated with maternal authority and paternal affection. In the families of less skilled workers the concepts of toughness and physical assertiveness often replace the educational tokens. Simple educational achievement may even be an indication of femininity in the boy and be obstructed or despised. To some extent this may account for some of the boys who seem to be withdrawn from school when within striking distance of state examinations.

Thus in adult life the gender role of the woman has a great deal more flexibility than that of the man. The woman may be homosexual and not condemned. She may be a nursing sister, teacher, civil servant, or public figure but does not become unacceptable because she is homosexual. Until very recently homosexuality in a man, if disclosed, would have barred him from many careers. As a teacher he is still conceived as a perverter of children and as a civil servant a security risk. A woman in a traditionally male job is to a degree honoured, a man in a woman's job is denigrated and suspected of being sexually odd. Social ridicule and rejection are effective sanctions in controlling gender-role behaviour but the formalities of the law are invoked to regulate the male. Gender roles are strongly reinforced by the mass media. Advertising exploits a polarisation of roles using the extreme "he-man" and seductive female stereotypes as sales promotion points. "For him the executive brief case, for her the Parker lady pen." Cigarette advertising is based on similar images of the dominant male lighting the cigarette for the passive accepting female.

There are marked gender differences in artistic motivation. Successful women painters and composers are almost non-existent although female art and music teachers abound. In Farnsworth's (1960) research by questionnaire on the artistic interests of adults, ballet was regarded as the most feminine talent and jazz the most masculine. Women were regarded as excelling in performance and appreciation; males were the creators.

In the end one comes to a concept of gender role and identity which is determined by the culture in which we live to a very large degree, the starting point is certainly the decision of the parents about their child's sex, boy or girl, but even this is not so clear cut as simply the possession or not of certain (external) reproductive organs. On this basis a long chain of powerful social forces are brought into play so that the child recognises himself irrevocably as masculine or feminine. From that point not only does the culture mould the gender role but the child actively strives to conform. There may be some genetic contribution to the child's skill in acquiring the "correct" gender but it is far from proven and at least seems quite buried in the massive and complex social forces. However it comes about, the point of major importance is the recognition that by gender role we mean an aspect of personality which is relatively independent of biological sex. The difficulty in accepting what is fairly obvious, especially in view of anthropological evidence, is itself likely to be a phenomenon of culture. Gender amounts to the display and personal acceptance of a role in society which functions as a badge of physical sex.

Failure to conform to the forces of this all-pervasive social conspiracy is a threat to a crucial aspect of the structure of social order. It may be perceived as an index of dangerous sexual perversity and this over-rides the other perhaps more parsimonious explanations that the significance of an a-typical gender may lie only in the direct rewards of that role and be fairly independent of sex. This seems to be the heterosexual transvestite picture. We have already seen some available evidence that most often transvestites may show sexual behaviour conventional to their biological sex and how at the same time they find rewards in a non-sexual feminine role. The fact that some cross-dressers are homosexual, impotent heterosexuals, or fetishists, tends if anything to prove the point that the transvestite primarily seeks the cross gender role largely irrespective of sexual interests and capacities.

CHAPTER 5

Three Transvestite Autobiographies

The concept of the multiple personality has been studied in psychiatry for a time which is certainly a hundred or more years. Morton Prince's celebrated study of Miss Sally Beauchamp (Henderson and Batchelor, 1962) is such a case. These people were usually regarded as suffering from hysterical syndromes involving dissociation of different facets of the personality. "The Three Faces of Eve" is a semi-fictional account of a lady who seemed to possess three different personalities such that she behaved as quite radically different persons in certain circumstances. Perhaps Stevenson's Dr Jekyll and Mr Hyde is the ultimate cartoon of the multiple personality.

The multiple personalities appear to be each more or less complete consistent wholes and quite different from each other, although all existing in one individual. Passing from one personality to another occurs in an apparently involuntary fashion and the separate personalities are seemingly ignorant of the existence of each other. Such cases are at least very rare indeed. Many writers are sceptical about their existence and, as Mayer-Gross et al. (1960) say, "It seems that these multiple personalities are always artificial productions, the product of the medical attention that they arouse".

The psychoanalytic concept of the *alter ego* is more a matter of developmental dynamics than the overt behaviour of an individual but there is nevertheless some implication of the duality of the self. However, when Money (1974) describes the transvestite as a person with two personalities, two wardrobes, and two names, the analogy with the multiple personality in

psychiatric literature is misleading. The transvestite will fluc-
tuate in his need to adopt one role or another but certainly will
not manifest any ignorance of his "other self". The transvestite
will refer to himself in the other role as "my sister" or "my
brother" but there is little evidence of any very dramatic
discontinuity. He will describe the transition from one role to
another as being primarily a cognitive act in cross-dressing and
secondarily as a period of settling down into the cross-gender
role in which "my sister comes". The period of "coming" is
essentially one of adjustment to the artefacts of the assumed
role much more akin to a sensation of relaxing the constraints
on the day-to-day self by choice. The transvestite may say that
his behaviour changes in subtle ways and that his voice becomes
uncontrollably more feminine. He will be unable to demonstrate the voice he believes to have when in his "sister" role and
to the observer the voices are only different as a result of
obvious conscious effort despite the individual's belief in almost
magical changes. Whatever be the truth about the mechanism
underlying the multiple personality, dissociation state, malin-
gerer, or otherwise, it has little in common with the apparent
dual personality of the transvestite. The duality of the transvestite is more a matter of his own fantasies than anything else
and he is much more a single integrated personality with a need
to move from one gender pattern to another according to his
choice. Moreover, the cross-gender role has to be cultivated and
learned and the transvestite has to adapt some part of his
existence around this role.

The process of creating the other role is not only one of acting, learning how to open a handbag, put a parcel on a shelf, to
modify verbal expressions and so on. It is also a schooling
of the individual's belief in himself not as a male in a female
role but as some form of true female albeit with physical
deficiencies. This schooling process is one of relentless rehearsal, practice, and experimentation not only in motor performance but also in self-regard. A large part of this seems to occur
in talking, writing, and socialising. Part at least of the transvestite's need to appear in public is to put his female role to the

test, to get evidence of his success and the practice that makes perfect, indeed it may be no more than that.

Transvestite writing is abundant, far more so than, say, that of homosexuals. It seems that again the transvestite puts himself on paper so that he and others can check "her" out, as part of the process for searching for the perfect "femme" role. There is, therefore, a wealth of autobiography and fantasy written by transvestites but it is difficult to evaluate. As Worden and Marsh (1955) comment, there is a remarkable similarity in transvestite autobiographies. Indeed they refer to "a severe and extensive disturbance of memory" in that transvestites seem to refuse to look at the past beyond the well-rehearsed and highly selected points which justify and buttress their feminine self-concepts. In many ways of course, we all show such a selective memory for those aspects of life which seem consistent with the way in which we conceive ourselves. In practice it does seem more than usually difficult to get the transvestite to enlarge on the areas of his life relevant to his masculinity.

In this chapter three autobiographies are presented. They seem to be typical of transvestites writing about themselves for no external gain. The motivation for the writing seems to be the search for a coherent feminine self. There is constant winkling out of all those circumstances which not only account for but rationalise the cross-gender identity. The transvestite will not only selectively recall and record details which show feminine traits from early life but he will also grasp at straws which justify his current feelings. It is more comforting to believe "this is as I always was" rather than "this is what I have become".

None of these people have ever sought the writer's professional help, none are currently under medical treatment, appear to be seeking treatment, or indeed have attempted to follow up offering these autobiographies some years ago — indeed rather the reverse.

The first case came to the writer as a short book which was written about 15 years ago at the instigation of a psychotherapist but failed to find a publisher. The subject was also a diarist of some distinction and has compiled a highly detailed account of his transvestite existence, a copy of which is said to be lodged with the Institute of Sex Research in America. I.V. wrote to ask for assistance with the disposal of the second copy of his diary but also offered his earlier book to be abstracted for this purpose. The section adapted deals with some parts of I.V.'s own life and transvestite experiences.

The writer has corresponded with and met I.V. who appeared to be a transparently honest and sensible person. He was a man well into his eighties. He earned a considerable distinction in his profession although one suspects his financial success was very limited. There could be no ulterior motive for offering his writings for the purpose of this publication. He seemed content with having practiced as a transvestite all his life although at one stage he sought psychotherapy for some reason which he did not discuss.

The second case is that of D.N. who wrote his biography "to help anyone studying transvestism". It reached the author through intermediaries and its writer was not anxious to enter into further correspondence. Nevertheless, as far as it has been possible to verify the account it appears reliable.

The third case L.S. is that of a highly qualified doctor of medicine in early middle age. In his male role he is a highly regarded and successful man. Again the autobiography was written without any apparent gain motive and offered for publication. The author met and corresponded with L.S. and is convinced of his sincerity.

Case I. I.V.

Comment

I.V.'s case is specially interesting in view of his age. He gives no details of his childhood other than that he was brought up in a middle-class home at the turn of the century, being educated at one of the leading public schools.

He describes an early incident of cross-dressing as a childhood

game and then later episodes in the guise of socially acceptable
fancy dress. Throughout, the approval of women, the girl in
the childhood episode, his fiancée's mother, his wife, his
daughter-in-law and later still his grand-daughter are all very
important as confidantes of his transvestism. This is not so of
the male figures of his life who barely seem involved. Although
his sons are aware of his transvestism he does not seem to
involve them and he feels they cannot understand. He clearly
seems more able to relate to the women around him.

The history shows the marked bi-polarity of his gender. When
he is on war service his feminine self is packed away and he
assumes an aggressive male role as a soldier. It seems as though
becoming the father of young children also allows him to suppress his transvestism. He infers that the situation demanded
that he gave up cross-dressing but it seems as if when his role
became more highly masculinised his cross-gender needs were
less compulsive.

Clearly his stage appearances amount to a testimonial to his
feminine self. The newspaper reports he savours as testimonials
to his femininity in contrast to other evidence of his masculinity — it is left to his wife to comment on that. Curiously
whilst I.V. kept a diary of his transvestism he also kept an
equally detailed diary of his exploits as a soldier.

In fact I.V. and his wife died within a few years of his offering this account for publication. His wife who died first did not
cease to support him. Her death left him a very lost and lonely
person and although he continued to regard himself as transvestite he could not bring himself to cross-dress again. He felt
that he had to put "Ida" to rest with his wife. However, for a
time after his wife's death his grand-daughter became his close
companion and support.

Extract from "Who Is Ida"

"The writer must now explain that his interest in transvestism
is because he has indulged in it for more than half a century; he

is now in his seventies and still enjoys it. A brief account of his own experiences may help the reader to understand why.

"I am the second of a family of five. When I was about seven, I and a little girl of about my own age once crept into an upturned boat on the beach and exchanged clothes, she putting on my jersey and shorts, and I putting on her cotton frock. The idea was not mine, but hers. 'The woman tempted me!' I cannot believe that this incident had any influence on my subsequent, much later, interest in women's clothes. Small boys are often fascinated by the prettiness of feminine clothes. Our elder son took a photo of his little boy, then aged about six, sitting up in bed in his mother's best nightie, which he had begged to be allowed to put on. This fondness for pretty things was, in his case, merely transient, and I never heard of him indulging in that sort of thing again. He grew up into a thoroughly masculine schoolboy.

"But as I grew into adolescence I began to become much more interested in girls and their clothes. Being of a rather shy nature, I soon found that very often their clothes interested me, even just to look at, far more than the girls themselves!

"When I left school and lived at home for a year or so I sometimes surreptitiously tried on some of the clothes (coats and skirts) that my mother kept in the wardrobe in my bedroom.

"When I left home to live in lodgings in London in 1909, I was able gradually to get together quite a respectable trousseau of women's clothes, which I put on in the privacy of my bedroom of an evening, or early in the morning. I kept them in a locked suitcase under the bed.

"The only times I ever wore these clothes other than in the privacy of my own bedroom was at dress-up parties at the houses of certain friends. But, though they may sometimes have wondered where a young bachelor had borrowed the clothes from, I don't think they ever suspected that they were my own. At these parties all the men dressed up as girls (if enough feminine clothes could be found for them) and all the girls as men. Even at my fiancée's home (a vicarage), we sometimes amused ourselves in this way. Her mother used to provide most of the clothes for the young men, especially corsets and under-clothes. All I can now recall is that her mother once told me, as she pushed the rolled-up socks that were my 'breasts' into place, 'Nature sets them farther apart than that!'

"In August 1914 the First World War broke out, and I was in the Army within a month. I lived in lodgings for a few weeks after being called up as a recruit; and I used to relax at the end of a gruelling day of 'square bashing' and lectures and so on, by getting into a few women's clothes that I had secreted in my baggage. When, in due time, I was posted away from there and later sent overseas, these clothes had to be packed away 'for duration'. If I was to die a hero's death on the battle-field, my other, feminine, self should die with me!

"But, though I was wounded in Flanders, I did not die; and my other self, too, survived for, so far, another forty-seven years!

"Before going to France with my regiment I got married; and when I returned home, after some weeks in a hospital in Rouen, I was able to resume my hobby in the privacy of our own house. By this time we had had our first baby, a boy, and five years later, a second boy. While they were babies I was able to continue with my dressing up in women's clothes at home, but when they were a little older we judged it prudent to give it up, except on very rare and very secret occasions. It would have been most confusing for the children to see me sometimes as their father and sometimes as a woman! Later on still, when they were away at boarding school, I was able to be my 'other self' more freely.

"When we left London and went to live in the country I used still to amuse myself, and my wife, by dressing up. One evening, when I was dressed up in my best clothes, for a joke we called on some friends across the road, two maiden ladies who were highly amused at our frolic.

"Shortly after that a young man in the village asked one of these ladies if she would act with him in a little sketch at the next village concert. She was far too diffident, but on the spur of the moment she told him what a good 'girl' I made, and suggested that he should ask me to partner him on the stage! So he came across to our house and asked me if I'd do this. He had never seen me as a 'girl', and so I invited him to look in the following evening to meet 'her', and when he came he gladly accepted 'her' as his leading lady!

"Thus was born IDA VIRTUE (I DIVERT YOU), the stage-name that I chose, and which we have ever since called my 'other self' whenever I am dressed as a woman.

"The sketch was a huge success; so much so that I was tempted to do more amateur stage work as a feminine impersonator. During the next few years I did quite a lot of it, not only in our village, but in the town hall of the country town, on the pier at the neighbouring seaside resort, with the resident 'Follies', and at many other places. 'Ida' got a wonderful reception wherever 'she' appeared, and got many 'rave notices' in the newspapers. 'She' was referred to as 'the beauteous Ida', who turned out to be, at the end of the concert, 'a well-known local personality'. 'The Great Ida Returns' was another headline. 'Mr ——'s jolly impersonation of a bright young thing, Ida, in a dainty evening frock, with feminine mannerisms to match' was the description in yet another paper. And 'The fascinating Ida made a welcome return' said one paper; while another spoke of 'his marvellous impersonation of a charming, if somewhat muscular but intensely feminine young lady' and went on to speak of 'the slim suppleness, the dainty allure, the perfect fluttering girlishness of this really remarkable performance'. Needless to say Ida did the thing properly, and everything she wore was genuinely feminine, underclothes and all. This was essential for I could not have 'felt the part' in anything but the correct clothes.

"For all the popularity that Ida enjoyed on the local stages, there was also some outspoken censure expressed by certain friends, who did not approve of my larking about in petticoats. This disapproval eventually became so savage that I felt it wise to give up my public appearances and from then onwards Ida appeared, as she still appears, only in the strictest privacy of our own home."

Ida's Wife Speaks

"I have known my husband for nearly sixty years and have always known of his fondness for dressing in women's clothes; but I have never thought any the less of him for that. As a man he is entirely masculine, and no one could ever call him 'sissy'. He served in the 1914/18 war in France (where he was wounded) and in the 1939/45 war at home.

"Until a sudden severe illness forced him to retire some fifteen years ago, his work took him all over this country and to the Continent. He has never allowed Ida to interfere with his work, nor with our normal life.

"I am quite used to seeing him about the house dressed as a woman and am never in the least scandalised nor ashamed of him for this. I know that he finds great relaxation and pleasure in this change of personality; and as he says he always feels so well then, I fully approve of it, and help him in any way I can."

Postscript

"Earlier this year my wife was so ill that I began to wonder what would happen if she were to die before I did. Who would wind up Ida's affairs, dispose of her wardrobe, for instance, and her diaries, and so on, if she were no longer here to do it?

"With some diffidence, therefore, I decided to confide in our daughter-in-law, Pat. We are very fond of her, and she is a sweet and intelligent woman. How would she react to this revelation about 'Ida'? It must be a bit of a shock to learn that your father-in-law, in his 75th year, is 'queer' enough to enjoy dressing up in women's clothes! Would she, like certain other friends of ours in days gone by, be nauseated at such an idea?

"However, it was so important to me to find someone to cope with 'Ida's' affairs when I died, if my wife predeceased me, that I plucked up my courage and broached the delicate subject to her. Let Pat now speak for herself:

"I have known my father-in-law very well for nearly twenty years. We live only a few minutes' walk from one another.

"Recently he asked me if I would consent to act as his executrix in a certain matter which, he said, he had kept very secret all his life. He warned me that what he was about to tell me might surprise me, or even offend me, but he begged me to try and understand. This sounded ominous and I braced myself for his confession.

"When, however, I learned what this was my immediate reaction was one of immense relief, for there had flashed through my mind quite unwarrantable suspicions of homosexuality or something equally horrible, which really would have shocked and disgusted me. I would have been most upset to learn that anyone so close to me indulged in that sort of thing.

"When he told me about transvestism, and how, all his life, he had enjoyed dressing up as a woman, in the privacy of his own home and the full knowledge of his wife, I could see nothing wrong in that at all.

"I had heard from my husband that his father used to go in for feminine impersonation on the stage when he was a young man and I had been shown photographs of him dressed as a girl.

"He lent me the typescript of his book to read and a few days later I was introduced to 'Ida' in person.

"I must admit that I was extremely surprised as nothing in his manner or appearance suggests his interest in feminine clothes, much less his fondness for wearing them. Now that I have seen 'Ida' dressed in her various clothes, I have no reason to alter my opinion. If, in this way, he finds relaxation, and feels happier and younger, I really cannot see the slightest harm in it. Indeed, I found it all most intriguing."

Case II D.N.

Comment

This report begins with the writer giving what he sees as evidence from his childhood connected with his subsequent transvestism. He lists three points: (a) mother suppressed his sexuality as being "wrong", (b) blushing was a physical attribute he possessed even as a child, (c) circumstances produced opportunity to dress up in feminine garments.

Cross-dressing then appears as a possible escape into a fantasy world free from the pressures of a male existence. It is associated with the common preoccupation with tight constricting clothes and he also recounts an associated experience of asphyxiation which had a sexual component. Mayer-Gross *et al.* (1954) referred to this phenomenon in association with transvestism and linked it with self-strangulation and suffocation for erotic ends. Very little indeed is known about this phenomenon. The transvestite undoubtedly sees feminine roles as submissive, weak, and restricted. Women's clothing is also restrictive, e.g. high-heeled shoes, corsets, or even the wedding ring (said to have its origins in the band placed round the wife's waist to make her the husband's captive). There is little to indicate that erotic masochism is materially more intense among transvestites than any other group. The anoxic experience described by the writer is not an uncommon one amongst adolescents. It is probably related to practices such as inhaling cleaning fluid and anaesthetic substances which are by no means uncommon but not a special feature of transvestism. Like many transvestites he asserts a sexual naivety concerning homosexuality in particular. In general this naivety appears more a matter of retrospective denial because the transvestite's feminine fantasy is in peril from assumptions of homosexuality. It seems as if the transvestite can best maintain the purely feminine fantasy by denying any acquaintance with homosexual desires. Few transvestites prove to be indeed unaware of same sex erotic behaviour in adolescence although, in fact, they may not draw together awareness of a variety of acts into a single concept and call it homosexuality.

D.N.'s reference to fancy dress and his refusal to dress as a "duchess" is an interesting reflection of his rejection of assuming the burlesque drag role. To do so implied the male underneath the dress far too strongly. It was only if the masquerade

was to be as convincing and as acceptable as possible that it
could contain any satisfaction. In contrast is the later
experience of a ragday escapade at university where he is pleas-
urably rewarded by a chance comment. The writer says he
married expecting his gender problems to be resolved and of
course they were not. He appears to marry in this hope, partly
in the belief that he would succeed in a supreme effort to be a
new man, partly that as a normal sexual life would become
available the gender dysphoria would be resolved and partly
as a justification for keeping the secret from his wife. In reality
the supreme effort is no more effective than other supreme
efforts, nor does the sexual activity resolve the gender difficulty. As D.N. found, wives resent the deception bitterly and
find themselves unable to express the fear and misunderstanding
that overwhelmed them on the discovery of the husband's
transvestism.

In his working life he has maintained the picture of the
executive which by many standards has given him a good
quality of life and hence been successful. There is no evidence
of a search for a less than wholly masculine image in his
employment and, in fact, he infers a great deal of pride in his
business world. Opportunities must have been open to him to
take reasonably lucrative work with some more feminine con-
notation, in the clothing, cosmetic, or catering industries. Even
though he reports being involved in advertising lipstick, he does
not seem to seek this total commitment to life with a feminine
aspect. Transsexual subjects seem to take a much more whole
time commitment in their occupations. Hoopes *et al.* (1968)
found, for example, amongst eighty-five transsexuals seeking
sex reassignment, twenty-one were employed as beauticians and
seven as female impersonators, whilst the list of other occupations includes wig stylists, secretary, floral designer, domestic,
doctor's assistant, etc.

D.N.'s visit to the psychiatrist illustrates the problem of
therapy quite well. Confirmatory advice "to carry on" was
accepted with pleasure while his comments on aversion therapy
reflect the current view that there is great danger in administer-

ing a therapy contrary to the desires of the patient. The fundamental ethics of such treatment are unacceptable and more likely to set up neurotic conflicts than to succeed. Psychotherapy failed to deal with the most pressing area of tension in this patient's life; that between himself and his wife. It is hard to conceive of therapeutic success where this crucial relationship was simply regarded as a secondary issue which would resolve itself if the transvestism was treated. It appears that a palliative session with the wife simply served to allow her to realise as fact what she felt were her worst fears. It is always hard for the therapist to appreciate that kindly reassurance is not accepted at face value. Reassurance is not infrequently seen by the relatives and patients as an attempt to divert the patient from the "real truth" and hence effectively confirms as true the client's false beliefs. It is very unlikely, of course, that the therapist intended to advise the wife that her husband was "a homosexual pervert". It is probable that in the session with her he did not see her as in need of inclusion in her husband's therapy, but only as seeking advice. The advice she is likely to have voraciously misconstrued.

The final section of D.N.'s account has a special significance. He has found some resolution of his needs for a female role in crochet work. Here is the sort of evidence found in most transvestites of cross-gender activity which is very hard to conceive as sexually motivated or fetishistic in nature. Few activities seem less likely to be stimulated by sexual excitement than the production of a crochet table mat. Nevertheless, D.N.'s feminine self can find some measure of expression of a gender role in such an activity. More than this the common ground which this seems to have created between the writer and his wife gives a valuable clue for therapy.

Autobiographical note by D.N.

"I was born in the 1920s in a middle-class home. My father was forty-two at the time and already settled in his ways. He had come from a large Victorian family and I do not think he ever really adapted to a small family.

My mother was some twelve years younger and I was her second and last child. My brother was three years older than me. I learned many years later that my mother's desire for a girl was so strong that she turned away from me for two or three days. Then, no doubt, she over-reacted. As a baby I had a serious illness — something to do with inability to feed. I believe this left me physically below average. Anyway, even at nursery school I didn't like football or 'rough' games.

"There are three points of significance in my early years. Firstly, I never masturbated as a youth. This is a fact, not an untruth. I can remember playing with my genitals at bedtime and my mother saying, 'What are you doing with your hands?' I blushed and said, 'Nothing' and ceased from then on having learned thereby that this was 'wrong'. Secondly, I blush very easily — even now. When I was about eight I was having lunch with my mother on a day when a very large funeral was being marshalled down the road. It must have been someone of importance, as it attracted quite a crowd, and I remarked to my mother that a lot of policemen were passing the window. She made some remark, intending it to be in fun, like 'Yes, I wonder who they are looking for?' Again, I blushed and from there on I blushed every time a policeman passed. Each meal time became a worry and I hoped to get through it without this happening. In those days the policemen sounded the beat with a slow, majestic tread. I am sure that no one knew the depth of my unease or they would have done something about it. Thirdly, the highlight of the Christmas holidays was a children's fancy-dress ball. I did not go as anything particularly girlish (nor did my mother ever dress me in girls' clothes), but they were silky garments with tight long stockings and, in the general excitement of the evening, felt pleasant. I spent most of the evening at the feet of the conjurer who performed several times and magic became my main hobby. I was sent away to prep. school at nine. I quite enjoyed prep. school, but in the evenings my thoughts went back to the 'tight clothes' and the pleasure they gave. Then quite suddenly — and it was as near to a 'revelation' as I will ever get — the thought came to me that if I could wear girls' clothes. I would not only get pleasure, but might find myself in a world where I did not have to play horrid games like football and cricket — and where blushing would not be such a problem — girls were, I knew, allowed to blush.

"Once the seed was sown, it developed, but how could it be put into practice? Clearly, such a thought had never occurred to anyone else nor could it be discussed with anyone.

"The last fancy dress party I was allowed to attend was when I was about eleven years old. I would have gone as a 'Rajah' in a costume my brother had outgrown, but we also had a Beefeater's outfit and I asked my mother if I could wear this instead — at least it had long stockings and something rather like a dress. This was agreed, but, alas, the date clashed with a theatre party which I was told I would prefer. Not for the last time, my desires were frustrated. There wasn't much I could do except dream and plan — all sorts of fantasies from being kidnapped and disguised as a girl to flying away like Peter Pan to a land where one could wear what one liked.

"In due course I was sent with extraordinary lack of parental wisdom to one of the toughest public schools in England. We played rugger three times a week and I hated every minute of it. I was really only happy in the moments when I could escape either physically for lone bike rides or in my mind. Oddly enough I met no homosexuality, nor even knew what it was until much later. There was only one mild experience which puzzled me. There was a craze at one time for taking twenty deep breaths and then exhaling, whilst someone squeezed the breath out of you. This produced a dizzy feeling and sometimes one passed out. I remember a boy suggesting we try this — he stood behind me and put his arms round me and squeezed with every breath. It gave me sexual excitement, which puzzled me but we didn't try it again — the school doctor stamped out the craze. Another thing I tried was self-hypnotism — I could get myself into a half dream world.

"My holidays were a blessed relief, spent mostly on my own

or with my mother. I spent many pleasant hours either writing or experimenting with conjuring tricks — I was quite good at the latter. Occasionally, when the house was empty I popped up to the lumber room and found cast-off dresses which I slipped on for a few moments. It was pleasant and did not give me an erection, as far as I recall. That only happened in bed.

"I missed out on opportunities to dress as a girl. I was never in school plays and once at a hotel where there was a fancy dress evening my father said he had gone to such a do as a 'duchess', 'Why couldn't I?' Somehow I couldn't agree — perhaps the word 'duchess' put me off. If he had said 'girl' I would have done so.

"One other point I remember at prep. school — I had a rather large pair of game shorts and someone on the playing field shouted 'Come on Skirts'. The nickname 'skirts' stuck as these things will. I didn't like it very much but I felt in some way it showed that other people could see that I really was a girl.

"So there I was at fifteen or sixteen, desperately seeking a way out of the problem. When I was confirmed there was great talk of confession one's sins. Everybody seemed to be expected to have a sin and I had no other to justify the name, except these 'naughty thoughts'. But I could not bring myself to 'confess'.

"I don't want to give the impression that I actively hated school — I don't think my character is such that I have enormous hates or loves. I had my friends, but no one very close and I found that I could sometimes amuse them, having a quick wit and an ability to make the amusing apt response. I was inhibited because if I became the centre of attraction I always blushed. Except that is, when I developed my talents as a conjuror — I could perform before an audience of friends, I suppose because I really felt confident about my subject — but this was at home, not school. There was no magical society at school and playing cards were forbidden. On the whole I was content to slip away by myself and dream up ways and means of becoming a girl, but without doing anything practical about dressing.

"It is not surprising that my reports usually finished up with remarks like 'needs to develop more self-confidence'. In retrospect this seems about as sensible as saying 'needs to mend his broken leg' without doing anything about setting it. I longed to have someone to talk to and why no one ever did try to help remains a puzzle. I suppose it was a conformist school and the boy who is bad at games just gets forgotten. My parents should have done more. I was a 'mummy's boy' and spent too much time with her. My father was ever pleasant and also could be great fun, but he lacked ambition, as my mother once said. This was the only slightly disloyal remark she ever made about him, although she had long been bored by his company. I can't recall them ever sharing a bedroom, let alone a bed except on holiday. Father spent his weekends in the garden or at his tennis club and was only occasionally rather unwillingly dragged into a family outing. He didn't take much interest in the modern world — it had stopped for him I suppose when that Victorian household broke up. Anyway, he had no point of contact and I found it hard to discuss things with him. Looking back I regret this, of course. Perhaps, we had more in common than we knew.

"At that time I was interested in ships and plumped for becoming a marine engineer. This was an absurd decision which should have been stopped. I was not unintelligent and was an above average mathematician and could have been influenced to be an accountant — which I now seem to be! My choice meant going to a northern university and I think that I was influenced by the fact that it meant leaving school a year earlier than usual. I couldn't face becoming a prefect, not because I funked responsibility, but because it meant doing things like standing in front of the house and reading the lesson at prayers. Besides, I would be in the impossible position of being a senior, yet sent to play games with the juniors.

"So I took the opportunity and found some freedom from school rules at university. Here on ragday came my one and only opportunity to don jumper and skirt and lipstick and walk around the town all day in high heels. I didn't dress perfectly and, of course, being a rag I was not intended to 'be' a girl, but how wonderfully free and easy it felt and what a thrill when I had my photo taken and the assistant said, 'Oh, I really thought you were a girl'.

"The move north didn't work out. I wanted to return to Science subjects and study from home, but I was persuaded by my parents to go to Oxbridge. Oxbridge was better, but what no one realised was that I had lost two years of study in the process so I could not really cope. I found more outlets in the Magical Society and joined two concert parties which entertained in the town and the Army and R.A.F. camps around. (The Second War had started.) Even then I missed opportunities to dress. One of the sketches we performed included a mock operation and I was the nurse. The producer decided to play it as a male nurse. Why didn't I protest? I dreamt about the crisp skirt and tight belt, but just couldn't bring myself to make the request. Educationally, however, I was a dismal failure — I fluffed the exams, and shortly afterwards joined the Army where I got a commission.

"I was always 'Diana'. I just picked a name which started with the same initials as my 'proper' name. I thought it might be easier if I ever came to need it. Diana grew up with me. I never wanted 'glamour' garments (except inasmuch as any girl wants pretty clothes) or what are now called 'kinky' things, only just the straightforward, normal clothes of a twin sister. Diana wore school clothes when I was at school and joined the A.T.S. when I joined the Army.

"My war was unexciting. I got into anti-aircraft and spent most of my time in the U.K. It was not until I was posted to a mixed battery that I was sexually aroused by any girl. There were two girls in the office and one of the other officers had paired off with one. The other, I suppose, rather threw herself at me. She attracted me and for the first time in my life I kissed a girl. I was excited by her and it all seemed perfectly normal. I was posted away and there was no depth in my feeling so I broke off our relationship. There were other girls from time to time, but nobody who interested me. We had the odd kiss and cuddle but no more. I can't remember how excited I got, but obviously not so much that I just had to have intercourse. I was posted to various gun sites, but saw little action and never during the heavier raids. My brother was killed in the R.A.F. and I felt guilty that I had not pulled my weight.

I have read how other transvestites found that military experiences suppressed their feminine desires. I remember keeping a diary at the start of the war and writing 'I must be a man' or something like that. I suppose this is an inevitable reaction for anyone with a sense of duty and responsibility. Nevertheless my imagination still toyed with possible ways of 'escape'. I imagined that I had been posted by one of those typical Army errors to an A.T.S. unit. Oh, well, must obey orders. I went to the 'Q' store to draw my clothes — skirts, khaki, blouses, khaki, knickers, bras, stockings. How smart I looked in my neat uniform: my skirt the regulation three inches above the knees or I would be ordered on a special assignment and trained to think, act and dress as a woman. To be honest I think that second one may have come along a bit later but it makes the point that my fantasy world continued.

"I was posted to India with nothing much to do. I went to the bazaar and bought a set of undies (everyone was doing that, of course, for wives and girlfriends) and make-up. We had separate sleeping quarters, so it was not difficult to slip these on probably with a jersey pulled up over my legs as an improvised skirt, and experiment again with make-up. Max Factor had just produced Pan-Cake make-up and it was rather nice to apply an all over foundation. It seemed to me that I could still look the part. Lipstick has a special symbolic meaning to me — it is the simplest outward sign of the difference between the sexes. Oh how nice it is to see that cupid's bow come out in its true colours! But on the way home I dumped the lot overboard. I have often done this, a firm resolve to mend my ways, even though I know that the thoughts will creep back in the wee small hours.

"I was back home, arriving I remember to a very damp reception, as my grandfather who had been living near our house in his declining months was just about to die. I took a training course and got a job in advertising and also met my wife. She was a nurse and a friend of her's had married a doctor cousin of mine. We were introduced and fell for each other and within six months were wed. It is a pity in a way that I married so soon after leaving the Army. All my life, with rare exceptions, I had been under some discipline — two years or so in a flat on my own might have given me a sense of freedom, although heaven knows what else would have happened. We were possibly attracted to each other by a sort of mutual naivety. We had some early little difficulties, but no more I suspect than most people. Later, my wife has chided me for not telling her of my 'peculiarities' before we were married. This is justified, but as I found it hard to tell anyone else it would be difficult to tell someone I was trying to impress. Besides, I genuinely felt that the 'normal' would drive out the 'abnormal'. Quite early on I once suggested that we should swop nightwear — pyjamas for nighties. We did this once, but I saw that Phyllis was horrified so I never dressed or did anything feminine in her presence again except very occasionally I lightly powdered my nose and touched up my lips so imperceptibly that she hardly ever noticed. These acts seemed so natural to me that it seems the right thing to do when one is in the mood. By contrast, even on those special nights, my wife removes all her make-up before going to bed. I wonder which is the more 'normal' behaviour? Phyllis has strong views on what is 'right and wrong'. Her own character and background is obviously not one that would tolerate my transvestism.

"I think I first tried on some of her dresses (never undies) when we were separated and our elder daughter arrived. Something must have been said about this on another occasion because at one point she gave me some old undies 'as a safety valve', but I cannot recall ever wearing them. We had a major row over this when she had a miscarriage and was away convalescing. I was alone at home and again popped into one or two of her dresses. She has been in hospital on several occasions, but I have always thought, both out of loyalty and because it is a worrying time for both of us, that I should not take the opportunity to 'change'. Because I cannot hide my unease I had to 'confess'. I then promised never to wear anything of hers again — a promise which I have almost kept. My wife's arguments are threefold. First, she wants to be married to someone who is 'all man'. I grant her that, although my impression is that this does not necessarily make a marriage any more secure. There is little risk of my being interested in other women. Secondly, she wants me to love her for herself alone. Thirdly, she uses the argument 'Suppose it was the other way round?' Apart from the obvious retort — 'If a woman wants to wear a trouser suit she can', I can only say to this that no matter what problem my wife had I would help her to solve it.

"After the birth of our second daughter my feminine instincts could be directed more usefully by helping to change, bath, dress, and generally play with the children. I was determined not to repeat my father's mistake of leaving them to their mother at weekends, but my desires were present — I recall trying some sample lipstick that came into the office for advertising and I had a skirt and various odd articles of clothing from time to time. The fact that it was 'verboten' and I am not awfully keen on having things hidden away in odd corners made my desires more a matter of wishful thinking than fulfilment. I joined an advertising agency and was thrown into the thick of the 'soap war'. I found myself in a world which I had never met before. It was a time when firms had plenty of money to spend on advertising and an era of big expense accounts. Even though by some standards my firm was modest in its entertaining budget, lavish meals and so forth were the order of the day. My first boss was a heavy drinker and to some extent I followed suit until I realised that it was not necessary — but there really was some need to keep one's end up by joining in the 'client entertaining' game. I did well because I am efficient, but I was bad at expressing myself and I became a backroom boy who had found himself in the front office! Nevertheless I found myself one of the seniors in terms of service in the firm. I was made a director and possibly this was my undoing. The firm was taken over by an American company. It became unprofitable, and the palmy days of advertising were drawing to an end. All of a sudden I was given three months' notice. I was absolutely shattered and felt as though I had tried hard to hold my place as a man in a man's world and had been rejected. I got another job, but my heart wasn't in it. After a couple of years I left to try to run my own business. However, with gathering economic storm clouds I finally absorbed myself inside another firm.

"Then after a time we made the decision to pack everything and leave London and settle in a lovely spot we both like in Shropshire. I now make my living in an accountant's office — which maybe is what I ought to have done all along. Financially we would have been better if I stayed working in the City, but my wife was sensitive about the fact that I had failed to make good and she felt she was having to put up a pretence with the 'Jones's'. Actually I had got on a slippery slope and it had been very difficult to get off it. Of course, I am no worse than thousands of executives who have come unstuck in the past ten years or so. In fact, I am in most ways better off. We have our dream cottage and my wife enjoys village life even if I don't.

"Opportunities to dress have been very restricted so that it is left for all practical purposes (occasional make-up sessions apart) to times when either I have the house to myself or I am away from home. This means that when such an opportunity looms on the horizon my wife is suspicious and I show my unease by blushing. Much the same happens after a separation, often in unspoken thoughts. It doesn't matter whether I have or have not dressed — the guilty look still comes. Unfortunately, it does not end there because this 'thing' is always between us — my wife calls it the 'ghost' that is always there, and at some periods of my life I have found it almost impossible to carry on a normal conversation without similar signs — particularly at mealtimes.

"It was really because of this problem that I finally decided, with her agreement, to see a psychiatrist. The sessions were quite helpful up to a point in putting things in perspective. His general attitude was 'It doesn't matter, it won't go away and so long as you keep it private get on with it'. We discussed aversion therapy which I had read about in the press as a cure for transvestism. Fortunately, he was against it — frankly I cannot see how it can work with a rational human being. (My thought was 'If he does make me do it, I'll insist on dressing really nicely — and if they make me sick, it will be worth it'. The aversion would, in my case, be directed towards the therapist!) However, I did not continue the sessions for more than three or four visits, as my wife also went to see the same man at his invitation and came back to accuse me of being a 'homosexual pervert'.

"I was doubly upset because I felt that she was no nearer to understanding the facts and because I thought that having gone to some trouble and expense to get myself sorted out, at least a little bit of co-operation on her part would be forthcoming. I think I went to see him once more, but obviously unless this was going to lead to a better understanding between myself and my wife it was not going to be very helpful. I read recently Virginia Prince's book *The Transvestite and his Wife* with surprise, learning that wives actually go with husbands to meet other transvestites and many husbands are free to dress at home, provided that neighbours and children don't know. Such freedom would be wonderful and probably leads to less dressing and I imagine less tension than in the homes of those where any 'deviation' is taboo.

"My wife also had a look at this book and said, 'If that makes me an "E" (completely intolerant) wife that's the way I intend to continue'.

"I have had one little breakthrough. Some time ago my wife got keen on crochet and I suggested that I also learnt. She agreed, 'Providing you do it sensibly and it's nothing to do with your silly nonsense'. I picked up the art and produced a set of dinner mats and a shawl. I find it very relaxing. My wife is quite content with the thought that 'lots of men do knitting and tapestry' providing I do not attempt to crochet myself a blouse, much as I would like to. It is nice to find common ground and (after a slightly tentative, hesitant start), something which is now accepted by both of us. Would that it could be extended."

Case III

Comment

Case L.S. is a middle-aged member of the teaching staff of a university medical school. Clearly his medical training is good ground for a careful look at his own transvestite problem and there is no cause to question the sincerity of the account. It is clear that in psychoanalysis he found some understanding of his transvestism, but although he found some satisfaction in this it is not clear what benefit came from therapy. Indeed he appreciates a lack of motivation for therapy and a desire to retain his transvestism. The case illustrates the psychotherapeutic difficulty of a patient whose presenting symptomatology is a firmly held means of avoidance of his fundamental difficulties. It seems that therapy must first ask him to relinquish his highly valued escape route and then take him back to face the issues from which he was escaping. Without great hope of a more satisfactory resolution of his fundamental difficulties it seems unlikely that he will be induced to make that step. There is a chasm between the rewards of his escape fantasies and the rewards of a mature gender-congruent role, and psychotherapy rarely seems likely to bridge it. He finds the explanation that his transvestism is a defence against being forced by his mother to replace her first husband, intuitively correct. It is particularly interesting that this is rather contrary to the more usual interpretation of transvestism that the powerful woman coerces the child into a female role (e.g. Stoller, 1970). One also notes the fact that some aspect of sexual anxiety is apparent in an early age in his preoccupation with his non-circumcision and his unwillingness to enter into competition with other males in games. It looks rather that in throwing himself into biology he could have been opting for a role like mother's husband rather than being forced by her. There is also the question of whether or not mother's first husband was, indeed, directly relevant to a problem occurring about 20 years after his death. It could be that L.S.'s own father first replaced the tragically lost first husband. Perhaps the father also opted out of this role throwing himself into biology and retreating into a silent and possibly secretive existence just as L.S. subsequently did. L.S.'s own father's retreat from the paternal role could be a more cogent factor in the formation of L.S.'s gender dysphoria. His father, particularly being present, would be a greater threat to him as a competitor in mother's affection and the deficiencies of father's role itself would be important. Certainly, L.S. seems to have achieved an incredible identification with father, particularly in the form of his career. Two questions are unanswered, of course. Why did this mother do this to three men? What happened to the brothers, did they find other escape routes?

Autobiographical Note by L.S.

"I am the first to agree that my home was other than usual. Mother, of a Bostonian business family, married twice. Her first husband died after only ten weeks of an unconsummated marriage and twelve years later she re-married. Her first husband was a doctor and her second, my father, also had medical interests. He came from a New England farming family, but was very much the 'Harvard intellectual' who had decided to enter medicine, but stopped short and became a physiologist. Both my parents had puritanical ideas, but of the two mother was the stronger and more dominant personality. She had a wealth of physical and emotional energy with an aptitude for running the home whilst father was very much the intellectual, quiet in manner and artistic in interest. There were three boys and I was the youngest. We formed a tight little family going our own way.

"There was a medical tradition in the family and it was quite clearly expected that I should carry this on as I had displayed some interest in biology. I entered medical school in due course. All went well until at about twenty-five years of age I began to have inexplicable difficulties with my work. This resulted in my having two years psychoanalysis. The situation improved and in due course I qualified not without some distinction. When I was twenty-seven I married, but my family standards permitted no great sexual intimacy before marriage. However, with our children we had a relatively prosperous marriage until my transvestism seemed to force us apart. Although effectively my marriage is now over there is no great rancour between us and we can meet on reasonable terms, even putting up some pretence of a happily married couple as we did at our daughter's wedding.

"My transvestite feelings were certainly apparent in my early teens. I recall vividly a geography lesson in which the teacher described a community in which boys were kept in dresses and with long hair.

"I resolved not to practise medicine but enter the academic world like my father, not only because of my anxiety about transvestism, but because of a fantasy revealed during my psychoanalysis. I had a fear about conducting physical examinations on a particular type of female patient. I had the fantasy that during the examination I would be seduced by a woman who had a striking similarity of age and build to my mother. It seemed that analysis explained my transvestism and my fantasy in this way. I imagined that my mother had attempted to re-create in me her first husband. In his place she had put my father and then she had given birth to me who she could build into a replica first as a doctor and then as her second partner. She had assumed a demanding, dominant position in constraining me first to become a doctor and then in forming a special emotional relationship with me. This deprived me of my integrity and threatened my right to be my real self. To escape from the threat of annihilation as a person and of the guilt of involvement in an incestuous relationship I escaped in the disguise of a girl. Curiously the family rather despised girls so not only would the disguise avoid the sexual relationship, but also free myself from the rather cocoon-like family. Needless to say, none of this was a conscious stratagem and it was only in analysis that I became aware of the process which had forced me into a girl role.

It seems that other things conspired to consolidate the

advantages of being a girl. In the mould of the middle-class professional family I was sent to boarding school from seven years of age. My family pursued me in the form of their powerful views and intensely held moral values and I was profoundly unhappy throughout. I adopted the attitude of despising team games which in the context of the boarding school was disastrous and I threw myself into biology at a level far in advance of my peers. I was also conscious of the fact that I had not been circumcised. I don't know why, but it seemed that almost all the other boys had been circumcised and this made me feel the odd one out. I suppose the fantasy of becoming a girl gave me escape from this agony also.

"There were only very occasional incidents of dressing in borrowed clothes before I married and the whole thing was really just a matter of fantasy. It seemed to me when about to get married that marriage would resolve all this because I would then have available a normal heterosexual existence. Indeed, for a time this was so and my fantasies grew rarer and weaker. My wife was a keen dressmaker and I tried to involve myself in helping her and taking an interest. This led, however, to my buying women's clothes for myself to wear as the opportunity permitted. The chances with children about and a wife who was not co-operative were few and far between, but opportunities did arise. On trips away from home I was able to stay in female attire for a full day every now and then. Earlier experiences and my adolescent fantasies had involved some sexual excitement, but with more opportunity this fetishism declined into a sense of relief at the regular satisfaction of the compulsion alone.

"I have met other transvestites and their wives and one of the latter told me that she had little difficulty in accepting me as a woman when I am in women's clothes. This seems odd to me as I am very tall, my hands are large, my beard is copious and my general appearance masculine. It seems to me that as I change my appearance my personality also changes.

"I have now been a transvestite for thirty-five years and my training must lead me to look at myself with a more than usually critical eye. It seems to be that explanations of transvestism have overlooked the dynamic aspects of the condition. It is as if the personality interacts with the pressures of the social and psychological environment, all the time shifting, adapting and learning ways of reducing those pressures, to enhance the sense of identity and integrity. The idea of the human personality as a reacting dynamic entity, always finding a path to a lower level of tension and a reduction in conflict is perhaps best conceived in Kelly's personal construct theory.

"I find physiological explanations of transvestism at best speculative and it seems from my personal life that no explanation based on hormonal imbalance, for example, is tenable unless it takes into account the unimpaired heterosexual drive in most transvestites. Similarly, there is enough experience to know that sexual depressant medication does not depress transvestite fantasies; indeed they might be enhanced.

"Transvestism is a compulsion. There is a build up of tension and anxiety until the compulsion is satisfied. It may appear that women's clothes are very specific objects like fetishes, but in reality this is not so simple. I appreciate the elaborate clothes of the Tudor nobleman, but they belonged to a man. If I go into a multiple store I may find a sweater on the male counter only differing from one on the female counter by the label in the neck. I am quite unequivocal in wanting the one which says '40″ bust' and not wanting that reading '40″ chest'. I can buy a patterned shirt with lace down the front, but I want a blouse with or without lace. A transvestite Highland Scot told me how much he disliked wearing the kilt and how his overwhelming preference was for a skirt.

"Suppose a simple cure was possible for my transvestism would I take it? I believe there is no such cure, but in any event I would not wish to have my escape route closed. There are difficulties and dangers in being a transvestite, but like other transvestites I find there are pleasures and some enrichment of experience which I do not wish to resign. The therapist must be confronted with the problem about how to attempt to cure the patient who does not wish to be cured. Should society, indeed, expect to insist on such a cure when it seems to the patient that the cure is an impoverishment. I grew up in a family where my parents muddled their gender roles and it may be expected that I can foresee the dangers to children in a family with a transvestite parent. It could be that transvestites should avoid parenthood, but this in turn probably means avoiding marriage. On the other hand, there is no evidence to show that children of transvestites are in any way incapacitated. A transvestite in a marriage relationship may develop a special role. He may take up a daughter-like role guided by and supporting the wife, doing the shopping and developing mature feminine interests. There may be little place for the wife though once the transvestite is fully developed — if there ever is such a point. Certainly a successful transvestite marriage requires an openness and an acceptance of the problem by both partners, particularly to ensure that the wife does not suffer a diminution of her role. Particularly, both should agree about their attitudes to having children.

"Transvestite jokes and entertainment suggest that in some way the drive may be present to some degree in every man. It may be a symbol of their partial awareness of the need to integrate a latent femininity into their culturally determined dominant masculinity. In transvestites perhaps this latent need is inflamed by particular developmental pressures. However, the transvestite must be only different in degree and all men need to find some level of personal integration to maintain their stability."

CHAPTER 6

Transvestite Writings

Autobiographies are a useful means of obtaining an understanding of the transvestite's self-concept. They tell us a good deal about how the individual sees himself and his relationship with society. However, it is a curious fact that transvestites show an enthusiasm for writing about themselves not only in autobiography, but in many other ways. It could well be that transferring the fantasy to paper gives reality to the fantasies which preoccupy the transvestite. The act of making a statement which has a separate existence which others can read is rather like the need to appear in public for a confirmation of the fantasy of femininity. For this reason, if treated with reservation, an examination of the non-autobiographical writings also contributes to the knowledge of the inner world of the transvestite which proves to contrast sharply with the reality of the autobiographies.

Writings with transvestite content have two main sources. There is a large body of "hard" and "soft" pornography with transvestite themes. In this context what we mean by pornography is writing with the prime intention of meeting a desire for a sexual experience in the reader. "Hard" pornography is that which dwells on what most people regard as perverse acts with a sexual context to a degree which would be judged upsetting by many people. "Soft" pornography is less direct, but concerns situations which the reader may turn into a source of perverse sexual excitement. In this latter category belong books which are presented in the form of serious works, e.g. books concerning the history of corporal punishment or torture, but

in reality are directed to the sexually perverse. Serious works
themselves can be used in this way as "soft" pornography, e.g.
naturist magazines.

It goes without saying that the origin of most pornographic
literature is unknown. It could be that pornographic literature
catering for fetishists is written by fetishists, but it is certain
that the majority is written primarily for commercial profit.
Much pornography can be written to a formula by any fairly
imaginative person no matter what the market. However, it is
unlikely that the context exactly defines the market. For example, the large trade in pornographic literature about les-
bianism is not consumed by female homosexuals nor by male
homosexuals. In this sense one cannot assume that pornographic commercial literature involving cross-dressing is written
by or for transvestites. This is particularly true if by transvestism we are speaking of a gender dysphoria rather than a
sexual disorder. A great deal of pornographic literature
concerned with cross-dressing has other themes. These are
usually masochistic involving beatings, tortures, bondage, and
all manner of fetishes. Such perversions certainly appear in a
vast array of people only a minority of whom are transvestite.
There is no reason at all to think that these deviations *en bloc*
are characteristic of transvestism. On the other hand, the man in
the role of the woman allows an implication of "humiliation"
which is perhaps the necessary basis for much of this perverse
material. Humiliation in the female role is not, as far as one can
detect, a transvestite phenomenon. In this sense pornography
based on cross-dressing can be a highly misleading source of
understanding transvestism.

It is difficult to generalise about "soft" pornography since
to the non-perverse it may have some degree of interest whilst
to the deviant it may acquire all manner of sexual significance.
The transvestite with some fetishistic feelings may find a "drag"
magazine sexually arousing whilst another transvestite would
find it simply a source of information.

The second source of transvestite writings is in the club
magazines of the many transvestite societies. In America there

are magazines which appear to have a more general circulation. These writings are clearly not "hard" pornography and the frank sexual content is almost non-existent. They do not appear to be designed to function as "soft" pornography either although, of course, they may be used as such just as the contents of any daily paper might.

So it may be that guided by the autobiographies, commercial pornography, if conservatively evaluated, may teach something about the sexual origins of the transvestite. Magazine writings on the other hand describe the conscious fantasies, preoccupations and the behaviour of the transvestite.

It seems that Stoller's (1970) paper on pornography and perversion which in part deals with "transvestite pornography" is based on the author's request to one transvestite to bring him "pornography to suit his transvestism". Unfortunately, there is little ground to suppose that Stoller's analysis of the one story from the one person is generally applicable to the erotic fantasies of all transvestites. Moreover, Stoller goes into the parallel between the fantasy and the personal history of the case and this proves atypical of transvestism.

The story concerns a student under force, with threats of violence, being bound and gagged, etc., by a group of fearful, aggressive women. He is obliged to wear female attire. The transvestite himself had been similarly treated as a child. The women in his life dressed him as a girl as a joke — as did the girls in the story. Beyond this point Stoller's interpretation of the pornographic story in terms of the transvestite's history is confusing. He makes the comment that the story illustrates that "never in transvestite pornography is a male turned into a female". Stoller's basis for this is not explicit. Certainly transvestite stories do include males turning into persons who feel and act and are accepted as women. On the other hand, the ultimate magical transformation or the realisation of being a genetic female all the time does not appear.

Stoller claims that his analysis of the story and case shows four components in the transvestite's fantasy:

1. In saying to himself, "See what a lovely woman I make"

the transvestite is turning the sense of being damaged by the females who forced him into the clothes into a triumph.

2. The comfort of "self-realisation" as the transvestite evolves a fully feminine role.

3. He has fantasies of revenge on these women which create an exultant sense of redressing the balance.

4. He identifies not only with the humiliated male in the pornographic study, but with the "masterful aggressor, the phallic woman".

The revenge motive Stoller finds in the fantasies of non-transvestite men which include "poisoning one's partner with ejaculate". However, the transvestite's revenge is found in getting an erection at his point of greatest humiliation at the hands of the phallic women.

"The transvestite in the reality of his masturbation is having the final victory over such a woman . . . he does win; he has survived. His penis is not only preserved, but now as he celebrates his sacrament, he feels himself no longer split." Stoller cites the same features found in "semi-perverse pleasures built on reaction formation". These semi-perverse pleasures are apparently such as automobile racing, acting on the stage, or competitive sport. All of which provide "acutely anxiety provoking situations of potential triumph".

Thus an imposing if implausible edifice is created on a tiny, shifting foundation. Indeed Stoller goes on to cite an entirely different story written presumably by a transvestite in a magazine which is quite benign and unlike the commercial pornographic story. "Charming stories of the happy, shy man and the happy, competent woman happily buying clothes and then the happy woman putting the lovely clothes on the happy man." Stoller asserts that the essential dynamic of pornography is hostility. This seems to be true. However, the transvestite's story is the antithesis in that it contains a total lack of hostility, indulging the fantasy of a world where all striving is "pure".

An earlier paper by Stoller (1967) is based on the cover of a book "published for transvestites". "There are two beautiful, monstrous-breasted stiletto-heeled women each with a phallic-like whip dangling beside her pelvis. They are bullying the poor, pretty, defenceless transvestite." He also draws on the interviews with "transvestites and their women". The women all share the attribute of taking a conscious intense pleasure in seeing males dressed as females. All have in common a fear of and need to ruin masculinity. The transvestite tricks these phallic women in the picture, and in reality, into thinking he is "a poor, cowering wretch, whilst he is, in fact, full of triumph and excitedly masturbating".

It is hard to evaluate Stoller's papers composed as they are on such scant tangible evidence, the immense clinical experience and the psychoanalytic formulations. Undoubtedly there is the logical abyss here that commercial articles which seem to be aimed at transvestites are pornographic in the usual sense, where those written by transvestites for other transvestites are not. There are, in fact, no good grounds to assume that the stories of phallic women are specifically erotic to transvestites, if indeed at all commonly so. Indeed the phallic-woman motive is found with some regularity in everyday advertising. A current advertisement for rum on the hoardings employs such a figure complete with dagger strapped to her bare thigh. Neither does Stoller's belief in the origin of transvestism in the maltreatment of the male child by the aggressive women apparently stand up to objective evidence such as that presented by Prince and Bentler which is reviewed in Chapter 2.

As Burich McConaghy (1976) comment, it is not obvious that Stoller's pornographic story would appeal to the transvestite. Certainly the phallic-female figure as appearing in Stoller's story is not commonly found in writings by transvestites, but it is not absent either. For example:

> She was wearing a black "wet look" mini-skirt, matching knee-length boots, white high-necked blouse and heavy earrings. Her dark hair was drawn back and tied behind with a single scarlet ribbon and her full lips were emphasised with a scarlet lipstick. She looked sternly at Robert

and said "In this household I expect absolute obedience at all times" (*Beaumont Bulletin*, Vol. V, No. 5).

However, it is significant that Stoller in this paper is speaking of a condition in which "the clothes themselves cause sexual excitement". Such a definition is different to his earlier one and would appear to be more closely a definition of a form of fetishism.

Furthermore, in this paper Stoller suggests that the physical measurement of a penile erection in the patient shown transvestite pornography would be an objective means of arriving at a diagnosis of transvestism. Logically this would only be so if transvestism was a particular form of fetish. Stoller does indicate a degree of facetiousness in this suggestion and would perhaps agree that such psychophysiological measures are by no means simple and in any case have no bearing on the gender problems of the transvestite as opposed to the erotic sexual responses. The deficiencies in this reasoning are probably clarified when one considers that Stoller is equally saying that the "normal" man must show no such psychophysiological response to this category of pornographic literature.

Biegel and Feldman (1963) took a wider sample of transvestite literature. They pointed out quite rightly that stories about transvestites are only a "tiny fraction" of all stories involving female impersonation. They might also have included the observation that stories have often been written about transvestites by non-transvestites and for a non-transvestite audience. Biegel and Feldman suggested the various groups of literature differed in motivation and treatment so that in non-transvestite fiction the disguise serves to deceive someone to obtain or avoid something essential to the plot with no sexual conflict. In the transvestite story female impersonation is the central theme with the hero experiencing elation or degradation and final persuasion to adopt the opposite-sex role permanently.

Whilst there is reason behind this categorisation, practice is less convincing. It is not possible to draw these lines. Non-transvestite literature, i.e. written by non-transvestites for a general readership, e.g. Bernice Robins' "Sunday Best", may find a great transvestite following. Equally the description of the transvestite story is by no means all-inclusive especially as transvestites can and do write stories which are not preoccupied with final acceptance of a permanent female role. These writers took seventy-three published novels and short stories and twenty stories unpublished but submitted for publication. The latter group came from an American publisher dealing with transvestite literature (Chevalier Publications). It is not clear how the seventy-three other articles were gathered except they were written by amateurs, presumably transvestites, and only of a standard that 'could not possibly pass for literature of any but the lowest standard". Some selection has obviously been made perhaps with the underlying assumption that transvestite literature is only that of the lowest standard. This may, of course, be true but the arbitrary selection represents a weakness in the research.

Biegel and Feldman find that in only thirteen out of the ninety-three stories does the hero experience any desire to cross-dress before he has actually done so. In all cases he does so against his will at the outset. This might be regarded either as excusatory or perhaps realistic. We are, after all, talking of a compulsion which is almost invariably surrounded with guilt in its early phase. The hero fights against fate, but in the end half of the stories suggest he will continue as a woman and the other half that he will adopt the transvestite double life. Again the writers' observations seem to be in line with real life that some transvestites progress to transsexualism and others remain stable and adjusted to the transvestite dual role. In almost all the stories the transvestite was subject to an external compulsion to cross-dress.

These authors do not accept that this idea of external compulsion is in agreement with reality but the point of disagreement is rather in the source of the compulsion. The transvestite and transsexual often say that life has played a dirty trick in giving them a male body with female feelings. Such seems to be the one real belief in an external compulsion, i.e.

the individual is at the mercy of a whim of fate. Moreover, the transvestite striving to find explanations often centres on external figures in his unbringing. It might also be added that the transvestite story without some theme of external compulsion and the transvestite's resistance might be rather hard to concoct. Certainly the ninety-three stories usually dealt with transvestites who found themselves perfect women and again the writers view this as invariably far from reality. They comment that no transvestites make "ravishing beauties". Factually they are incorrect in this, some do succeed both in real life and on the stage in appearing to be attractive women. It is rather the transvestite's own insistence on adopting the pose of a "ravishing beauty" which is a departure from reality. In reality very few women are indeed "ravishing beauties". This is a very rare achievement for a woman and in any event mostly in the eye of the beholder! As has previously been remarked the transvestite adopts a model which is not simply that of the average woman, but attempts to assume the characteristics of what he regards as the most feminine of women. Nevertheless many transvestites and transsexuals make quite acceptable "passable" women. For example, April Ashley worked as a female model appearing in major fashion magazines and one of the author's transvestite patients is employed as a demonstrator of ladies clothing in a fashionable store. At any rate the generalisation from this finding to the assumption that transvestites must feel adequate neither in the male nor female role is somewhat unjustified.

This research emphasises that the two major coercive forces pointed to by researchers studying transvestism, genetic and the experience of being forced to dress in female clothes as a punishment, are relatively rare in fiction. Biological forces only appear as an afterthought and "pinafore punishment" was involved in only one of the ninety-three stories — and this a story where the hero is homosexual and ceased to cross-dress. However, in Prince and Bentler's (1972) survey "pinafore punishment" is not mentioned by more than a few transvestites. For some reason Biegel and Feldman regarded this as an explanation which is a favourite of transvestites in clinical interview. Generally clinical impressions do not agree with them.

Forcible coercion in the hands of the powerful woman appears in about one-third of these ninety-three stories, apparently Stoller's phallic women who appear as strangers, stepmothers, and aunts demanding service. Some of the stories turned the woman into a lesbian lover or the transvestite becomes cared for by a man or another wealthy transvestite. Indeed in some cases the woman castrates the transvestite (Stoller denies such stories occur). In some cases the mother figure keeps aloof whilst the transvestite hero mixes at an intimate and not a sexual level with sexually evocative girls. After demonstrating his asexuality he returns to be accepted by his mother. This type of story is related to transvestites who frown on sex and, in fact, are characterised by a low sexuality.

"Conditioning" or the transvestite hero having been dressed as a girl, cuddled and told he was lovely, etc., did not appear frequently in Biegel and Feldman's stories. Indeed they agree that though this is an attractive explanation of transvestism it is rarely true in real life. A variation of the theme is that of "mother really wanted a girl" so that in fiction mother's wish is fulfilled by the hero's change of sex. Twenty-five per cent of the stories seem to have embodied this theme, possibly because it has a "guilt-soothing effect on the reader". In ten of the stories persuasion rather than coercion was the format. Cross-dressing usually involved altruistic themes of helping others in some way and the altruism is highly rewarded in affection and attention from mother.

It is not clear how Biegel and Feldman found incest to be a theme except in a symbolic way. "Having given up his masculine strivings — the boy — can enjoy mother's love without fear." It is true that such a theme would bring to mind the origins of the oedipal situation, but the writers go on to say that forced or voluntary castration in the stories mitigate the incestuous meaning. However, in psychoanalytic terms the castration fear would originate in the incestuous desires of the oedipal situation. Logically castration would not be associated with an amelioration of the oedipal guilt.

The process of "dressing" is an important point made by these writers rarely mentioned in other works. The process of dressing for the child is in many ways the most positive continuing attention and physical contact with mother. It is a warm, intimate, and dependent exercise which is lost with maturity. Dressing, therefore, may acquire a special meaning and transvestite literature continues to refer to the feel of clothes, the detailed examination of them and the precise process of putting them on. Dressing as a process must then evoke "the blissful past" perhaps. For example:

> The dressing continued, a cream brassiere matching the panties next: bending forward in a typical feminine gesture he expertly fastened the straps behind his back. Finishing, he went to the mirror and critically examined the effect. A satin "van ralte" slip was next. Liza insisted that this material was the only one that gave a fluid line and flow to the outer garments. The outer garment was superb, a completely original yet classical style. It was a fabulous cream gaberdine, the material just right for the rather changeable Sydney winter climate. It was top stitched, the bodice semi-fitted with six straight pleats across the bustline, these all stitched down. Long, skinny sleeves and the same pleats on the skirt. These were not stitched but released to flow into a gently flared skirt. Two long strands of large cultivated pearls loosely knotted around the neck completed the outfit. Liza fitted the same wig he had worn the previous evening. It was still perfectly set and only needed the slightest touching up to make a perfect coiffure.
>
> The shoes were cream kid leather shoes, again cut in a classical court style, the low cut vamp flowing smoothly into a one inch platform sole. The heels were four inch and perfectly completed the classical look that the style of dress sought to create. (From *Feminique* — magazine of the Sea Horse Club of Australia. "Don't Judge a Book by it's Cover" by Trina Taylor.)

An odd finding in this research is that about half of the stories mention young girls flipping the transvestite's skirt, stroking his thighs, kissing him affectionately, showing their underwear and other "minor sexual intimacies". This sort of theme is absent in other samples of transvestite fiction which rarely involve this form of frank sexuality.

One has to view Biegel and Feldman's research with as much reserve as Stoller's because of the uncertain origins of the material. It seems to have involved transsexual and homosexual themes denied by Stoller and not apparent in the two studies to follow.

In the case of commercial soft pornography one must enquire what the effects are of the need to produce stereotyped stories for a reasonably wide market. How far are such "fantasies" a valid representation of the transvestite's personal fantasies and how far they are simply a concoction expected to play on the fantasies of transvestites and many other groups? These are problems for which an answer has not been found. Buhrich and McConaghy (1976) take issue with Stoller, and Biegel and Feldman, and it is clear that the difference in the research findings is largely a matter of sampling. Unlike the other researchers Buhrich and McConaghy sampled the magazine literature of transvestite societies. These included the Australian magazine *Feminique*, the British *Beaumont Bulletin*, and *Transvestia* from the U.S.A. None of these magazines would normally be regarded as pornographic, although, of course, they include a fair number of stories about transvestism written by members of the societies, they do not contain frankly sexual or erotic material. Indeed, references to sexual issues seem rather rarer than they do in the average woman's magazine.

Almost without exception stories in these magazines elaborate on the fantasy of how a boy becomes a beautiful girl and magic, supernatural, or even science fictional themes appear. It is a curious fact that any kind of reference to surgical intervention or even accidental injury to sexual organs seems to be missing. The main figures in the stories simply achieve the appearance and emotions of the opposite gender. Equally, no fantasies of marriage as a woman, sexual relations, having children, even of kissing or physical contact appear. However, the transformation is almost invariably into an attractive young person and never into an elderly housewife.

Buhrich and McConaghy found that Stoller's phallic woman, aggressive and frightening, did not appear in these stories. Women were generally shown as sympathetic and helping. Even where women coerced the transvestite this was done rather in the context of someone who knew what was best and not as a person exerting a ruthless authority. This is not entirely true as shown by the previous excerpt from such a story.

In the analysis of Buhrich and McConaghy of twenty-eight stories there are thirteen of the type where the main male character has to cross-dress for some accidental reason. In four cases the cross-dressing is against the wishes of the main character, but it emerges that he finds his true self in the female role. In ten stories a woman is a helpful initiator who teaches him how to dress and apply make up and behave as a woman. Buhrich comments that in this context no sexual interest appears although in four stories he marries the girl who helps him to dress and lives happily ever after. In eight stories the transformation is depicted as complete, women admire him, men compete for his attention, and even his male friends do not recognise him. He is able to be another person. Transsexuals do not appear to indulge in story writing of this kind, but judging from the numerous autobiographies (Jan Morris, Roberta Cowell, etc.) one would not expect transformation themes as much as a belief that the transsexual achieves only the right to be his female self (or her male self) rather than to become another person of the opposite sex. In seven stories there was an extensive and meticulous description of clothing and the hero becomes a remarkably beautiful woman. Buhrich and McConaghy record reluctance to cross-dress, e.g. soldiers sent in women's army uniform to spy, etc., in nine stories and in five he is made to appear in public with a fear of discovery. However, his fear of discovery is always gratifyingly unfounded.

Attention is drawn to the fact that hypotheses about the

appearance of mother figures as of major importance in transvestite fantasies are hardly borne out. More often than not the woman is specified as fairly independent, e.g. as a new stepmother, a shop assistant, a girl at work. Of course, there is sufficient ambiguity in the hypothesis to argue that the transvestite does specify the independence of the female figure just because of the guilt which would be aroused by consciously admitting that her significance is that of a mother figure.

The most pervasive feature in this literature is its stereotyped nature. The literary level is weak and there is a consistency of expression which is almost unrelieved. The hero never "puts on a dress", he always "slips into something comfortable". The stories are always of a fairy-tale quality even if they do not resort to magic mirrors and mysterious potions. There is invariably the theme of the miracle of a strongly male hero emerging instantaneously as a beautiful woman. It is rare indeed for stories to be based on the real-life efforts of the transvestite to acquire the skills to "pass". Buhrich and McConaghy make an interesting comparison between their group's stories and the reality of the lives of thirty transvestites. Table 10 is abbreviated from Buhrich and McConaghy's paper. It is clear there is a vast difference. In fiction the transvestite is a reluctant man persuaded into the role of a woman and assisted by enthusiastic women around him. He sometimes marries one of these women who readily accepts him. He successfully passes as a woman in public, often escorted by males and is never detected. He sees himself as permanently in the female role in a world in which transvestism is not uncommon. Sexual implications are avoided. On the other hand, in reality the transvestite initiates his own cross-dressing very much alone and usually at the outset feeling the problem to be suffered by only he himself. He continues despite the opposition of others, sometimes only passive, and only informs his wife after marriage. The wife has difficulty in coming to terms with the transvestism. His brief spells of cross-dressing only infrequently take him into public and then in constant anxiety about detection. The sexual component in his

TABLE 10   *Comparison of transvestite fact and fiction (abbreviated from Buhrich and McConaghy, 1976)*

	Fact (30 subjects)	Fiction (20 stories)
First cross-dressing	Secret, at own initiative	Reluctant but persuaded
Assistance	Alone — parent or wife not enthusiastic	Always assisted by women who are enthusiastic
Public appearance	Never — or avoiding places where friends might see him	Passes successfully. Close friends fail to recognise him
Escorted by males	Very rarely	Often
Marriage	Wife informed after marriage if at all and has difficulty in accepting	Married woman who helped him to cross-dress and they are very happy
Sexual arousal	Always in adolescence and often in adulthood	Not mentioned
Orientation	Heterosexual	Heterosexual
Duration of dressing	Brief, often through lack of opportunity	Permanent
Incidence	In adolescence believe themselves to be alone	Not uncommon

transvestism is strong in adolescence and sometimes stretches into adulthood. Both fact and fiction declare the transvestite's insistence on his heterosexuality.

Discussion of transvestite fiction and pornography seems no more likely to reflect the preoccupations of all transvestites than say homosexual pornography and fiction represents those of all homosexuals. To bring this into perspective the contents of several magazines issued by transvestite groups have been examined. These magazines are *Beaumont Bulletin* from Britain, *Feminique* from Australia, *Transvestia* and the *Femme Mirror* from the Phi Pi Epsilon Society in the U.S.A. The first of these was most readily available and hence was examined in the greatest detail. A complete series of magazines from 1971 to 1975 was made available by the Beaumont Society.

The articles in the *Beaumont Bulletin* are clearly divided into two categories. Firstly, those typical of any club magazine written by the secretary, editor, and section organisers. These were more or less regular business reports, editorials and so on. Secondly, there were articles apparently written or submitted by members which did not belong to the routine format of the magazine. For the purpose in hand it is the second group which most truly represents the concerns of the transvestite.

No article in the twenty-five issues would be regarded as pornographic in the sense of being obviously designed to promote any perverse sexual excitement. Indeed reference to any frank sexual matter was exceedingly rare. Photographs were published, but were all of transvestites in conventional poses presumably intended to resemble photographs of the average woman in the family album. Wives often appear in these photographs also. The articles were not easy to categorise. On the one hand the content was often mixed and on the other it was sometimes hard to determine, say, whether or not an autobiography was better categorised as fiction. Table 11 gives the breakdown obtained. The major single contribution is found to consist of rather academic discussions, particularly about the nature of transvestism. About one in five of these articles concerns wives and discusses how a wife might be told about her husband's transvestism or the articles are written by wives themselves describing their anxieties or acceptance of transvestite husbands.

The law also figures prominently. The articles more or less evenly distribute into three categories.
1. Statements of the law under which transvestites might be prosecuted.
2. Accounts of brushes with the law in which the police had acted with kindness and understanding.
3. Accounts of conflicts with the law in which transvestites had been subjected to ridicule, loss of employment, etc.
Unlike literature from other minority groups there is a singular lack of the vituperative articles directed at the police and the law. Rather they reflect passive complaint when things go wrong and gratitude when they do not.

TABLE 11. *Classification of articles in transvestite magazine*
(Beaumont Bulletin)

Type of article	No. of articles
1. *Serious discussion*	
(a) Nature of transvestism	18
(b) Problems facing wives	11
(c) The law	9
(d) Reprints	7
(e) Conference reports	3
(f) Transsexualism	2
(g) Hormones	2
Total:	52
2. *Literary articles*	
(a) Poems	17
(b) Autobiography	11
(c) Newspaper cuttings and book reviews	10
(d) Fiction	7
Total:	45
3. *Accounts of transvestite behaviour and advice*	
(a) Make up, dress, etc.	19
(b) Public appearances	14
(c) Electrolysis	7
(d) General	2
Total:	42
4. *Club matters*	
(a) Specific social activities, parties, etc.	16
(b) Club organisation	14
Total:	30
5. *Miscellaneous*	8
Total number of articles 177	

Matters relating to sex change including the use of hormones to produce feminisation are relatively rare. This is consistent with Prince and Bentler's (1972) finding that transvestites were not greatly concerned about sex reassignment.

Fiction forms part of what has been called "literary" articles in Table 11. This is a small part though and, in fact, the number of contributions recorded was largely composed of the serialised part of one story. Autobiographies were the more common, but of course they were hard to evaluate and being brief were selective and optimistic. A relatively large number of short poems was generally relevant to transvestism, but was restricted to no particular form. They included a few comic limericks, but no salacious material.

The third largest group of articles consisted of advice giving articles about transvestite behaviour. The largest part of these concerned matters like how to apply cosmetics, fashions, suppliers of women's clothing in unusual sizes, shops which were prepared to welcome transvestite customers and so on. Articles about exploits "going out dressed" were mostly accounts of incidents in which transvestites were "read" or trapped in situations where they might be discovered. There was a consistency about this theme which suggests that there may be some seeking for just this pattern of experience. An almost Cinderella element appears in the way in which the beautifully dressed transvestite walks out and returns bedraggled, all composure gone and in fear of disclosure. The advice giving seems to be rather repetitive and almost invariably includes the warning that night time is not the time for "a girl to go out alone".

Articles concerning the electrolysis of facial hair are partly purely technical advice and descriptions of the somewhat painful process, but also include comments on how to obtain what is essentially a service provided for women.

Articles relating to club matters have no special features other than the rather ponderous use of feminine names and pronouns. Members always seem to be prettily attired ladies or girls and never well-dressed women. Social events are featureless, apparently having their value in the opportunity "to dress". As one correspondent expresses it "Society gatherings tended to take the form of pre-Renaissance Mothers' Union/ Womens Institute meetings sans knitting!"

Other sources of information about transvestite fantasies can be obtained from studies of dreams and from projective test material. Karpman (1947) studies the dreams of one transvestite patient in great detail. He makes an unusual comment on the

sexual component of cross-dressing in that he insists that transvestism and masturbation are "univerally concomitant". This is
not universally accepted in the present state of knowledge.
However, Karpman says that the transvestite may not masturbate for several hours after cross-dressing, but ultimately either
masturbates — or urinates as masturbation and urination are the
psychic equivalent. It would, of course, be surprising if several
hours cross-dressing was not universally concomitant with urination alone! He analyses fifty-three of his patients' dreams and
says that the common theme is that of masculinised women and
feminised men. Women are usually equipped with a penis and
have no breasts while the patient himself is entirely a woman,
able to receive a male organ. He dreams of men making love to
him as a woman passionate and receptive. Karpman regards this
as a homosexual fantasy despite the fact that the relationship
depicted in the dream is explicitly heterosexual. The argument
is complex because the "masculine traits displayed by him
appear as a defence reaction developed to overcome his basic
femininity". His transvestism is seen as an attempt to maintain
a fiction of heterosexuality although homosexual. The patient
is a married man with a family, as Karpman argues most transvestites are, and the interpretation illustrates the difficulty of
understanding the concept of homosexuality as it is employed
in psychodynamic explanations.

Worden and Marsh (1955) report the results of the Thematic
Apperception Test as applied to cross-dressers seeking sex reassignment. In this test the subject is asked to create stories
around a series of pictures. In all probability the subjects were
mostly transsexual, but the findings appear to reflect a number
of points relevant to transvestites also. The authors comment
on the concept of femininity which is an over-generalisation of
restricted aspects. They comment that it is like the child who
says "I want to be a fireman because they ride on fire engines",
but does not take into account the dangers and difficulties of
the work. They find that cross-dressers conceive femininity in
two ways:

1. A woman is a person who wears pretty feminine clothes

and is admired specifically for this.

2. Female social interaction is seen as unilateral involving admiration of the transvestite by others and relationships based wholly on appearance.

Interestingly, Worden and Marsh also found that their subjects stated directly that they hoped sex reassignment operations would leave them sexless so that they could feel "free and clean". This observation may be some clue to the significance of the contrasting writings described by Stoller. On the one hand, Stoller's stories seem to be violently erotic whilst on the other hand some appeared to be banal and without sexual awareness. Perhaps it is part of the transvestite fantasy to escape from the pressures of male sexuality possibly exacerbated by guilt aroused by its deviant content. The banal stories may well reflect the transvestite's concept of femininity as being largely depicted as simple, asexual, passive and "pure".

Buhrich and McConaghy quoted a number of outlines of transvestite stories, but no complete stories have apparently been published in the professional literature. In view of the special qualities related to the transvestite feminine fantasies the following two transvestite stories and a poem are quoted as typical.

ALL FOR THE BEST by Jackie

Like most newly engaged couples, Tim and Jean were up against it. Marriage meant a home and a home meant money — lots of it. Both wanted to begin marriage and a future together in their own home and as they both said many times a home wasn't a home without a family. So they were saving very hard.

Tim had a job as a design engineer and he was firmly anchored in digs in Manchester whilst Jean was in her last year of a teaching course at college in London. This really made weekend visits very difficult without the almost mindless expense on hotels for Tim. Evenings seemed so long for both of them and to Jean the girls at college all seemed to be taking things so lightly whilst she was aching to be with Tim. He spent his time either at work or writing long emotional letters to her to bridge the gap between them. Facing the loneliness was enough but inwardly he felt a terrible uncertainty about himself, he eternally longed to be able to talk freely to Jean and know that she would not desert him.

Jean's last letter had caught him between a wild dream and desperate anxiety. She had casually joked that if only he had been a girl he would have been able to stay weekends at the college, just like the girl friends of her companions. The warden was generous about allowing them to use the rooms of students who were home for the weekend, but visitors were to be girls only — the warden saw to that with a beady eye. He found his hands all of a tremble and he let his eggs and bacon go cold during his reverie. Neither was it all far from his mind for three days until he decided to write in answer.

"Darling it is so rotten for us when I could come to stay if only I was a girl. It is so unfair. How's about you turning me into a girl? Ha, ha!" He felt that if he put it that way Jean might take it either as a joke or a serious hint. Either way he might sound out what her reaction might be to the truth about himself. By the time he had posted the letter it had begun to feel more like a desperate gamble and his world would be shattered if she was angry.

No reply came for several days. One idea chased another through his mind. Was she upset, might she be angry, what might she think of him if she guessed? Then the letter arrived. "Darling Tim," it began, "what an idea you've had. I bet you could get by as a girl if I helped you." Tantalisingly she said no more but little at a time the pair worked out the details. Tim was in a constant state of suspended excitement. As *the* weekend drew near he could hardly contain himself.

He would meet her at a station outside London with the firm's car. She had promised to bring some of her own clothes and buy him some undies and a girdle. She asked him to bring shoes and a wig — he wondered why. He was hurtling through a state of uncontrollable happiness, not just at the thought of being with her but because he had been wrestling with the need to tell Jean about his love of feminine things. He didn't like the term at all but he had known for years that he was transvestite. To resist his feminine self was agony and at the same time spending all those hours in the privacy of his own room as a woman seemed to be such a happy and content experience. He felt it might all go if he was married but half wished that it wouldn't and the other half feared what it might do to Jean if it didn't. Now a perfect solution seemed possible.

He met Jean as arranged, his heart pounding — he almost feared she had set it all up just to trap him somehow, although he knew that was nonsense. Then she came bouncing out of the station towards him wreathed in smiles carrying her small suitcase. They parked in a quiet country road and the transformation began. Tim tried to pretend it was all new. She was very patient with him, handing him the garments one by one. She fastened the lacy bra for him and helped him get the matching slip over his head in the confined space of the car. He rolled the pair of sun mist sheer nylon tights up his legs without thinking whilst she smiled cryptically. He then eased his feet into the pair of dainty court shoes he had brought with him. He then put on the check skirt and smoothed away the wrinkles around his hips, then the mushroom coloured sweater. Jean then set to work with the make up she had taken from her own bag and put on him the wig. Somehow she worked the wig into a style which was so much more attractive than it had ever seemed before. Gazing at himself in the mirror he could hardly believe that he was the happy girl in the mirror. He had never noticed before how long his eyelashes were or the peculiar feminine pout of his lips. His feeling of joy was only part of a sense of new found oneness with Jean.

"You really look attractive Tim", she said. "Oh heavens that won't do, Tina it will have to be."

As they drove along to the college Tim's confidence grew — especially when a lorry driver whistled down at him when they were held up by the lights. They left the car in the college car park and Jean watched her new found cousin walking along beside her. "You look perfect Tina, relax." Tim felt on a plateau, everything he ever wanted seemed to be coming true. At last they reached Jean's room and Tim flung himself untidily into a chair. "Oh no you don't Tina, you never know who will come in. This weekend Tina you are and Tina you stay, Tim got left behind somewhere up the M1. Sit up properly, cross your ankles and put your hands gently together in your lap."

Just then the door burst open and in rushed a red-haired girl.

"Hey Jean, have you still got . . . oh sorry!" "Come in Liz. I want you to meet my cousin Tina who's staying in Margaret's room tonight."

"Hello", said Liz. "To be honest I saw you come in a few minutes ago and I thought I had better come and size up the opposition before the dance tonight." Tina ventured a demure "That will be lovely" to Liz's offer of an invitation to the dance and as Liz prattled on he began to feel that Tina was there to stay. Liz had the idea that Jean and Tina could make a foursome with Alan and Roy but Jean stopped that short by saying they had tickets for the theatre.

"News of my dishy cousin will be all round the college now Liz has got hold of it." said Jean. "Prepare to repel hungry males!" Tina hadn't thought of that but Jean laughed. "That's one lesson a girl has to learn, and you haven't much time Tina. Still you've certainly made it if you have got Liz worried."

Jean smiled at Tina as one girl smiles at another. "Now you won't need to hide things away when we are married darling, Tina will be welcome too, she's such a smashing girl!" Tim was aghast. "You. . . . ." They took each other's hands and felt very very close and in love.

THE UNKNOWN WOMAN . . . Shirley

There she sits, neat and prim,
Confident in her own woman self.
Legs Black-stockinged
Peep beneath navy polka dotted dress
And slip into patent, plum, sling back shoes.

Clear and fresh,
Perfume wafts around her person
Face prettied with a little make-up
Head adorned with a French style cut
Was there anything lovelier.

Presently she will arise
Trip across landing and stairs,
And make her way to quieten
Her pet parakeet,
Confident in her own woman self.

If one knew she were not female
Would it make any difference
Would she be scorned and ridiculed
For her belief in free dress?

Oh! hypocrites of mankind,
Who would do the same.
If they had only half the nerve
of this poor creature.

CONVERSATION ON A STAIRCASE . . . *Penny*

The Escort tripped over the hem of his dress for the hundredth time and only saved his nose from being driven into the mossy steps of the staircase by frenziedly flapping his wings. Peter's full skirt wrapped itself suddenly round his knees in the ensuing gale and down he went. Unhappily lacking wings (for the moment he hoped) he was unable to save his nose from the fate that the Escort had narrowly avoided but richly deserved.

"Hey!" Peter protested angrily, "for Chri. . . . ."

"Ah!" said the Escort, lifting an admonitory finger, "not here. If you don't mind."

"Well — hell, why can't you lift the hem of your dress and see what your feet are doing? It's getting boring. You have got feet, I suppose."

"Of course I've got feet," said the Escort primly. "Nice feet as it so happens. A lot nicer than yours," he added with a rather sickening smirk.

"Anyway," he went on "I can't lift the hem of my dress because if I did I would have to let go of you, which I am not allowed to do. Regulations, you understand."

"No, I don't," said Peter. "I think the whole thing is quite barmy. Incidentally," he went on, "do I get a dress like that when we get there?" He rather envied the Escort's beautiful attire which was not unlike the garment he had been gazing at wistfully when the bomb went off in the shop.

"Well, I don't know," said the Escort doubtfully, "it depends on your duties. Now this," he added with another of his smirks, "is only issued to flying personnel. It was just unfortunate that they didn't have my exact size."

He looked at Peter sharply with a slight frown.

"Anyway," he said, "you're a woman . . . though my instructions were . . ." He shrugged his wings and looked slightly puzzled.

"Well — er," Peter began.

"Women have different duties where we are going," the Escort went on, "— we'll be there soon, by the way, just another couple of aeons — and they wear trousers and suits and travel on commuter trains and things — hey! hang on, you have gone as white as a ghost — um — in a manner of speaking. What's the matter?"

"Just one of my turns," mumbled Peter, clutching the balustrade. "Suits, you said? Trains?"

"Yes," continued the Escort brightly. "You see, everyone who comes here does exactly the opposite to what they did down there. So you see, as you were a woman, you'll be a man here. Get the idea? and of course, it's the other way round for men. Rather fun really."

"There's something I should explain," said Peter shakily.

"Explain," said the Escort. "Explain what?"

"Well, I am not actually a woman," Peter began.

The Escort tripped over for the hundredth and first time, but on this occasion did not succeed in saving his nose, to Peter's intense satisfaction.

"Not a woman?" said the Escort, rubbing his nose and looking up at Peter. "But your clothes . . . hair . . . make up . . ." He scrambled to his feet, momentarily displaying a flash of silken stockings and a beautifully hemmed slip.

"Now, look here," he said severely, "don't mess me about, otherwise there will be trouble when we get to the Guardroom. You'll be issued on arrival with a pin stripe suit whether you like it or not. And a shirt. Tie. Black shoes. Oh yes, and an umbrella, though I can nver understand why — it never rains."

"What do men get issued with?" Peter asked.

The Escort's face softened. "Ah, well," he said, "we . . ." He stopped and glared at Peter. "Never mind," he said, "you know, the sort of thing you've always had. Now, come on or we'll be late."

"Now just wait a minute," said Peter. "You seem to have some very quaint ideas about what men and women do. For a start, women already wear trouser suits and a lot travel to work on trains. I am jolly sure that not many of them will want to go on doing that — travelling on trains, I mean."

"Really!" exclaimed the Escort, almost tripping over again, "are you sure?"

"Of course I am sure and furthermore . . ."

"I suppose you are going to tell," the Escort interrupted, "that men wear skirts."

"Some do," said Peter. "And a lot more housekeep and so on."

"I'll have to report this," said the Escort firmly, "there's going to be trouble. Terrible trouble."

"So I can take it that there will be no problem about my wearing what I like when we get there?" said Peter.

"What — you mean dresses and things?"

"Yes."

"Oh! You won't be able to do that, most certainly not. No, no. The system can't be changed just like that. There's all the Rules you see. And one of the Rules is that if you turn up as a woman, then you will be a man when you arrive. It's your fault, you shouldn't have dressed like that."

"Why not?" said Peter indignantly.

"Well . . . I don't know really, but it does upset the Manufacturer when he finds out that people aren't happy with the way He made them. He does try terribly hard to please, you know."

"Well, He didn't please me. Anyway, what's going to happen now. I am not going to spend the rest of Eternity in a pin stripe suit."

"It is all rather unfortunate, I agree," said the Escort, scratching his beautiful hairdo with one delicately extended finger. "It would have been better," he went on, "if you had gone to the Other Place — you know, the one Way Down There."

"Why?"

"Well, everybody stays as they are on arrival — that's the point of the place, you see. So if you had turned up there instead of here, you'd stay just as you are for eternity."

"How do I get there?" demanded Peter eagerly.

"Here, hang on — you wouldn't want to go there," said the Escort with alarm, "it's not nearly as comfortable as where we're going — though the central heating is more efficient, I believe. It couldn't be worse than ours," he added gloomily, "I have to wear my electric knickers most of the time up here."

"I like it warm," said Peter. "How do I get there?"

"Well, it's quite simple. You just slide down the balustrade here and . . . hey!

come back — at once!"

In a flash Peter had wrenched himself from the Escort's grip and leapt on the balustrade.

"I'd rather spend the rest of Eternity in hell as a woman than be a man Up There," he shouted. "Goodbye!" and off he sped with the speed of Light into Infinity.

"Drat her — him — her. Oh! knickers!" The Escort was truly vexed and stamped his foot, tearing the hem of his beautiful flying suit in the process.

CHAPTER 7

The Transvestite and the Law

West (1974) quotes Ullerstam, a Swedish physician: "coupling of inferior personality and moral turpitude with unconventional sexual interest is an unjustified slur, perpetuated by the ignorance and prejudice of psychiatrists." Whether or not this is a valid accusation of psychiatry, it most certainly depicts a confusion which is perpetuated in society by a wide range of both professional and lay people. There is a general and intense conviction in most of us that those whose sexual feelings are unusual, or even those whose behaviour we believe to be sexually abberant, are in some ways necessarily immoral and inferior. This deep belief leads to the use of laws to condemn and control at all costs in terms of prejudice rather than reasonable understanding. With this context the law and its application can come dangerously near to distortion and misuse.

The concept of the law specifically framed for the prosecution of well-defined antisocial acts is a naive one. Laws appear to be made with specific objects in view but become general principles for the management of diverse forms of behaviour in many cases. The Official Secrets Act, laws relating to Conspiracy, and the Public Order Act of 1936 are clear examples. The former was put on the statute book in the context of the First World War and the latter to control Fascist parades in the thirties but both are open to use in quite different contexts.

Similarly we have a mass of ubiquitous law which seems to serve as and when required. Law relating to obstruction does not require that anything or anyone be obstructed in the

normal sense of the word. Possessing housebreaking implements
does not require the specialised tools of the burglary trade, a
plastic library ticket might well be sufficient for a conviction if
in the possession of a "suspected person".

What makes the law viable is its responsible use by the police
and the courts in the interests of society. The legal machinery
must be maintained in a state of equilibrium by the good judgment of a large number of people. Recent talk of a police pay
dispute raised the suggestion that police might seek to prosecute
all observed motoring offences. This sanction would immediately have created social chaos. The "law-abiding citizen" is a
myth for we can only stay within the spirit of the law, we can
never hope to be within the law itself.

Transvestites have particular difficulty with the law in many
countries because they are frequently prosecuted when in fact
there are no laws apparently relevant to cross-dressing in public.
The crucial issue is not if the behaviour of transvestites breaks
specific laws but if the social control of transvestite behaviour is
properly and justly exercised by the use of existing law. Moreover, it is society itself which determines if this is the case. If
society is offended by a minority it exercises a right to be protected from that minority. On the other hand the offence may
originate in false beliefs and misconceptions which can only be
regulated by social education and in turn this process modifies
the law.

The *Journal of Homosexuality* reports a legal wrangle in the
City of Chicago. The city's "Public Moral Code" prohibits
"Wearing clothing of the opposite sex with intent to conceal his
or her sex". Following the prosecution of two transvestites this
law was challenged on the grounds that it was unconstitutionally
vague, denied equal protection under the law, and was an
improper use of police powers. A similar action in the City of
Columbus had been successful but in that city the clause about
intent to conceal sex had not been included.

The Chicago judge declared "It was not enacted to regulate
the manner in which one may dress. Rather it appears to
prohibit conduct of a homosexual nature. . . ." Despite the

amendment of the law relating to homosexual practices many years ago, the judge ruled that homosexuality "was not a fundamental right" and that it may contribute to moral delinquency! A large part of the concern of the judge seems to have been the misbehaviour of transvestites in "public ladies' facilities" which could hardly be conduct of a homosexual nature. This is an example of ill-founded law and its application, which is probably immune from rational argument but on the surface of it would seem to exempt transvestites who publicly declared themselves in some way such as wearing a badge.

Some illogicality is apparent in the law related to transvestism from early times. Bowman and Engle (1957) discuss the condemnation of cross-dressing from three possible sources which have little to do with transvestism as we know it. Firstly, some religions involving the worshipping of idols also required cross-dressing amongst the followers. (This might be said of the Christian religion to some degree if one thinks of the effeminate dress of the bishops.) Therefore, idolatry and cross-dressing were seen as associated and the former was controlled by outlawing the latter. Secondly, there have long been rules and conventions about the conduct of war and it is readily apparent that if men stooped so low as to dress themselves like women, they might unfairly obtain an advantage in battle. (The Scots and the Greeks at least did not respect this convention it seems.) Thirdly, it seemed that permitting a person to dress in the clothes of the opposite sex might encourage homosexual behaviour which was more vehemently proscribed.

It is difficult to keep Judaic law in proportion because of its apparent severity and the way in which its emphasis differs from the laws of modern Western civilisation. For example, it was forbidden for men to view themselves in a mirror except to shave, since to do so would be equivalent to feminine vanity.

The law has also arrived at a position which discriminates between the cross-dressing of men and women. Bowman and Engle report an attempt in a California court to prosecute two women for cross-dressing. Whilst a strict application of the law indicated that they were committing an offence, the court found them not guilty on the grounds that it would be unreasonable for any woman who chose to wear trousers to require a police permit. Nevertheless transsexual women living as males live in an identical manner and, for example, act in as provocatively sexually assertive a manner as a genetic man would. Bowman and Engle also cite the case of a married couple who were both transsexual. The wife wished to become a man and the husband a woman, in fact they wished to reverse their roles in the marriage. Both sought sex reassignment surgery and hormone therapy. The wife had her wishes readily granted and the husband was refused.

The law is implicated in the sex reassignment question in a rather vague way. For example, in Norway it was decided that the transsexual could legally have his testicles amputated but not his penis. In America the question of whether or not surgery is legal depends on its infringement of the "Mayhem Statute". This law had archaic origins forbidding the cutting off of any part of a soldier's body which may be required for fighting. Perhaps it may be in some way relevant to the male's warlike capacity but the law on this point does not seem to have been adequately tested. The whole question of surgery for transsexuals tends to be shrouded in a degree of mysticism and occultism absent in all other discussion of operative procedures. Even the plastic surgeons Laub and Fisk (1974), with extensive experience of transsexual surgery, speak of their personal difficulties in carrying out the operation, in near-Biblical terms.

The law traditionally regards man and woman as irrefutably distinct but still does not define this difference. Science finds otherwise, that there is a grey area where the indices of sex are ambiguous. Where the sex of the individual is in question there are decisions of expediency and there is a multiplicity of ways in which the "correct" sex may be chosen. The male to female transsexual Renée Richards attempts to secure the right through the courts to play in women's tennis. It seems that some courts uphold her right whilst others do not. Tennis authorities like other athletic institutions insist on a definition of sex by karyotyping or chromosome study. Medically this is a

limited definition with quite distinct deficiencies which are
likely to become more acute as scientific knowledge grows. A
group of people of no small size cannot be regarded as typically
male or female by chromosomal standards, despite the fact that
their social behaviour is indisputably that of a man or a woman.
The exact equivalence in terms of sex between the surgically
corrected testicular feminisation syndrome and the operated
male transsexual has no legal solution since the unalterable
birth certificate of one shows the sex as female and the other
as male. It appears to hang entirely on the presence of mind of
the doctor at the birth in declaring the sex "not completely
formed yet" to allow time for consideration about what might
amount to sex reassignment at birth. If the child is surgically
feminised then "she" would be registered as female and become
legally female.

The divorce proceedings heard by Mr Justice Ormrod in 1970
exposed the problem. A male to female transsexual, Mrs April
Corbett (formerly Miss April Ashley), had been "married" to a
Mr Corbett, but the marriage had foundered and Mr Corbett
was seeking a divorce which Mrs Corbett was to contest. The
divorce action was not in fact heard because it was necessary to
decide first if a marriage had existed at all. The court heard a
great deal of medical and other evidence about Mrs Corbett's
sex because the marriage could only be considered legal if it
was decided that she was female. In the event the judge ruled
that because she was shown as male on her birth certificate, and
had been declared male at birth, she was not able to enter a
legal marriage with another male. Therefore no divorce could
take place either. Whatever Mrs Corbett's (or Miss Ashley's)
psychology, whatever her style of life or even the appearance
of her sexual organs, she remains whatever her birth certificate
says she is.

Various social agencies co-operate with the re-registering of
sex, e.g. Income Tax and Department of Health and Social
Security. However, the process is simply one of framing
documents in the way in which the individual wishes to be
known. Any person may be known by whatever name he or she

chooses, be it male or female. Re-registration in this sense is governed entirely by the birth certificate, since the change of documentation does not mean that the person who was formerly shown as male, and now as female, has female legal rights. The male to female transsexual still is taxed and has pension rights as if she was male. The birth certificate is, of course, the document which cannot be legally altered, unless there is a purely clerical error. Generally the authorities in England do not seem to involve themselves in any medical debate about whether the individual is transvestite or transsexual providing the request to re-register is bona fide. It is not the case that re-registration is conditional on sex-reassignment surgery.

One cannot doubt the correctness of the Ormrod ruling in the legal sense but it is likely that the birth certificate will be shown to be increasingly fallible and possibly an unfair standard by which to determine a person's gender. It might be questioned whether a medical first impression is more valid than a life-long personal conviction. We may be entering a hornet's nest of litigation particularly as liberal ideas increasingly blur differentiation of male and female roles.

Ormrod's position as a judge in this case is odd in that he is also a medical man and was dealing with essentially medical evidence. Doubtless he was skilful and insightful enough to disentangle his roles in the case but transsexuals would feel some lack of justice in their being seemingly unable to escape from a web of "medical justice". Although a non-medical judge might have found more dificulty with the medical evidence perhaps the judgment would have seemed more credibly consistent with the views of the common man.

Different countries have widely different attitudes towards the use of the law for the prosecution of transvestites. It appears that both Denmark and Holland have laws which are specifically relevant to the transvestite and yet they are amongst the most tolerant countries. It could well be the case that a law specifically prohibiting some form of behaviour is less likely to be invoked than ones of more general applicability — like laws concerning public disorder. This could be because a defence is less difficult when the law exactly specifies the nature of the crime. A law which depends heavily on an opinion of what the offender intends to do rather than what he actually does, or what the outcome of his behaviour is likely to be instead of what the outcome is, almost completely deprives the individual of a defence. It appears that he can only demonstrate his innocence by demonstrating his intent was not that attributed to him and this is usually either impossible or very difficult indeed. Certainly the individual is in the position of having to prove his innocence since the court assumes his guilt apparently.

England has no law specifically prohibiting transvestism. Much the most commonly used law in prosecutions is the common law offence of "behaviour likely to cause a breach of the peace".

Common Law including the offence of "breach of the peace" is that which is unwritten law not arising from Acts of Parliament for instance. In many cases common law has been established for centuries. The relevant definition of "breach of the peace" is as follows: "The Queen's Peace, or shortly 'the peace' is the normal state of society, and any interruption of that peace and good order which ought to prevail in a civilised country is a breach of the peace." It goes without saying that such a statement admits all manner of questions, such as who decides what constitutes a "civilised country" or how is the normal state of society assessed. When using phrases like "normal state" the law often gives the impression of identifying normal with the ideal or perhaps even the idyllic. The normal state of society seems to be taken as the state where petty thievery never occurs, where man never curses his neighbour, where workers never strike nor employers profiteer, and where women never have affairs with the man next door. Alas all such things are the true normal state of society in most civilised countries and the disturbance specifically arising from a man wearing the clothes of a woman, by any standards, is no more than a ripple in rather turbulent waters.

The law does not infer that the offender is causing a breach of the peace, only that he is judged likely to. Should a com-

plaint be made by a member of the public there is little doubt
that the prosecution would be successful even if the witness
was in no way upset or disturbed by the observation. Some
years ago a transvestite in a city centre was set upon by a gang of
youths who in other contexts would have been called "hooli-
gans". The transvestite was prosecuted apparently because he
was regarded as provoking the youths. The gang who actually
created the disturbance were not prosecuted. In another case
a policeman and his wife were shopping one Saturday after-
noon and the wife "spotted" a man dressed as a woman and
pointed him out to her husband who arrested the transvestite.
A transvestite (who was also a policeman) was prosecuted when
he was found sitting in his car in the early hours of the morning
on a lonely stretch of the sea coast. The parked car raised suspicions in the minds in the police patrol car which went to investigate. The outcome of such prosecutions are minimal as far
as the conviction itself is concerned but devastating personally
since many of the offenders lose their careers and often their
families.

A number of laws designate sexual behaviour as "insulting"
behaviour. For example, the offence of indecent exposure requires proof of the intent to insult a female. There is also the
general offence of "conduct likely to insult a female" which
may be invoked if a complaint is made about a male transvestite
— particularly if seen entering a ladies' lavatory. Laws of this
kind are not consistently applied and behaviour such as "kerb
crawling" by men searching for prostitutes creates a great deal
of public unrest in some areas and manifestly is behaviour likely
to cause a breach of the peace but prosecutions are relatively
rare. It seems to hang on the fact that it is intuitively understandable to the point of being reasonable that a man should
seek a prostitute. It is not understandable that he should want
to masquerade as a woman, whatever the public consequences.

Curiously transvestites are in some danger from the laws
relating to prostitution. The pointless behaviour of transvestites
who go out at night, often away from the main streets, with
nowhere in particular to go, very often looks like the behaviour

of a prostitute, to the distant observing policeman. Add to this some preference amongst transvestites for rather garish dress and the necessity for heavy make up and the image is complete. When the policeman has approached, made an accusation but found that he is dealing with a male, he cannot simply withdraw without looking foolish. If he does not choose the "breach of the peace" law he may well argue that the transvestite is the male equivalent of a prostitute, a homosexual who is importuning. Again the evidence for such an offence may be very nebulous. Stone's *Justices Manual* used to cite the possession of a powder-puff as acceptable evidence that a homosexual act had taken place. Radzinowicz (1957) quotes "artificial reddening of the lips and face" as acceptable evidence of importuning. Smiling at another person particularly in a public lavatory, or the length of time spent in the lavatory may be crucial and indeed the only evidence for a prosecution. This is, perhaps, rightly so but the law is exceedingly hazardous in this respect.

The Public Order Act, 1936 is something of a red herring since its use is by no means as common as often alleged. Although really concerned with the disorder of public marches and the violent demonstrations of Fascists in the thirties, it has an apparently wider applicability. It declares a summary offence has been committed if there is a "visible representation which is threatening, abusive or insulting with intent to provoke a breach of the peace or whereby a breach of the peace is likely to be occasioned". There is a general belief that this Act could be used to prosecute transvestites but it would at least be unnecessary in view of the common law offence of "breach of the peace". It could, of course, be appropriate to a political transvestite movement like a public mass parade of transvestites similar to those held by homosexuals. It might just be a cause of prosecuting the organisers of transvestite gatherings which although intended as social meetings could be interpreted as "political".

It seems that there are also by-laws and provisions like the Metropolitan Police Act, 1839 which may be invoked in the prosecution of a transvestite but the consequences are very limited in the purely legal sense. The prosecution of transvestites is most unlikely ever to result in imprisonment.

For the transvestite the immediate consequences of a confrontation with a policeman are two-fold. In the best of all worlds the policeman detecting a transvestite will look the other way unless a real disturbance is likely, in which case he will challenge the offender. If he does challenge him then he will probably take the rational course and tell the transvestite to go straight home and stay off the streets. If there is some disturbance or if the transvestite is outrageously dressed, he might decide to take some action. He might also be put in a difficult position by the transvestite who chooses to argue the toss about his "rights" and refuses to go home. The policeman may then ask the man to come with him to the police station. Officially this is a simple request and the constable cannot take the man until he has made a formal arrest and explained why he has done so.

Unfortunately the practice is a little different. The transvestite being challenged is usually fearful and upset to the degree that he complies with the request which is probably phrased and issued like an order. If he is able to state his right not to go on request the policeman may opt for a charge on the spot or he may settle for cautioning the offender. He may also press his wish to take the transvestite to the station and in practice laws like those relating to resisting arrest help him to do so. Such strategies might be legally dubious but from the transvestite's point of view the matter is solely one of his word against the policeman's and if there happen to be independent witnesses they are unlikely to be prejudiced in his favour.

He may not be charged even after being taken to the police station but in the process his aplomb will be gone and police stations are public places. He will be kept in the station for some time, probably questioned about his activities and the police will reasonably want to know and collect information about him. In public interest matters may be pursued about sexual offences and the like which are highly offensive and distressing to the transvestite but necessary within the understanding of the police. He may be closely questioned about sexual offences, assaults on children, etc., on the belief that his behaviour is sexually motivated. He may not be allowed to leave in female clothing and to collect his clothes a constable may have to visit his home and inform his wife. The general mêlée may well result in the transvestite's behaviour becoming public knowledge even if the police do not prosecute.

Such a picture may infer injustice but it must be set in the context of the fears of the individuals the police are duty bound to protect. It is no matter that those fears are irrational or based on mistaken assumptions, the legal system has to protect the public from the threat. This is a hard fact of life that the transvestite must live with. No matter how innocent his behaviour might be he must have regard for those who do not understand it and this involves the majority of the public, the police and other legal figures.

There are a number of guidelines the transvestite should be expected to follow, not to escape detection but to allay the anxieties of others:

(a) He ought not to go into public places in a way which arouses suspicion. Solitary, unlit streets late at night are neither a proper place for a lone woman nor a lone transvestite. There are constraints on the behaviour of a woman not applied to a man. Generally a man can go where he likes and when he likes. He may go to the cinema alone, or lounge around the street corner waiting for something to turn up. If a woman does such things she is an object of suspicion, behaving out of pattern and instantly a point of interest. Equally the transvestite becomes subject to public curiosity and his behaviour will provoke questions like "Where is she going?"; "Why is she not in a hurry?"; "Why does she walk on the unlit side of the street?"; "Why does she stop to look in a shop window when the shop is closed?" and so on.

(b) The transvestite concept of feminine dress is quite often unsatisfactory. Usually it fits the fantasy better than the figure. So a middle-aged transvestite may not appear in colours appro-

priate to a teenager. He may not wear red plastic high-heeled
shoes, a short skirt revealing somewhat unfeminine legs and a
wig appropriate to a film star. At the other extreme there are
more experienced transvestites who dress themselves in such a
degree of quality and taste as to invite special attention — even
jealousy.

(c) Make-up is a problem for the transvestite. Usually he has
a beard to cover which calls for a thick opaque layer, perhaps
even of stage make-up. This is in itself significant of something
about a woman which arouses suspicion. If she is naturally an
attractive person with the exceptional features of a model a
heavy make-up may be acceptable. If she is older and at best has
lost her looks then she is contemptuously regarded as "mutton
dressed as lamb" but if she is younger she is simply "cheap"
and probably sexually cheap also. The transvestite is therefore
forced into wearing make-up rather more like that of a prostitute than an ordinary housewife. He often adds to this effect by
using artificial eyelashes, too much lipstick and too much
jewellery. A wig often seems to be particularly inappropriate
and out of keeping with the individual's own colouring.

(d) If he is challenged, he is then responsible for demonstrating his good faith and innocent intent. To deny obvious fact
and to have no evidence of identity only arouses fears of mal-
intent and a demand for legal action. The transvestite should
consider how he is going to justify himself to the policeman or
passer-by. If he has medical or legal documents acknowledging
him as a transvestite this goes some way to demonstrating some
public good faith. Even if he has a letter from a friend of standing, a photograph taken with non-transvestite friends or a
transvestite society membership card, these are all testimonials
which may help the enquirer to feel less perturbed by his
behaviour.

It is a matter for the individual professional worker to decide
how far he can involve himself in the threat of the legal process
to the transvestite client. There is a perfectly good case for
arguing that the wishes of society are really perfectly clear,
transvestites are not wanted on the streets and in public places.

There is no absolute need for the transvestite to appear in public and it is behaviour which cannot conceivably be regarded as so compelling as to be irresistible. In this case the transvestite might reasonably be told to behave himself and stay indoors or take all normal legal risks and consequences. These hazards can be fully explained to him.

On the other hand, it could be that the "ease" of the transvestite is to be balanced against the unease of a minority of the general public. The view can be taken that given reasonable standards of behaviour on the part of the transvestite his needs can be supported to some extent, at least, as far as needless prejudice is concerned. This means in effect that the person concerned with the transvestite in any way, general practitioner, clergyman, solicitor, psychologist, social worker, psychiatrist or whatever, may declare his acceptance of the transvestite's behaviour. He can issue some note which the transvestite can use as evidence to people who may challenge him. Various writers regard this as a medical certificate, e.g. Anchersen (1956), and according to Bowman and Engle (1957) such a medical certificate was a legal document accepted by the police in Germany. However, even a medical certificate has no legal value in England and is simply a testimonial in no way different to that which might well be issued by any other responsible professional person. Some transvestites have carried the matter to the point of changing their names by deed poll as a means of justifying their behaviour. Essentially the operated transsexual is no more immune from prosecution than the transvestite.

The form of any such certificate should simply be an open letter covering the following main points:

1. Stating the writer's professional relationship with the transvestite.
2. Expressing confidence in his good general behaviour.
3. Emphasising that transvestism is not a sexual deviation likely to involve or endanger others.
4. Offering to provide further information and help if needed by any responsible person.

5. Stating the period for which the certificate should be regarded as relevant.

The transvestite should be expected to maintain some informal contact whether under active therapy or not. This is clearly necessary for the certificate to carry any great credence and this must imply that the certificate should relate to periods of not more than 1 to 5 years. It goes without saying that the certificate should not be issued unless it is accurate and true. The temptation to be "generous" in this respect is in every sense counter-productive.

Some transvestite societies have attempted to use such certificates. A society in France, no longer in existence, certainly distributed a certificate signed by a professional consultant, as part of its membership card. If these were actually used and how far such a general licence was accepted is not known.

Finally, some comment might be made about possible legal changes which might make the transvestite less liable to prosecution. Could it be that transvestite groups could seek a change in the law as the homosexual groups did? The fundamental difference, of course, is that for transvestites no law exists to be changed, as it did for the homosexuals.

In some areas transvestites approach local police for advice and solicit tolerance but it is hard to argue against prosecution for behaviour which is not itself against the law. If behaviour of any kind results in a public complaint the police must act to satisfy the complainants in some way and cannot be expected to promise to do otherwise.

The homosexual groups made great play on "coming out" or publicly declaring themselves as homosexual. They adopted badges and slogans like "It's good to be gay" which desensitised the public to the idea of homosexuality so that resistance declined. Such groups have occasionally incited transvestites to similar activities without appreciating an important difference in attitude. The transvestite does not proclaim "It's good to be transvestite" because he does not think it is. His fantasy is "It's good to be female". The acknowledgement of himself as transvestite is something he wishes to deny not to publicly recognise. In this sense it is hard to envisage strong openly active groups of heterosexual transvestites taking the same course as the homosexuals have done. Equally it is hard to see their political efforts being as effective in altering the functioning of the law and perhaps that is unjust.

CHAPTER 8

The Treatment of Transvestism

Papers appear in the learned journals reporting the treatment of transvestism by all manner of means. Regrettably most suffer from the deficiency of an imprecise concept of transvestism. Most case reports are concerned more with an empirical symptomatic treatment than with transvestism itself. The writers are satisfied to report the effects of therapy on cross-dressing as a symptom without probing any more deeply into its nature. Almost no studies of therapy directed towards transvestism as a gender dysphoria, perhaps other than in psychotherapy, are available.

Within this very broad concept of treating cross-dressing, almost all forms of common psychiatric treatment methods have been reported to be effective in treating single cases. Electroconvulsive therapy was used by Liebman (1944) to treat a young coloured American homosexual. He was admitted to hospital in a psychotic state. He wore beads and a crucifix, had flowers in his hair and wore lipstick and rouge. There was no suggestion that he wished to be regarded as a woman, except his unusual garb and a list of Christmas presents which he had written including some articles of female clothing. After treatment with E.C.T. his behaviour became less bizarre, he was judged no longer transvestite or psychotic but still an effeminate homosexual. He was discharged from hospital but a few months later was reported to be running wild and drinking a lot of whisky. He was returned to hospital, according to Liebman because he still showed homosexual desires and the police charged him with "Idleness". He was again treated with

E.C.T. before being discharged to face charges of theft, breach of the peace, and resisting an officer. Liebman concludes that E.C.T. was effective in the treatment of the psychosis and the transvestism but not the homosexuality. There is inadequate evidence in this report to regard the patient as even a cross-dresser and there is no evidence given of a gender problem beyond his homosexuality. Whilst E.C.T. may have had some therapeutic effect, it seems to have been implemented primarily as a means of treating the psychosis and no argument is presented to explain its effect on what was interpreted as trans-vestism.

Eyres (1960) reports two cases, one treated with E.C.T. the other treated with the Reiter Sedac high-frequency electric current. The first case was initially treated psychotherapeuti-cally but deteriorated into a depressed state. That depression was effectively treated with E.C.T. No suggestion is made that the transvestism was in any way modified. The second case was treated at the outset with "damned medicines" and then as he was becoming increasingly anxious and tense he was treated with the Reiter Sedac technique. Stoller (1966) has referred to this case as treated by E.C.T. but it is inadequately described and it seems more likely that another rather uncommon treat-ment was used. According to Philpott (1966), in treatment with the Reiter Sedac "the patient remains awake and accepts excitation up to the limits of comfort for the first phase of the treatment and this is followed by a low stimulus sedative (inhibition) phase. This conditions in the normalisation of both excitation and inhibition." It seems as if an electrical stimulus changing polarity each 10 seconds is given between the back of the neck, head, and arms. In this case there were twenty-nine treatments of 1 hour each. The benefit of the treatment is said to be the experience of relaxation, and the tension and anxiety which the patient reported seemed to diminish. Again it is not reported that the transvestism was materially modified.

Some writers have employed psychotropic drugs. Pennington (1960) reports a case of transvestism again with scant clinical description, whose response to a régime of treatment with nialamide, meprobomate, and chlorpromazine was a complete success. The patient reported that his previous transvestism seemed like a bad dream. Pennington justifies the therapy in the following terms: "Since earliest times it has been recognised that changing brain chemistry produces altered behaviour; the treatment of our transvestite was carried out with that thought in mind." One can only feel that if only that thought had been in mind the treatment was based on little short of profound optimism.

Ward (1975) treated a case of "sexually arousing cross-dressing behaviour", which he identifies as transvestism, with lithium carbonate. The patient was also diagnosed as suffering from a manic-depressive psychosis and the therapy was directed solely at the treatment of this aspect of the problem. Ward saw the cross-dressing as secondary to the psychosis and the success of the therapy suggests that this formulation was correct. However, clinical judgment would not suggest that either fetishism or transvestism are commonly secondary to any other psychiatric disorder.

Hormone preparations have been employed in the treatment of transvestism. Administering oestrogens as a sexual depressant has a reasonable rationale in cases where deviant sexual drives are apparent. Foote (1944) reports how stilbestrol is of value in treating patients with mixed sexual deviations. He goes on to argue that as most psychiatric conditions have "symptoms in common which do not require enumeration", stilbestrol may be of wider value in psychiatry than just in treating sexual deviation. Some transvestites and transsexuals claim that oestrogens have an antidepressant effect but it seems likely that this is only a secondary result of the sexual-depressant and feminisation effects. Jones (1960) reports two cases of transvestism treated with stilbestrol. The first was much the more typical transvestite and obtained "great relief" apparently without feminising effects from quite a small quantity of stilbestrol. The second case was clearly a transsexual who used large doses of stilbestrol specifically to obtain feminisation.

Physical methods of treatment have been recommended also. Epstein (1961) is a worker who adopts the view that transvestism is not normally associated with orgasm. He links both fetishism and transvestism with brain dysfunction. He presents five cases with temporal lobe electroencephalographic abnormalities but does not discuss the fact that the majority of transvestites do not appear to show such abnormalities. Hunter *et al.* (1963) report a similar case of temporal lobe epilepsy arising in a transvestite. Mitchell *et al.* (1954) describe a temporal lobe lesion surgically treated resulting in "relief" of the patient's transvestism. Yet a further case of temporal lobe dysrhythmia is reported amongst a series of sexual deviants treated by Feldman *et al.* (1968). One is bound to add that this group of reports appears in a period in which temporal lobe dysfunction seemed to have a somewhat ubiquitous quality and the reports have not led to any more concrete findings.

Thompson (1949) holds some extreme views about the physical origins of some sexual disorders. His hypothesis is that as with problems like Parkinsonism, sexual problems result from some lack of normal control in specific areas of the brain. Hence "the cure is the finding and removal of areas or centres which emit the abnormal discharges". The argument seems to lead to the expectation that E.C.T. would be beneficial. Working in a Californian State Hospital he gave E.C.T. to a small group of "sexual psychopaths", mostly homosexuals. They were patients who were detained until it could be certified they had been "treated and cured". Thompson says that the treatment "was undertaken with the realisation that no other form of therapy would help" and the "patients' requests for electroshock therapy were very urgent". This is hardly surprising as they had apparently been in hospital without hope of discharge for 6 to 10 years! The results of treatment were poor as far as the sexual disorders were concerned but Thompson seems to have been sustained in his belief about the cortical centres of abnormal discharge.

None of Thompson's cases were transvestite but Lukianowicz (1959) refers to his work with hope. This appears to be intended as a serious comment on treatment of transvestites but many would not find it easy to accept as rational. He refers to "all the horrors" of sex reassignment surgery and the possibility that they can be superseded simply by a brain operation. His analogy with leucotomy is less than persuasive and one's experience of transsexuals, let alone transvestites, is not that they would grasp with great enthusiasm any surgical removal of sections of their brains! This may be an area in which the patient and the medical man cannot be in accord and the course of action depends on the capacity of one to influence the other against his judgment.

Many writers, whilst expressing pessimism about treating transvestism successfully, are inclined to be ever optimistic about the results of psychotherapy. Ostow (1953) says, "No psychotherapy less than intense prolonged and classic psychoanalysis and its derivatives. The general aim of the term has for insistence on the intensity, duration, or the particular form of psychotherapy. There is no evidence whatever beyond the conviction of particular practitioners that either the theoretical basis or the administration of psychotherapy are of general significance.

Psychotherapy as a concept is closely linked to psychoanalysis and its derivitives. The general aim of the term has broadened immensely so that Cawley (1976) can now refer to the general practitioner, with no training or aspirations to formal psychotherapeutic skills, simply talking to his patient, as conducting psychotherapy. Equally behavioural techniques have become part of "behavioural psychotherapy". It is probably fair to say that the *raison d'être* of psychotherapy is the fundamental postulate that human beings have a capacity for change which is motivated at a cognitive level. That is the individual as a result of a desire to change can indeed change and the process can be mediated by the intervention procedures of a second person. The argument rests on a belief which is so basic that it cannot be relinquished. This belief is that of the individual's ultimate responsibility for his actions, at least outside the limits of severe incapacitating illness.

Psychoanalysis in the classical form appears to predominate in the literature as a means of treating transvestism. There seem to be no accounts, for example, of Rogerian or Jungian psychotherapy and only one of Adlerian orientation (Deutsch, 1954). More fashionable therapies like Gestalt therapy or Transactional Analysis appear not to have been attempted.

The difficulty in describing the psychoanalytic approach lies in the tendency to self-fulfilment in the system. This is best illustrated in a paper by Prince (1954) who refers to Stekel's description of transvestism as "a mask for homosexuality" in the face of evidence of normal heterosexual behaviour, including marriage, and parenthood amongst transvestites. He cites Ellis as pointing out that Stekel's argument amounted to saying that anyone who had not yet murdered, robbed, or raped was no less a masked murderer, robber, or rapist. It is just that "he has not gotten around to it yet". The journal editor sees fit to insert a footnote. "The author errs here. What Stekel really maintained is not that the transvestite has not 'gotten around' to being homosexual, but that, despite his overt heterosexual behaviour, his unconscious attitude is homosexually orientated. This can be verified only by the psychoanalytic method of exploration which, unfortunately, neither Ellis nor Hirschfeld applied." Had the editor given Prince the facility to reply he would surely have responded "O.K. so the transvestite's homosexuality can be known only to the analyst. It cannot be known to the man himself, nor his wife, nor his employer. Nor can it be observed in any other way. Indeed it looks at present like an unassailable psychoanalytic fantasy which perhaps at best we must keep in mind as awaiting more convincing proof from evidence available to those outside the system."

It seems almost impossible to discuss the contribution of psychoanalysis to the treatment of transvestism in this context. Otto Fenichel's paper (1930) is clearly "front runner" in all later psychoanalytic studies and Fenichel himself explicitly disregards the belief of Hirschfeld, Ellis, and Nacke that transvestites may be classified as heterosexual, homosexual, narcissistic, and asexual. He does so on the ground that as the classification is only in terms of manifest expression it is of "no meaning". Fenichel then proceeds to the assumption supported only by psychoanalysis that all transvestites are fundamentally homosexual. It is, he says, what psychoanalysis will suspect "And the analysis of transvestists entirely confirms this suspicion". (The terms transvestist, transvestitist, and transvestitism were formerly sometimes used.)

The acceptance of Fenichel's interpretation of transvestism is often without due regard for the fact that he was speaking at a time when available case material was very restricted. Transvestite patients were usually highly complicated with many other problems and not by any means typical of the people we recognise as transvestites nearly 50 years later. In particular Fenichel was unaware of the existence of the transsexual group as a material part of the cases he referred to as transvestite. The earliest attempt at sex reassignment came at least 5 years later than Fenichel's paper was read (1929). It can then be recognised that Fenichel's insistence that the transvestite in effect cries out "Love me . . . it is not true that this wish of mine places my penis in jeopardy" cannot have the general applicability he assumes. It seems all transsexuals if not a number of transvestites willingly put their penises in jeopardy. It may be, of course, that the analyst does not find this the incongruity it seems to be at first sight. Rosen (1964) indeed says that the transvestite can "experience his entire body as a magnified phallus when dressed as a woman" and the female clothing surrounding it represents a vagina. Fenichel refers to a case of Ellis's where castration was sought but the wish was effectively cancelled by the putting on of women's shoes and ear-rings. He is aware of attempted self-castration cases but can offer no explanation of how they would fit into his formulation without his having the opportunity of examining such cases in analysis.

Fenichel describes the psychoanalysis of a transvestite case of incredible complexity involving considerable sexual difficulties of many kinds. He found the case entirely supported

his psychoanalytic expectations. He begins at the point where
he posits a close relationship between fetishism, transvestism,
and homosexuality. Freud said that the fetishist was unable to
accept the fact that the woman lacked a penis so that he could
only make love to a female who he has supplied with an illusory
penis. Equally the passive homosexual (described by Fenichel
as "feminine") cannot love a person who lacks a penis. He
solves his castration anxiety by identifying with his mother and
looks for a new object love which may be himself. Fenichel
says the transvestite is both fetishist and homosexual. He identifies himself as a woman with a penis but also believes in the
phallic nature of women. Because he has identified himself
primarily with his mother or her substitute he avoids coitus
with her by his fetishistic love of her clothes which he wears to
bring them into contact with his genitals. Fenichel says this is
why the garment should have been used and should retain the
warmth and odour of the woman's body but this is entirely
untrue for the vast majority of transvestites who make considerable play on possessing their own wardrobes. Fenichel then
argues that the garment is a symbolic penis which he wishes to
display to refute the idea of castration — Rosen, of course, says
that the clothes represent a vagina, perhaps regarded from
inside. As the transvestite has so far identified with his believed
phallic mother he must also be in a position of self-love and
intense narcissism. Primal sadism may be turned against the
transvestite's ego such that he may be driven to a masochistic
relationship with the phallic woman.

Analysis shows that as with the passive homosexual, father
becomes the object choice. In effect he says to the father "Love
me, I am just as beautiful (in the phallic sense) as my mother".
Superficially, Fenichel says, the transvestite is saying much the
same thing to his mother and in both cases he is denying that
there is danger of castration from either mother or father. On
the surface the transvestite may appear to express a need for a
masochistic "lesbian-like" relationship, "to be in the relationship of the slave to her mistress". Fenichel also points out a
further superficial level of identification with the role of a little

girl. This secures the advantages of a regression to childhood. He says that it is often found that a sister has at an early period become a mother substitute such that this identification has occurred. This, of course, is not in accord with the facts as they are now apparent.

Fenichel sums up by saying that the picture is common enough in other conditions and that it has not been possible to say what has caused the crucial belief in the phallic woman to be retained. Nor is it clear why transvestism itself should be the result in specific cases. What has occurred in his particular patient he recognises as due to special environmental factors and in particular the characters of the family members who seem to have thrust the role upon him.

Fenichel is aware, therefore, that although he is sure of the relevance of the castration complex to transvestism, little else can be said about its origins. Perhaps this is because he is reporting the only case he has examined psychoanalytically – it could be so. Equally he does not indicate that analysis was a successful treatment in this particular man. Gutheil (1954) comments on the accusation that psychotherapy has not been successful, that it doesn't matter. Poor results do not mean the concept of the etiology is wrong. It only means we must investigate what caused the failure and learn from the mistakes and make improvements. "In most cases", he says, "the lack of success may be attributed to the patient's uncooperative attitude." This is more than generous to the psychoanalytic formulation and Gutheil appears to be avoiding recognition that whilst the inadequacy of the etiology is not proved, failure of therapy is just as likely to be from such a cause as from the patient's attitude.

Stoller (1966) agrees with Gutheil about the patient's motivation.

Although he may ask the psychiatrist to cure him of his transvestism, what he is really asking is to be cured of his pain. He generally does not consider his transvestism as painful. Quite the opposite it is most enjoyable; what it

stirs up in others is what leads to pain. So when the transvestite discovers that the doctor's goal is the removal of
the syndrome, the patient leaves. . . . Practically speaking,
the amount of guilt felt by the transvestite is insufficient
to galvanise the treatment once he learns how to deal with
society.

Stoller is quite clear in his summing up of the results of psychotherapy with transvestites. "In no case in which the descrip-
tive material is that of a real transvestite is it clear that the
patient has lost his perversion — either the sexual (fetishist)
aspect or the gender (the desire to pass as a woman)." Nevertheless he reports cases of two boys with the symptoms of true
transvestism being analysed together with their mothers with
some success — although with inadequate follow-up. Stoller
adds that although such treatment has promise it requires a
revolution in the attitudes of parents and is "terribly time-
consuming".

Peabody *et al.* (1953) also propose that "the analytic
approach or psychotherapy with emphasis on dynamic understanding and guidance offers best results". Their three presented
cases provide no great support for this claim. Clearly the
authors favour the hospitalisation of transvestites, ostensibly to
relieve stresses on the patient and on the family but there is no
indication of the nature and extent of the psychotherapy
carried out. In any event the success reported is anything but
clear cut.

Certainly the most comprehensive study of psychotherapy
with a transvestite is that described by Barahal (1953). The case
is that of a female who is also homosexual and in all probability
would now be regarded as a transsexual. However, Barahal's
paper gives a detailed session by session account of the therapy.

With the best will in the world one can find little in psychotherapy as a cause for optimism in treating transvestism.
Frankly most transvestites do not wish to undergo psychotherapy as many writers have observed and perhaps this is the
major problem for any form of psychotherapeutic intervention.

Bowman and Engle (1957) place their faith in "intensive and prolonged psychotherapy" but recognise "there are no reported successfully treated cases". However, their faith is based on a curious hope that techniques may be found to make the patient more accessible to psychotherapy. Such a notion seems not without objection and in the extreme methods like high doses of psychotropic drugs or E.C.T. are open to use in rendering patients more accessible to therapy. Treatment orders might also be included as means of inducing acceptance of treatment in a mentally ill patient but we are not here concerned with this degree of disorder and it is a moot point whether or not a technique to change a patient's attitude to treatment can be other than an infringement of his absolute right to accept or reject therapy. It seems that if methods of changing attitudes to psychotherapy fall within the sphere of psychotherapeutic techniques they are in danger of being unacceptably devious. On the other hand, if the methods are to employ drugs, brain operations, E.C.T., or legal sanctions then one has to view Bowman's hope with great concern.

Edelstein's (1960) case is the only one reported in which hypnosis was used. Unfortunately the case is one of polymorphous perversions with a marked tendency to transvestite fantasies rather than a typical case of transvestism. Edelstein also broadly adopts Fenichel's analysis of the dynamics although the case is so unusual. Other members of the family were transvestite and the patient had fantasies of necrophilia, gerontophilia, and coprophilia (sexual excitement associated with dead bodies, old people, and excrement) most certainly not characteristic of transvestites. He had also been treated previously by psychoanalysis, sedatives, hormones, and E.C.T. Indeed Magnus Hirschfeld himself had treated him unsuccessfully. Edelstein makes the important point about the use of hypnosis which was persistently demanded by the patient. His whole personality was structured around "passive feminine wishes". He desired to be ruled over as part of what he saw as a feminine role and in hypnosis he was achieving total subjugation. Edelstein adopted hypnosis as a last resort but felt that in hypnosis the patient's dreams and visual fantasies were orgastic. It would seem that although the patient offered something in return by partially responding to post-hypnotic suggestion, the hypnosis could have been more reinforcing of his gender dysphoria than effectively therapeutic. In this respect Edelstein's case is somewhat similar to many transvestites and points out a fallacy in employing hypnosis.

In more recent times most interest has been directed into attempts to treat transvestism along "behaviour therapy" lines. On occasions the treatments have attained little more than a veneer of respectability from a place under the fringe of behaviour therapy. Some reports have provoked strong emotion, hostility, and condemnation, some of which has come from therapists adhering closely to behaviour therapy principles. There is no clear line of demarcation and, to clarify the contribution of behaviour therapy as properly conceived, it is necessary to look in some detail at the principles of behaviour therapy.

Behaviour therapy seems to be established from two streams of activity. These two sources were, firstly, long-established techniques like the "bell and pad" treatment of enuresis, or some forms of aversion therapy. Secondly, there was the extension to therapy of the increasing knowledge of learning which had a sound experimental basis.

The various established techniques seem likely to have been founded on a "common-sense" argument of the kind "If the boy wets the bed what you need to find is a way of waking him up when he wants to urinate"; or "If a man drinks too much it will put him off if somehow drink sometimes makes him feel ill". There is little in the origins of these techniques to think the reasoning was more sophisticated. They took no great ingenuity to devise although it is true that many contemporary therapies, e.g. E.C.T., do not have their origins in sound theory and depend mostly on clinical assessment of their results rather than a knowledge of their action. The significant point about techniques like the "bell and pad" was that their success was demonstrable objectively and because of the success they persisted. Other "common-sense" methods did not produce results and vanished, e.g. the Weir Mitchell Technique of treating war neuroses with rest and an incredibly rich diet. The success was also apparently explicable in learning theory terms but not only this, it seemed possible to improve the method by the application of established experimentally based information.

Much the same process continues. A technique such as implosion (Boulougouris and Marks, 1969) in which a phobic patient is induced to experience the highest possible level of anxiety without avoidance, has obvious origins in the age-old practice of throwing the anxious swimmer "in at the deep end"; the nervous soldier right back to battle; or the fallen rider-to-hounds back into the hunt. As "implosion" the technique acquired a loose psychodynamic justification and then a more objective analysis as a learning process and was absorbed into the methods of behaviour therapy.

The development of a profession of clinical psychology, particularly in Great Britain, from graduates in experimental psychology brought with it a demand for an objective therapy. Eysenck (1960), though not himself a practising therapist, most clearly enunciated the fundamental postulates of a learning-based therapy. Behaviour therapy was to be a technique of dealing with symptoms as learned habits by methods in which hypotheses could be formed and tested by objective measurements. Clinical acumen and judgment were not felt reliable enough to guide such a therapy. The hypotheses would be founded only upon sound experimental knowledge. Whatever the merits of psychodynamic approaches, behaviour therapy would eschew any consideration of the "unconscious" because it was not accessible to direct observation. The interpretation of symbolism and the formation of transference would be equally irrelevant. Indeed the conscious historical origins of problems would hardly be important because the method would treat the symptoms which exist in "the here and now" and not underlying causes.

It was in this latter area that behaviour therapy found its feet. The psychodynamically orientated therapists in particular issued dire warnings of symptom substitution. A characteristic analogy was that if you treated the spots of measles the illness did not go away but new spots would break out elsewhere. If a neurotic symptom was simply extinguished, since it was an upshot of unconscious processes, a new symptom must replace it because the underlying neurosis had not been resolved. Indeed this was the infallible consequence according to established psychodynamic theory and not a few stood by expecting glaring and disastrous symptom substitution to occur. In fact no clear case of symptom substitution associated with behaviour therapy has been reported. This is not to say that the argument that the removal of the symptoms was a removal of the neurosis has been accepted, it has not and indeed it is often the patient who has most difficulty in accepting this orientation of behaviour therapy.

The problem was depicted in rather devastating fashion by J. B. Watson in his paper about "little Albert" (Watson and Raynor, 1920). Little Albert was a year-old child who was taught to fear a white rat by presenting it to him and at the same time clanging a metal bar behind his head. The fear generalised to many furry things including a seal skin coat, whch also aroused fear in Albert. Watson comments:

> The Freudians 20 years from now, unless their hypotheses change, when they come to analyse Albert's fear of a seal skin coat — assuming that he comes to analysis at that age — will probably tease from him the recital of a dream which upon their analysis will show that Albert at 3 years of age attempted to play with the pubic hair of the mother and was scolded violently for it.

It would at least be hard to conceive that psychoanalysis would dredge up the true explanation that the fear was a simple learned response with no deeper meaning.

Unfortunately Watson's experiment, together with the use of aversive stimuli, tends to be over-identified with behaviour therapy practice. Watson was not, in fact, concerned with therapy and in most respects his experiment seems callous and quite indefensible. Equally, in the lee of behaviour therapy, methods have been applied which appear to owe a great deal more to the vindictiveness of a frustrated therapist than they do to the principles of behaviour therapy. It should be axiomatic that a therapy based on learning processes does not employ disruptive stimuli which impair the individual's capacity to learn. Learning is a tender process which does not occur efficiently in a terrified, sick, or ill-motivated patient.

It is also true that behaviour therapy employs more techniques based on rewards and pleasant stimuli than on noxious ones. Simply, this is because learning is more easily and predictably manipulated with rewards than with punishments.

Behaviour therapy has not always applied techniques which are simply derived from "common sense". For example, the extinction of tics (e.g. nervous repetitive head movements) by massed practice, is based not on suppressing the tic but actually exercising it without reinforcement so that the habit becomes extinguished, the extinction process having a sound experimental basis.

Apart from Rogers' Client Centred Therapy perhaps, behaviour therapy is the only psychotherapeutic method which stands or falls on the evidence of its measurable success. It is inappropriate to justify a therapy based on experimentally verifiable fact by nebulous intuitive generalisations. However, there are many weaknesses. At the outset much of the evidence must be drawn from animal studies and there is a logic gap in its application to humans. It is not possible to totally disregard the therapist–client relationship or the informal process of reinforcement of some of the behaviour going on in any therapeutic session. The syndrome very likely is not confined simply to quantifiable habits. Behaviour therapy has not limited itself to treating wet beds or tics which can be counted, or to psychophysiological responses which can be measured. A sexual response might be measured, albeit somewhat uncertainly, by the penile plethysmograph but a gender role preference cannot. Social skills training may depend in part on the timing of the client's capacity to listen in conducting a conversation but it is equally dependent upon the less objective assessment of his warmth and sincerity. Many have doubted the wisdom of the behaviour therapist's diversified objectives (e.g. Hamilton, 1973) partly because they seem to have outstripped the experimental basis of the original model. However, the origin of a therapeutic hypothesis can be seen as a less important component than the perception of a syndrome as the result of learning and the principle of adopting clear hypotheses and goals for each individual case. The broader concept is more satisfactorily termed "Behavioural psychotherapy".

The major change which is brought about in the diversification of behaviour therapy into behavioural psychotherapy is the re-admission of the therapeutic relationship. It almost goes without saying that therapy conducted with a patient who has formed no bond of confidence or trust with the therapist is overwhelmingly likely to fail. Even more so if the client's motivation for therapy is uncertain or absent. The fundamental postulates of behaviour therapy brushed these factors aside, apparently in the assumption that dimensions like motivation were also capable of experimental control. In this respect the foundations of behaviour therapy were apparently in error and this fact is of profound importance in the application of behaviour-therapy methods in the treatment of transvestism.

The vast majority of cases of sexual disorder treated by behaviour therapy have been treated by aversion methods. (The author is fully aware of the objections to conditions such as homosexuality and transvestism being referred to as sexual disorders. In the present discussion the term is retained simply because it reflects the orientation of the therapy being described, in this context it is almost impossible to avoid.) In a standard work on behaviour therapy methods in general, 20% of all case studies concern sexual problems. Every one of these comes in the section on aversion methods and in fact 39% of all cases of aversion therapy quoted are cases of sexual disorder. Generally the argument seems to be that there is no alternative therapy but as this is manifestly untrue one wonders if behaviour therapists have been seduced into adopting society's orientation towards punishment in such cases. Meyer and Chesser (1970) quote the case of a transvestite in a discussion of ethical problems in behaviour therapy. They envisage a transvestite seeking treatment who shows anxiety, guilt, and depression. His family, wife, and work are affected and psychiatric treatment would, suggest the authors, relieve his anxiety and depression with drugs. He would then be assisted to come to terms with his transvestism by behaviour therapy using desensitisation or by psychotherapy. Attempts would be made to adjust the family feelings and then his cross-dressing might be modified by either insight therapy or aversion therapy. This analysis is by no means exhaustive but it points out the role of aversion therapy as an alternative part in a complex programme of treatment. It also makes one painfully aware that in practice aversion therapy has been reported as almost the sole therapeutic effort made and disproportionate attention has been paid to the aversion therapy component.

The reason for this might well be that the model for the treatment of transvestism was simply an extension of aversion therapy as carried out with homosexuals. Aversion therapy was seized upon avidly as a ray of hope in an era when homosexuals were under grave legal threat. It offered a technique which had a face validity which seemed to make therapy rather than imprisonment an acceptable course for the courts and indeed it had some success in modifying the behaviour of homosexuals (Feldman and MacCulloch, 1965). The clients were more often than not respectable, honest citizens in terror of imprisonment, desperate for help to save the fabric of their ways of life. Aversion therapy served for a few years but with changes in the law relating to homosexuality the ethical questions changed. The severity of the law has rapidly been forgotten and it is largely from ignorance of the demands at the time that the condemnation of aversion therapy treatment of homosexuality comes. It would not have been either rational or welcomed by the clients concerned if aversion therapy had been withheld in anticipation of the objections to be raised, out of context, 20 years later. The legal threat to the transvestite is still present but more easy for him to avoid.

The model of aversion therapy as applied to homosexuals in particular but to others who committed sexual crimes such as paedophilia, exhibitionism, etc. (but very few if any rapists!), was available to apply to transvestites. It depended upon the linking of a noxious stimulus with the deviant behaviour. Ostensibly the patient was to learn an "aversion" or even a conditioned "nausea" response. It is doubtful if any stable aversion or nausea was ever in reality achieved. Although the rate at which a sexually deviant act would occur might be drastically reduced, no paedophiliac ever reported nausea on meeting a child, nor homosexual report a distaste for his gay friends.

The noxious stimulus employed was either a chemical vomiting agent or an electric shock. Both had difficulties within the context of aversion therapy. Vomiting agents are unpredictable in their effects and timing. Very little indeed is known about the optimal strength of electric shock, its timing, or indeed the most suitable form of shock. Equally, little is known about adaptation to shock or risks of establishing masochistic responses.

Aversion therapy divides into two models, classical conditioning and avoidance conditioning, although Feldman and MacCulloch (1971) indicate that as far as homosexuality is concerned there is little to choose between them. In classical conditioning the patient is effectively a passive agent. He is first presented with a stimulus associated with his transvestism. This may be a picture of himself dressed as a woman or perhaps a significant word such as "bra". This stimulus is then followed by a shock usually given to the hand or arm. The argument was that the fear aroused by the shock would be associated with the clothing so that the patient would feel ill at ease wearing it subsequently. Alternatively the treatment would result in the clothing becoming a conditioned stimulus for anxiety arousal. This conditioned anxiety response would appear in real life and act as a second order reinforcer of the act of avoiding female clothing. This would be because the anxiety aroused by the clothes would diminish as the transvestite discarded them, thus reinforcing the avoidance of them.

Eysenck (1963) proposed a further explanation, that the conditioned anxiety response was an arousal of the sympathetic nervous system. Sexual responses involve arousal of the parasympathetic system and it seems that the sympathetic and parasympathetic responses are incompatible. This is another way of saying that at a physiological level one cannot be anxious and sexually aroused at one and the same time. This argument did not attract a great deal of support but pointed to the important fact that the anxiety resulting from aversion therapy was hardly ever within the limits of conscious awareness. The patient attempting to cross-dress would perhaps say his hands felt clammy or he was breathless but never that he felt afraid or worried.

Avoidance conditioning was particularly employed by Feldman and McCulloch (1965) on the basis that classical conditioning as normally used was not believed to be the most stable or rapid form of learning. Avoidance conditioning is a form of the wider learning model known as instrumental conditioning. This implies that the subject is able to exert some active control over the learning process. Effectively in aversion therapy it means that the patient is able to do something to avoid some of the stimuli or shocks if he opts for doing so. In classical conditioning he receives all stimuli and shocks prescribed by his therapist. In avoidance conditioning practice the patient might be presented with a picture of an article of clothing and it would be possible for him to avoid some of the risk of getting a shock by switching off the picture. It almost goes without saying that the patient learns to do so very rapidly and this avoidance is hard to extinguish. What is less persuasive is that this response of switching off the projector is specially relevant to real-life behaviour, like that of ceasing to wear high-heeled shoes, stable though it may be in the therapy situation. This criticism of avoidance conditioning is made by Rachman and Teasdale (1969) but answered by Feldman and MacCulloch (1971) in the empirical terms that it does generalise because the treatment is successful. Of course, this is an inadequate reply since the avoidance response may not be the operative part of the therapy at all. Feldman *et al.* (1968) quote an attempt to improve on the face validity of avoidance conditioning by using apparatus where a mercury switch, mounted on head gear which the patient wore, served to switch off the pictures. Thus the active avoidance response would be looking away. In fact this is no more convincing since the elimination of homosexual behaviour must be a great deal more complex than a conditioned gaze avoidance.

Rachman and Teasdale (1969) arrive at the conclusion that Feldman's concentration on an avoidance model was not essential. "We are suggesting that the effective process operating in the Feldman and MacCulloch procedure is not the development of a motor avoidance response but the classical conditioning of anxiety to the homosexual stimulus." Feldman's (1971) failure to show avoidance conditioning superior to classical conditioning supports this view.

Feldman also incorporated refinements in the therapy by spacing treatments, variation of shock level, randomisation of delay between stimulus and shock, the omission of shock from a random number of "trials", and so on. Such refinements are clearly indicated by the experimental evidence for an optimum conditioning rate and stability of learned response. Others have further attempted to improve the process by the use of central excitant drugs, e.g. Barker *et al.* (1961).

So it seems that attempts to treat transvestism and other sexual disorders by aversion are characterised by two important factors. The first is the degree to which the treatment is actively designed within the framework of behaviour therapy and how far it simply appears to belong there fortuitously and is in reality based in quite alien thinking. The second is the degree of sophistication of the use of learning theory principles within the treatment. In fact, few if any treatments using vomiting agents can have been properly conceived within the tenets of behaviour therapy and they seem to have been carried out despite the considerations of learning theory rather than in line with them. This must be so because of the insuperable difficulties in controlling the timing and intensity of this type of noxious stimulus. Neither are the effects of such drugs on learning adequately understood and the attempts to correct for the central depressant effects by the use of arbitrary doses of dexamphetamine sulphate are based only on optimistic guesswork. So that it is the therapies employing shock which are most precisely defined but even here the difficulties abound particularly in the application of aversion therapy to transvestism. One of these problems is that any aversive stimulus can be considered punishing at its commencement, i.e. when the shock is switched on, but its cessation is also a positive (rewarding) reinforcer. Consequently if a series of shocks is administered to a transvestite whilst he removes his clothes, a series of effective punishments and rewards takes place. Even worse than this confusion of reinforcements, it is more than probable that undressing is held up whilst the patient is receiving a shock because he is distracted. Thus the process is one of undressing being followed by punishment and staying dressed being followed by positive reinforcement. It should also be remembered that positive reinforcement is more effective and predictable than punishment. Thus the net effect of discontinuous shocks given in this way would be to reinforce staying dressed in female clothes. Figure 10 illustrates this point.

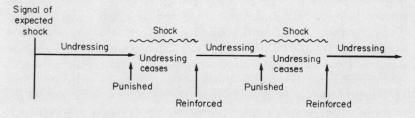

Fig. 10. Pattern of reinforcement and punishment in aversion therapy.

The picture of aversion therapy is therefore very complex and by no means as simple as first appears. A few cases have been reported as successes but very many unreported treatments have been attempted and failures rarely justify the writing of a paper for publication.

The use of vomiting agents in the treatment of sexual disorders in recent times is mostly derived from a paper by Raymond (1956), rather prior to the formulation of the behaviour therapy concept. Raymond treated a man with a pram and handbag fetish. The patient's room was filled with prams and handbags and 2-hourly treatments with apomorphine were given day and night. Eventually the patient was discovered "sobbing uncontrollably" and begging for the articles to be taken away. This treatment is, of course, incapable of satisfactory explanation by learning theory.

The model was borrowed by Glynn and Harper (1961) for the treatment of a transvestite who was in danger of prosecution. Nausea and vomiting was induced 2-hourly for 4 days and nights and the patient was obliged to cross-dress and wear female clothing throughout the nausea. The patient is recorded as successfully treated as far as a 7-month follow-up is concerned.

An early report was given by a group of co-workers, Barker, Blakemore, Conway, Lavin, and Thorpe (Lavin *et al.*, 1961; Barker *et al.* 1961; Blakemore *et al.*, 1963; Barker, 1965, 1966) in which it appears that two distinct cases of transvestism were treated. The first case is described in Barker *et al.* (1961) and is that of a typical transvestite. It is reported that his marital sexual relations were regarded as always satisfactory. The treatment used apomorphine and emetine as vomiting agents and an arbitrary quantity of dexamphetamine sulphate was used to enhance conditioning. The drugs induced nausea and vomiting. During this period the patient was shown slides of himself dressed in female clothing and a tape recording describing the putting on of female attire was played to him. This procedure was repeated at 2-hourly intervals for 6 days and nights and the outcome was that the patient ceased to cross-dress regarding his transvestism as a "ghastly nightmare".

The authors are fully aware of the fact that the result has no simple explanation in learning-theory terms and confess themselves "unable to demonstrate the precise mechanisms which alleviated the symptoms in our patient".

Barker (1965) compares this case with that described by Blakemore *et al.* (1963) in which an electrical aversive stimulus was used. The transvestite stood on a grid through which an electric shock could be given to the soles of his feet. The patient commenced dressing in his female clothes and after a given signal he received a series of irregular shocks until he was undressed. The authors regarded the treatment as a success because the patient ceased to be sexually satisfied by cross-dressing. The advantages of shock seem apparent in the comparison of these cases but for the reasons already pointed out the effectiveness of the therapy is again not conclusively explained in terms of learning theory.

Morgenstern *et al.* (1965) described an investigation designed to predict the outcome of behaviour therapy. An extensive battery of tests was given to nineteen transvestites who were offered aversion therapy. After testing six of the number withdrew. The remaining thirteen were admitted to hospital and were given thirty-nine treatments of apomorphine aversion therapy at the rate of three sessions a day. An attempt was made to bring on the peak of nausea and vomiting just as the patient completed his dressing. The writers infer that this was successful. The patients seem to have remained dressed until the end of the session and the nausea had passed.

The patients were evaluated over follow-up periods of 8 months to 4 years by interview. Of the thirteen treated patients all were said to have shown some improvement but six relapsed. All patients claimed that dressing did not give them the pleasure it had previously done. This statement from "cured" patients is explained by the fact that all patients attempted to cross-dress once spontaneously within 1 month of completing aversion therapy. This episode was described as an attempt to see if there was any satisfaction left in cross-dressing.

Unfortunately no details are given of the patients themselves and one cannot guess how far the improvements were confined to fetishism. It is not clearly stated but it seems that family pressures and threats of court action were the factors which led to treatment, i.e. few if any could be regarded as seeking treatment purely on their own behalf.

A test of verbal conditioning was included amongst the test battery given. The results are stated in a rather complex manner but the impression is that the authors regard "verbal" conditioning as discriminating between cured, relapsed, and failed patients. "Non-verbal" conditioning did not discriminate. The authors might perhaps have discussed whether or not verbal conditioning could have been more relevant to the conforming verbal reporting in the follow-up interview than to the cross-dressing behaviour. The criticism that aversion therapy has been more effective in establishing a pattern of verbal reporting rather than a change in the behaviour under treatment is not uncommon and is hard to refute. Perhaps this is a cynical view but it should not be totally overlooked and Morgenstern's research could be seen as lending it some support. In an alternative terminology maybe the response learned is a verbal strategy of not declaring one's impulses or exposing one's private behaviour!

Shirlaw (1961) claimed that the whole performance of the aversion régime when vomiting agents were used was irrelevant. The results claimed by the various workers could be obtained just by treatment with apomorphine alone. Shirlaw claimed that the drug had a specific action of a chemical nature "curing" transvestism. It was also recommended as quite effective in treating psychotic and neurotic patients.

Oswald (1962) reports the treatment of a case of transvestism using Raymond's technique which failed but he attributed the failure to the patient's age (37 years). He comments on two other treated cases of transvestism, also unsuccessful. Only a rubber fetishist seems to have responded. However, the details reported of a treatment which seems to readily result in "schizophrenia-like" hallucinations and paranoid thoughts must simply be regarded as disturbing if not distressing. This is especially so, perhaps, in the context of a paper which places such emphasis on the patient–therapist relationship.

Pearce (1963) reports the treatment of a transvestite by

Lukianowicz which he euphemistically describes as an unconventional technique. The patient's wife would help him to put on her dress everyday and then she was instructed to watch him masturbate in front of a mirror in her presence. It seems the patient reported "After a few days of this disgraceful procedure I became heartily sick of the whole pathetic situation. I became so disgusted with myself that the mere thought of putting on female clothes and masturbating became nauseating, and made me feel very foolish and deeply ashamed of myself. I developed a real and profound aversion for female clothing and masturbation." Treatment was also followed by a period of impotence it seems, but there is little information on the case available as Lukianowicz seems to have avoided almost all involvement in the treatment. It could, one supposes, be argued that humiliation was being employed as an aversive stimulus in a classical conditioning process but this does seem to be a technique which left a lot to be desired in both theory and practice.

McGuire and Valance (1964) presented a number of cases of sexual deviation who had been treated by having the patient operate his own shock device used *in vivo* when he was sexually aroused in a deviant way. Although they did not specifically report a case of transvestism treated in this manner, McGuire *et al.* (1965) made a valuable contribution to the theory of sexual deviation with specific reference to transvestism. They recognised the value of orgasm as a powerful behavioural reinforcer. Stoller (1968) makes a very similar observation.

McGuire hypothesises that deviations in sexual behaviour may occur through "accidents of our first experience" so that masturbation in particular has an important part in shaping sexual behaviour. That is to say a fantasy stimulus perhaps at first only remotely related to sexual arousal may by chance become associated with orgasm and acquire increased sexual-stimulus value. The fantasy is likely to be shaped into a necessary part of the sexual fantasies. If fantasy of contact with, or the wearing of, female clothing, or garments of similar material, etc., is associated with masturbation, the sensation might be "shaped" into a sexual stimulus. One strong justification for such an argument is that masturbation is clearly likely to be a most powerful reinforcer whilst "guilt feelings" which largely underpin psychodynamic hypotheses are at best weak and unpredictable.

Oddly enough society appears in some ways to regulate its institutions occasionally by witholding sexual gratification. Just such a case might be the traditional insistence on premarital celibacy. Surely the wedding-night ritual of allowing intercourse for the first time must have some of its roots in a need to reinforce the stability of marriage as an institution. The apparent liberalisation of views of premarital sexual relationships could quite easily be linked with the decay of marriage as a social institution; although unprovable, the hypothesis is intriguing.

It is interesting too to speculate that if the origin of transvestite fetishism was as McGuire suggests in the chance shaping of sexual stimuli, early transvestite experiences would be fetishistic — as indeed they are. However, one might also expect that the fetish might be extinguished in a fair number of cases, i.e. shaping out the cross-dressing as a sexual stimulus leaving behind a cross-dressing pattern as an autonomous habit no longer experienced as erotic. It may also be that if a gender dysphoria precedes the sexual-reinforcement phase, the fantasies are in any event much more likely to be cross-gender fantasies simply because such a non-sexual fantasy would be the more common. Such an explanation is, of course, very incomplete but raises some interesting considerations.

Given the importance of orgasm in shaping up sexual stimuli, it is quite clear that the process should not be ignored in therapy. McGuire proposed that the patient could extinguish the transvestite stimulus by controlling and avoiding the fetishistic fantasy during the period immediately preceding orgasm particularly in normal intercourse. Certainly this would be a rational strategy in the treatment of the transvestite fetish although there does not appear to be a report of any case in which McGuire's suggestion has been successfully applied.

Brierley (1965) (quoted by Feldman and MacCulloch, 1971) presented a report on a series of thirty-four unselected cases in which the cause of referral to hospital was a sexual deviation alone. Most of the cases were offered treatment by a classical conditioning technique. The series included seven cross-dressing patients.

The technique of treatment was to present the patient with a series of pictures which he had himself chosen to represent the female clothing which he found specially attractive. Each picture was presented for randomised periods of up to 30 seconds. The shock which followed was either immediately after the picture was withdrawn or delayed by a variable period of up to 15 seconds and a random number of pictures were not followed by shock. An interval of 1 minute occurred between "trials".

It was clearly observed and reported by the patients that the shocks administered were not themselves the cause of anxiety. It was the anticipation of the shock which contained the strongest aversive element, whilst the shock itself appeared almost as a relief followed by a strong sense of relaxation. The shock used was described as "rough shock". It had been found by trial with volunteers that various forms of electrical discharge felt different. The choice was made according to four main needs:

1. No physical danger of burns or other injury.
2. An experience of discomfort at low levels of electrical energy.
3. Acceptable for continuous stimulation of up to 1 second.
4. A minimum of adaptation to the shock over the time it would be used.

Interrupted D.C. (Faradic) shock of the type obtained from a trembler coil or older type of physiotherapists' battery-powered stimulator using a 6-volt battery was the most satisfactory on these counts. Electronic devices producing the same wave forms did so with greater precision and the shock felt more predictable and the rate of adaptation was high. The mechanical machine with its arcing contacts was, within limits, unpredictable and the shock was felt as rough and prickly, hence the adaptation rate was likely to be lower.

Sinusoidal (A.C.) shocks felt confined to the surface of the body and were unpleasant, rather than having the startling quality of the Faradic shock. Perhaps the difference was somewhat analogous to the difference between an ache and a pain. Continuous D.C. shock was rejected because of the danger of skin burns and also because it produced quite violent muscle contraction which could be injurious if used at an aversive level. D.C. discharges from a condenser could be safely used at an aversive level but were only possible at very short duration, i.e. milliseconds. D.C. square waves have been employed in aversion therapy but they are unsuitable in the same way as continuous D.C.

The seven cross-dressing cases reported were as follows:

1. Transvestite aged 21. History of adolescent delinquency. Attended at wife's instigation only. Moderately co-operative. Eight weekly treatment sessions during which the patient reported that cross-dressing ceased. No follow-up since patient ceased attending. Later found to have relapsed.

2. Transvestite aged 37 employed as a senior prison officer. Attended at wife's instigation only. Quite unco-operative with therapy in any form. Aggressively demanding to continue his transvestism.

3. Transsexual aged 17. Co-operative with treatment and three sessions were undertaken. Emotionally very labile and in a state of such general distress that aversion therapy was discontinued by the therapist.

4. Fetishist aged 14. Charged with stealing ladies' underwear and referred by court. Unco-operative and refused to attend for counselling.

5. Fetishist aged 14. Charged with stealing ladies' underwear. Not considered suitable for aversion therapy on account of immaturity. Attended for counselling. No further offences during 2-year follow-up.

6. Fetishist aged 34, specific to mother-in-law's clothing. Attended because of family pressure but quite co-operative. Seven weekly sessions. No further episodes during 6 months of treatment and follow-up.
7. Fetishist with cross-dressing aged 27. Numerous other profound sexual deviations including inducing prostitutes to indulge in sexual acts with dogs, trading in pornographic photographs, etc. Five aversion therapy sessions at 2-weekly intervals specifically directed at interest in pornography. Patient reported all sexually deviant activities greatly diminished but therapy still continuing at time of the report.

In this series aversion therapy had nothing to contribute to two of the three cases who could be said to have clear gender-identity problems. The third case seems only to have been helped for a short period of time. The two fetishists treated by aversion therapy were regarded as responding but the follow-up was quite inadequate in one of these. In comparison ten homosexuals were included in the series and offered similar treatment. The results indicated a material response in six cases and the four others were unwilling to undertake therapy.

Clark (1965) employed an avoidance conditioning model but with the variation of presenting his stimuli by tachistoscope in the form of words and pictures and also including an unshocked relief word unassociated with transvestism.

Feldman and McCulloch (1965) reported his application of avoidance conditioning to the treatment of homosexuals but later (Feldman *et al.*, 1968) reported the treatment of two transvestites. The first case is interesting in that it seems to be the only case reported in which there has been hysterical dissociation. It is not a case in which there is a consistent dissociation related to the feminine and masculine personalities, but an episode of amnesia occurred perhaps as a result of impending bankruptcy. Nevertheless, after the amnesic experience his female clothing was found in the boot of his car. Unfortunately the report omits any discussion of this interesting aspect. The patient seems to have been primarily fetishistic making no attempt to pass as a female, his activities being largely a matter of cross-dressing and masturbating in front of a mirror. Avoidance conditioning employed photographs of the patient in various stages of cross-dressing. Photos of his wife were employed as a relief stimulus presented when the patient avoids the shock. In this case the cross-dressing disappeared and the patient improved his social position. Feldman described this as an undoubted success.

The second patient was treated similarly but without the relief stimulus. He was again a fetishistic transvestite who had gone out at nights dressed as a woman but Feldman feels he had "no desire to be or act the part of a woman". Going out dressed was apparently purely sexually motivated. In this case it is specially interesting that marital sexual relationships were reinstated but he also returned to cross-dressing but without the sexual stimulation aroused by clothing. It would seem therefore that the effects of aversion therapy could be interpreted as effectively dealing with the erotic fetishistic component but leaving the gender dysphoria. Of course this is the familiar picture of the mature transvestite who has moved out of the fetishistic phase of his early transvestism.

Feldman's view of transvestism and transsexualism seems to be that of the established behaviourist. For example, he says (1971) that "We consider transsexuals as homosexual by definition". Whilst his definition of homosexuality is not completely explicit, one presumes that what is meant is that the transsexual is a person capable of a sexual relationship with another of the same biological genetic sex. It is very questionable whether this view suffices without consideration of the individual's gender identity, i.e. if his relationship is perceived as that, say, of a woman with a man as opposed to a man with a man. On the whole it seems that transsexuals see themselves as consorting with heterosexual males who value them as women. It would seem very unlikely that aversion therapy with transsexuals conducted as if they were simply homosexual would achieve an acceptable goal.

Marks and Gelder's (1967) research was an interesting experimental investigation of aversion therapy with transvestite patients. There were five treated patients and unlike many other writers they point out that the group was not necessarily typical since they showed strong fetishistic features.

> Patients with fetishism and transvestism characteristically experience their abnormal desires as a mounting urge producing tension which is only released when the abnormal desire is indulged. In our patients this indulgence involved sexual excitement and usually ejaculation but other patients found wearing clothes satisfying itself without overt sexual stimulation.

This was an important issue since Marks and Gelder were specific in directing their treatment at the fetishistic component. For example, they used a penile plethysmograph to measure sexual arousal. (The penile plethysmograph is essentially a device for measuring the change in size of the penis in the early stages of an erection. The most commonly used form employs a fine silicone rubber tube containing mercury which fits around the penis and as it is stretched by the change in circumference of the penis the column of mercury changes resistance which can then be detected.)

All the patients were regarded as highly motivated and regarded as well-integrated personalities. Two had previously been treated by apomorphine aversion conditioning without success. (One notes that one of these was markedly masochistic in his sexual impulses.)

Two patterns of aversion conditioning were employed. The first followed, roughly, the routine of Blakemore et al. (1963). The patient would be instructed to begin dressing, then up to 120 seconds after starting he would receive a signal indicating that he would receive a shock at random intervals until he discarded the clothing. Twenty per cent of trials were in fact unshocked. The other pattern of aversion therapy was new in that the patient was instructed to produce clear stable fantasies associated with women's clothing. When they felt they had attained such a fantasy they signalled and the signal was followed by a shock sufficient to dispel the fantasy. In both régimes the patient was allowed to select the level of shock himself and was warned that it need not be chosen to be very painful.

Two pieces of evidence were collected from two of the five cases. In one case the response shown by the plethysmograph was clear enough to compare the results of aversion therapy directed to just one article of clothing, say "panties". A fantasy of a female nude was also incorporated but not of course shocked. After a session concentrating on the one garment it was found that the penile-response latency to that fantasy was greatly increased, i.e. it took a much longer time for an erection of a given degree to occur. The emphasis could then be changed to another garment with the same result whilst the increased response latency to the previously shocked garment was maintained. In this way aversion therapy could work through the array of individual garments and, of course, the response latency associated with the nude remained unchanged. Thus it seemed that aversion therapy was quite specific in suppressing the sexual arousal to a specified stimulus and the degree of generalisation was remarkably small.

Changes in attitude to the garments were investigated using the semantic differential method of Osgood (1957). One patient devalued all the clothing before aversion therapy commenced but another showed clear changes specific to the garment being treated as occurred in the experiment with the plethysmograph in the previous case. These results are shown in Marks and Gelder's figure reproduced as Fig. 11.

It was not the purpose of this report to pronounce upon the quality of long-term outcome. However, relatives seem to have regarded the results as generally favourable except that all patients reported some increase in irritability, in one case lasting 6 months. There was no evidence that other sexual deviations were substituted for the fetishes eradicated and no symptom substitution.

A follow-up report came in Marks *et al.* (1970) which dealt with twenty-four cases 2 years after treatment. The cases they divided into two groups of twelve, twelve transsexuals and

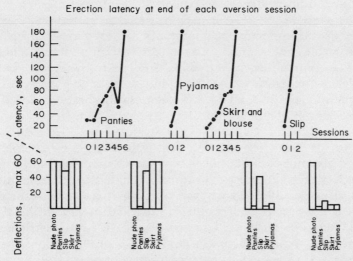

Fig. 11. Specificity of autonomic changes.

twelve transvestites, fetishists, and sado-masochists. One presumes that the patients include those reported in 1967 but the data seem not to be entirely consistent since it is stated that none of the patients devalued the concepts concerned in their deviation whilst on the waiting list, whereas one had done so in the earlier paper. Half of the transvestites, fetishists, and others in the second group continued to engage in the deviant behaviour after treatment but with less enjoyment. Three others cross-dressed a few times after treatment.

The figures are difficult to conjure with because the transvestite group is such a polyglot affair including even a patient with a fetish for lame women. At best nine cross-dressed but all seem clearly to have been fetishistic. The transsexual group also appears to have included some unusual cases, e.g. a fetishistic transsexual with a fetish for one-legged women. In contrast it seems that another group which was untreated, (eleven out of twelve had rejected treatment) included four of the transvestites who seem to have been recognised as not fetishistic.

The overall change in deviant attitudes measured on a 7-point scale was little more than one point. This amounted to a return to a mean score which the writers interpreted as a neutral attitude. This they regarded as similar to what one would expect of "sexually normal men" but there is no good reason to assume this and it is a type of generalisation best avoided when considering sexual behaviour.

Marks *et al.* are obviously very aware that a great deal hangs on the case selection and the fact that there is no completely agreed classification of transvestism and transsexualism. This is important for the present purpose in that it is necessary to be as clear as possible whether the research is relevant to the type of person under consideration and defined in Chapter 1. Marks *et al.* were obviously far less concerned with or constricted by the precise definitions and it was more important to them to demonstrate a general point about the long-term outcomes of aversion therapy as applied to groups of sexual deviants. In this respect the evidence of some success for faradic aversion in the treatment of the sexual component of the disorders is sound. The research also has considerable methodological qualities which make it more convincing than most other reports.

Perhaps the most impressive report of the application of behavioural techniques to the treatment of gender disorders is a single case study. Barlow *et al.* (1973) adopted primarily a technique normally referred to as social skills training. This might best be described as a method based on the analysis of behaviour into essential elements which can be taught by means like modelling, behaviour rehearsal, and video feedback. This package of methods has a great deal of flexibility in the therapeutic methods it uses, some of which, for example, owe as much to Client-centred Therapy as they do to learning theory.

Barlow *et al.* treated a case of transsexualism but in many respects the model should serve quite adequately for the treatment of transvestism also. The patient was a 17-year-old man who had sought help largely motivated towards sex reassignment. Because of his age immediate surgery was not possible and he was induced to accept treatment because in the long term he could always seek surgery at a later stage. Indeed he must have felt that if he went along with the attempt he would add some weight to his plea of the necessity of the sex reassignment. However, he seems to have been caught up in the therapy and persisted with a deal of enthusiasm as progress occurred.

In the first stage an attempt was made to treat his homosexual orientation by aversion therapy and including the "fading" in of heterosexual stimuli. However, the attempt was unsuccessful. Various objective measures of response including the penile plethysmograph were employed.

Attention was then turned to social skills training. Specific components of motor behaviour in sitting, standing, and walking were attacked. Video feedback with analysis and discussion was extensively used and the patient was treated for 30 minutes each day. Extensive praise and "verbal feedback for errors" were used to reinforce the desired behaviour. Independent raters showed an increase in his masculinity and the patient himself found that he was far less an object of ridicule in everyday life. Any improvements were found to be strictly in the area of behaviour being treated and not general.

The next stage was to deal with more complex social behaviour. By modelling and rehearsal he was induced to adopt male-role behaviour, increasing eye contact, initiating conversation, and demonstrating affect.

Voice training was then attempted since he had a naturally high and effeminate voice. A male recording was made of sentences like "A good looking woman turns me on". The patient could repeat these sentences and the playback analysed. He was also trained to keep his thyroid cartilage as low as possible, monitoring its position by feeling with his finger. After 3 weeks of daily sessions a close acquaintance failed to recognise his voice on the phone.

Having had some success in masculinising his behaviour attention was again turned to his homosexuality. First an operant technique was used. He chose from *Playboy* a number of female pictures which were least unattractive to him. He was shown these pictures and asked to fantasise a sexual involvement with the girls. When the fantasy was clear he signalled and the picture was replaced by one of a series of pictures which he found very pleasant, these were usually pictures of food or animals. He also received lavish praise from the female therapist. He began to report more heterosexual fantasies and his transsexual attitudes measured on a simple scale began to change.

The response to the opposite sex was then strengthened by a classical conditioning routine using his homosexual sexual feelings as a reinforcer. He was shown first a picture of a female nude as a conditioned stimulus, followed by a picture of a strongly arousing male nude as the unconditioned stimulus. The attraction to females increased.

It was then necessary to extinguish the homosexual arousal and at this stage he responded to electrical aversion and covert sensitisation methods. His behaviour in general improved, he became more confident and talkative, and a year later he had a steady girl friend with whom he could enjoy mild petting.

No other such dedicated attempt at treatment either of a transsexual or transvestite appears to have been carried out. Barlow *et al.* admit that the case was unusual because of the patient's original willingness developing into enthusiasm and declare the case "not necessarily prototypical". On the other hand, they feel that the change can only be attributed to the therapy because "We may assume that luck, growth or placebo effects do not produce a change in transsexuals". This is not necessarily a safe assumption particularly in an adolescent youth. Even transsexuals sometimes seem to change their orientation, a fact which does not fit closely with theory but is nevertheless real.

CHAPTER 9

The Management of Transvestism

Following on a chapter devoted to the somewhat disappointing studies in the formal treatment of transvestism it becomes necessary to consider broader possibilities of how the transvestite might be helped and their implications. Because areas of helping are considered which can hardly be properly identified as "therapy" we will simply regard these techniques as "management".

The overall picture of therapy with transvestites is that there has been a multiplicity of shots in the dark and we have to take into consideration what are likely to have been large numbers of unreported abortive treatments. Aversion therapy has laid better claim to be effective in a limited way than other techniques, because it has paid better attention to careful appraisal of its effects. Unfortunately aversion therapy has not always been carried out in either aesthetically or ethically acceptable ways and also it has been ill planned and not in true accord with the theoretical basis claimed.

Certainly the constant interest has been in fetishistic cross-dressing, occasionally with some acknowledgement that this is not a necessary part of transvestism. Indeed the present argument is that fetishistic cross-dressing is meaningfully regarded as an independent phenomenon from transvestism. Only one of the treated cases found in the literature in which behaviour therapy was employed (Barlow *et al.*, 1973), and perhaps the cases treated by psychotherapy, can be said to have been treated for the core problem of gender dysphoria. No psychotherapy report has specified the gender problem as a focus but it is not in the nature of traditional psychotherapy to do so in any event. It could be said that psychotherapy was more likely to resolve the gender problems than most other therapies would.

Many writers (e.g. Hamburger, 1953; Anchersen, 1956; Bowman and Engle, 1957) take the unequivocal view that all forms of therapy are ineffective. This is a view probably supported by the experience of Money in cases of hermaphrodism where an attempt has been made to change gender identity.

Certainly the evidence presented by Prince and Bentler (1972) suggests that this is largely the position felt by transvestites themselves. In their study of 504 transvestites the results shown in Table 13 were obtained. Of this group 24% had in fact sought psychiatric help and only 9% had gone into treatment in any depth.

TABLE 12. *Psychiatric Treatment in 504 Transvestites*

Sought psychiatric help		24%
Undertaken long-term treatment		9%
Evaluation of treatment		
Waste of time and money	53%	
Better understanding	42%	
Temporary cure	5%	

This may have been because most were not offered active treatment or because the aims of the treatment were rejected by the transvestite. It has to be remembered that only 1% of the sample gave as a plan for the future of their transvestism "trying to restrict myself and hope to stop it". 22% expected to continue things "about as they are" and 72% said "hope to be able to expand my activities more" or "trying to develop my feminine self more fully". In this respect it looks as though at least 23% of the sample must have gone into treatment under external pressure and neither in the hope nor confidence of being "cured". This amounts to saying that over 95% of the treatment group were not personally motivated towards therapy. Indeed this is the impression one obtains from many reports on therapy with groups of transvestites, e.g. Pearce (1963), where it is rare indeed to find a patient coming to therapy simply because he wishes to change his transvestite behaviour in the direction of normalisation. Many do, of course, come with a personal request for sex-change.

Of the people who went into long-term therapy just above half regarded it as futile and "a waste of time and money" whilst 42% felt that they had gathered some better understanding. Five per cent said that it had effected a temporary cure. These figures should be translated into percentages of the entire transvestite group. They mean in fact that only 1.2% of the entire group found some temporary relief. Oddly this is about the percentage who wanted and planned to "stop it" but one could expect just such a result from the simple effects of suggestion rather than fundamental therapeutic change. The sample does not include any cases who have been cured, for obvious reasons, but if such cases were by any means numerous one would have expected far more cases of transient relief.

An interesting sidelight is the fact that Prince and Bentler found that where the cases were divorcees, those who told their wives before marriage about their transvestism tended to go to a psychiatrist more readily. This might indicate a willingness to share information about their condition and perhaps a lower level of guilt in these cases.

We are, therefore, concerned with a condition which at present appears incapable of being "normalised" in its more profound aspects but there is some scope for the elimination of deviant fetishistic arousal where it exists. Moreover, few transvestites are motivated to lose their transvestism even though they may seek to escape guilt aroused by society or a release from the erotic component. What then might be offered?

The first question to consider is whether or not we can productively answer the problems posed by the transvestite within the concept of therapy. Is the notion of treatment appropriate or are there personal and social issues which do not fit within this frame of reference. Clearly aversion therapy, as an example, is designed to induce a pattern of behaviour based on a belief in "what the normal person does". One must ask, then, if we have the knowledge which really entitles us to select such a model for the patient. There are many known disorders or quirks of sexual behaviour. Kinsey and others have estimated that roughly 15% of adult males have been homosexual exclusively for 3 or more years. Add to this figure a few per cent for transvestites, transsexuals, and clothing fetishists, then a few more for those who are sado-masochistically inclined, the impotent, the sexual athletes, and so on. We then are seemingly talking of 20, 30, or perhaps an even greater percentage of normal people and we must wonder what our concept of "normal" is all about. Could it simply be the myth we all believe about the rest of society and can therapy with such a goal really be expected to succeed?

The danger may be that the relative failure of therapy may stimulate just such a conviction that therapy is irrational. If there is a rational goal then it must be pursued. It seems, however, that in the present state of things five important conclusions can be drawn:

1. The outcome of attempts at therapy are related almost entirely to the sexual component of cross-dressing behaviour and even in this area are not entirely convincing.
2. Few attempts at therapy orientated towards congruence between gender identity and biological sex have been made.
3. Consistently transvestites are depicted as unwilling to relinquish behaviour they find pleasurable.
4. There is no evidence that transvestites show greater evidence of psychiatric disorder than the general population. Their level of real-life adjustment and achievement seems at least adequate.
5. Where depression and anxiety are features, it is likely that these arise from conflict aroused by social condemnation, which is founded mostly in misunderstanding and irrational hostility.

Figure 12 represents an outline of possible courses of action. Three groups are included, fetishists, transvestites, and transsexuals. It would be incorrect to regard these groups as entirely

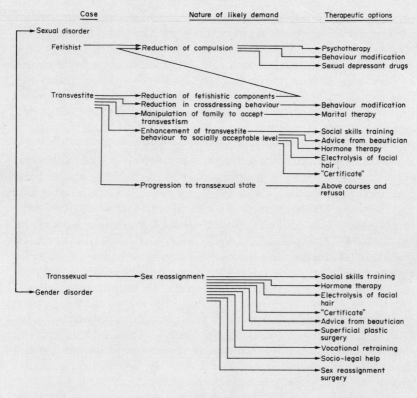

FIG. 12.

distinct rather than being interrelated by degrees of sexual erotic involvement with cross-dressing and by degrees of gender dysphoria. Broadly the more a patient exhibits a primarily fetishistic problem the more likely a form of therapy directed at normalising his sexual behaviour would be acceptable and effective. The more the problem has transsexual features and is one of gender dysphoria the less hope there is of effective normalising therapy and the less the individual will seek or accept such therapy. In the middle range remnants of fetishism may remain and the individual may well wish to be free from them.

In this case he may accept therapy providing it is clear what the focus is. This is a problem for psychotherapy in accepting the patient's willingness to resolve only a part of what the therapist sees as his disorder.

There is no point in evading a good deal of social pressure against aversion therapy, primarily on the grounds that the therapist is inflicting pain as an agent of society which chooses to condemn the harmless behaviour of a minority group. Such a case could be argued but, be that as it may, there are other models of behaviour therapy open to exploration.

Covert sensitisation is a technique close to aversion therapy (Cautela, 1966) but one in which the patient has absolute control over the process. The client is trained in relaxation techniques and during relaxation he is asked to visualise his fetish as clearly as possible. He would then be asked to signal when he feels he has reached as clear and lively an experience of his sexual deviation as possible. He is then immediately asked to imagine an unpleasant experience, e.g. nausea, headache, presence of a policeman, ridicule, etc., such that the unpleasant fantasy dispels the sexual excitement. The model is, of course, a loose replication of the aversion regime but using the patient's own fantasies. This has a severe disadvantage in the lack of control over the stimuli which is demanded by the classical conditioning model. On the other hand, the client can use and practice the procedure at home for an indefinite period.

A somewhat similar process is the technique described by Homme (1965) which would be equally applicable to fetishism. The patient is here taught a control technique using an incompatible fantasy. The fetishist might follow his deviant fantasy with one which would suppress his sexual arousal, e.g. his wife and family accusing him. In addition to the success of displacing the deviant fantasy with the covert stimulus he would be rewarded and reinforced, e.g. by a cup of coffee. The fantasy which dispels the sexual arousal becomes in effect a conditioned covert operant.

Unfortunately neither technique seems to have been used in the treatment of clothing fetishism and in general there is no sound evidence of the effectiveness of covert techniques. Biofeedback methods have an advantage in permitting some external control. Again a biofeedback approach to fetishism could have much in common with covert sensitisation. The client could be asked to imagine a hierarchy of sexually provoking objects or situations during which his level of autonomic arousal is monitored and relayed to him, using, say, penile plethysmography or psychogalvanic response. The feedback can be either visual or auditory. The client learns to maintain relaxation and control arousal by observing his psychophysiological response. The provocation may be increased in intensity as the patient acquires effective control. Certainly sexual deviants can develop control by this technique within a treatment situation but how effective the control is in the real-life situation is hard to say.

A rather different approach is offered by the hypothesis that a deviation such as fetishism might be mediated by learned anxieties about heterosexual behaviour. The fetishist may use his fetish in fantasy to obtain an orgasm during intercourse—this is a not uncommon report. It appears almost a cultivated erotic touchstone to save him from the danger of impotence and hence is strongly reinforced. Thus it may be that the fetish may respond to attempts to resolve the heterosexual anxieties by the conventional techniques of marital therapy.

McGuire's (1965) suggestion of distancing the fetishistic arousal from orgasm and, as it were, extinguishing it by non-reinforcement, is also an approach which has apparently been neglected. The method seems entirely plausible even if excessively dependent on the patient's individual dedication to make the attempt.

There is, therefore, no shortage of relatively untried methods besides the traditional forms of aversion therapy for attacking the problem of fetishism in transvestites.

At this point the picture changes. The transvestite's motivation becomes uncertain and he is often in opposition to attempts at more radical therapy. Given some degree of motivation "to be a man" which is rarely found, it appears tempting to suggest techniques of reinforcing his masculine role. This proves abortive because one does not find clinically any material evidence of deficiencies in the way he conducts himself as a male. His "masculine self" does not appear deficient unless it be that there is a degree of compensating masculinity obscuring the anxieties he experiences in the male role. The apparent high success academically and economically which at least three studies have reported seem to support the hypothesis that the need for feminity is somewhat counterbalanced by a striving for masculinity in the transvestite's male role. Problems of this nature are dealt with in techniques like social skills training (Falloon *et al.*, 1977) and fixed role therapy (Kelly, 1955). It seems unlikely that long-established gender-identity problems could be resolved by such techniques although Barlow *et al.* (1973) indicate a good deal of hope if the subject is motivated.

In terms of Fig. 12 this is the limit of the true "normalising" therapies and all the remaining areas of Fig. 12 relate to a different style of activity. This activity is one of aiding the individual's adjustment to his transvestism and not one of making moves to eradicate it.

The transvestite's heterosexuality poses the second problem. More often than not the transvestite subject is married and also has children but it is not surprising that there are stresses and strains in the marriage. These strains are imposed both by the transvestite and his wife as a result of the sort of contract they have made or failed to make to cope with the transvestism.

The marriage may well be a perfectly satisfactory one in all respects. The wife has married an average sensible man who fulfils his heterosexual role as a husband quite adequately. She then begins to realise that unaccountable things are taking place. She finds lipstick on his clothing, she smells perfume not her own when she returns from visiting a friend. He is not quite convincing when he tells her what he has been doing on the day she went to visit her mother. Her natural fear is that another woman has caught his interest. If she accuses him he will not admit to her suspicions of course and he will be unable to explain away her evidence. She will be angered by his inability to put her mind at rest. If she does not accuse him but bides her time and nurses her wrath for the time when she finds evidence of his infidelity, the day of reckoning never comes.

It is by no means always the case that the wife discovers her husband's transvestism, at least she may not do so for many years of marriage. The disclosure may come in a variety of ways. The wife may realise that her clothing is being disturbed. Garments she knows she has washed and ironed have clearly been worn. A fastener on a bra or a zip on a dress is unaccountably broken. What at first was a mystery builds up into an inescapable explanation which she cannot understand or accept, mostly because she cannot link such behaviour with her apparently quite normal husband. She may find garments not belonging to her or make-up obviously hidden under the seat of his car, in the attic at home and so on. Her husband may begin to put forward excuses for wearing female clothing. He may suggest a game of "I'll wear your nightie and you wear my pyjamas, just for fun".

A transvestite patient told his wife that his colleagues at work had formed a dramatic society and that he had been chosen for the star part. The play was to be Charley's Aunt. The society provided him with an extensive wardrobe and he had to practice at home how to wear the women's clothes, how to put on his make-up, and behave as a woman. At first the wife accepted this with amused incredulity since he had never been interested in acting before but as the rehearsals stretched well into their second year she felt something was amiss! She enquired of his workmates and found that no such dramatic society had ever existed.

This case illustrates the irrational subterfuge but also hints at the importance which transvestites can place on their acceptance in the guise of a woman by their wives. This transvestite was an intelligent university graduate but placed himself in an impossible position on a direct collision course in order to incorporate his wife into his transvestite practices. Indeed such an almost conscious committal to a situation in which the transvestism must ultimately be exposed is not uncommon amongst transvestites, as if chance must be allowed to dictate the exposure and not his own responsible judgement.

The transvestite may also openly confess himself to his wife. He hopes she will understand and allow him to cross-dress to some degree at home. His ambition which he is likely to pursue relentlessly is that she will accept him as a woman. He may wish to share the housework or take up feminine hobbies, like needlework, with his wife's help.

Almost invariably the transvestite will regard his problem as something which will vanish once he marries so that there is no need to tell his fiancee. In fact it does not vanish just like that and if it is in abeyance for some time after marriage, sooner or later it is probable that it will reappear. His wife, of course, feels she should have been told because she would then have had the choice of not marrying someone who was less of a man than she thought. Even if she does not acknowledge that her anger is based on the feeling that she has not been allowed this choice she will feel that she has been deliberately cheated. Her husband could hardly have taken the marriage vows in good faith so she will feel that the marriage has become a sham.

Other marriages do possess more openness than this. Some transvestites have informed their wives before marriage. Alternatively they make a convincing and determined effort during marriage which may not cease until the feelings have been explained to and accepted by the wife. Neither should we forget that a material percentage, perhaps 10%, of transvestites only become aware of their transvestism during mature years when the marriage may already have taken place.

The outcome of the transvestite's disclosure might be classified as follows:

1. The wife is completely unaccepting. She demands that the husband be treated and/or ceases to feel transvestite needs or she will break up the marriage.
2. The wife endeavours to encapsulate the transvestism. The husband is allowed "to get on with it" if he locks himself in his bedroom and never mentions it to her again and she never sees him cross-dressing.
3. The wife gives partial acceptance without participation,

that he can cross-dress within the home on certain
occasions with her permission, providing it is known only
to the pair of them. If there are any children they must
on no account know.
4. The wife participates in that she allows him to share in
housework, helps him to improve his appearance and will
take some interest in his feelings, but she is unable to
treat him other than as her husband.
5. The wife is totally accepting, being prepared to regard
him as a sister and call him by a female name. She only
opposes his transvestism when she feels he would endanger
their security.

There is, of course, no means of knowing just how wives
distribute into these categories. Neither is there any available
information about why seemingly adaptable, stable, and
competent wives are sometimes highly accepting and sometimes
entirely unable to cope with a transvestite husband. This is an
important and unresearched area.

The transvestite's wife, in addition to some feeling of having
been duped, raises all sorts of doubts. In particular she is afraid
that he is homosexual and is going to take part in sexual affairs
with his own sex. At best he may well no longer wish to have
sexual relations with her unless, she fears, he does so in some
"peculiar" way. She feels that perhaps he may wish to break up
the marriage and perhaps make his own life as a woman. She
may also, of course, regard him simply as a very odd sexual
pervert whatever his good points and whatever his actual
behaviour, so that he cannot be acceptable as a husband. She
may too feel that his needs are some comment on her sexual
adequacy.

Stoller (1968) has alleged that no transvestite marriage is
successful but this has already been refuted in Chapter 2.
Transvestite marriages seem to survive more or less as well as
those of non-transvestites. Also their marital sexual adequacy
does not seem in question. Stoller (1967) has described three
different types of woman in the transvestite's life based on the
treatment and evaluation of thirty-two "transvestites and their

women". Unfortunately he again depends somewhat on the same pornographic book jacket as the one on which he bases other work. One cannot but think that he places excessive value on this one doubtful shred of information. Nevertheless his three categories are:

1. "The malicious male hater" who is a ruthless angry competitive woman who hates all males. She humiliates men whenever possible. "The sexually important women in his life have the power. They are physically strong; they have beauty's power; they are equipped with those phallically shaped whips, sharp heels and boots, they hang those bosom bombs heavily over his head, they are cruel and haughty; they are sure of themselves, their gigantically voluptuous bodies are strong, hard, slim, long and smooth i.e. phallic."

2. The succourer is the type of woman who makes the co-operative transvestite's wife. She is feminine and gentle with men and is warm and affectionate. She can support even with enthusiasm a transvestite husband and even teach him how to dress and behave as a woman, mostly because of the need to succour all other creatures. These needs do not coerce her husband into transvestism nor does she seem to influence her sons to become transvestite.

Stoller argues that the sting in the tail for the succourer comes when she realises that she has nurtured and taught so well that another perhaps more efficient woman has entered her home, in the shape of her husband. The conflicts and jealousy arising from this outcome being the fate of such a marriage.

3. The "symbiote" is the third woman important to the transvestite in Stoller's view. She is not important as a wife as much as a mother and is included here simply for completeness. She is strongly bi-sexual and her feminity is of a boyish quality. She has a persistent feeling that she is a "nothing or neuter" which expresses the underlying state of depression which she experiences. The outcome is found in her sons who feel an overwhelming sense of

feminity which leads to their spontaneous cross-dressing.

It is very difficult to relate these figures to individual transvestites although there seems to be some element of truth in Stoller's observations. The phallic woman is, as Fenichel said about the woman-with-a-penis fantasy, important to many men and really is too non-specific to transvestism to have great significance as far as the genesis of the condition is concerned. Certainly the women of the second group, the succourers, who can and do adapt their lives to their transvestite husbands with real enthusiasm and participation are surprising in their number. Of course, it is not behaviour which has only one admissible explanation in terms of an overwhelming need to succour. It could well be that the wife's devotion is as much to the practical need to maintain the family and home. The adaptation may be realised by her as Hobson's Choice, if she does not adapt there is a threat of unknown quality to her marriage and family security. One cannot ignore either that once the disposition to accept in some degree the husband's transvestism is established there are certain advantages immediately apparent to the wife. Her husband may become more domesticated and shoulder more domestic responsibilities. He may develop interests which are closer to her own and involve himself more closely in her life. His transvestism itself may be some guarantee of his fidelity— at least she may believe so. Most importantly, however, she is given a fairly high degree of power over her husband by catering for his needs.

It is unlikely that many transvestites can attain such a degree of proficiency either in their ability to impersonate a female or in their practical abilities in the home to arouse jealousy in the wife. He may arouse jealousy by showing her that he has reached the point where he can partially detach himself from her. She may thus feel that he has attained some degree of separate existence and that she has been again cheated by finding that his dependence on her was a deception. It has led to losing part of him, just what she feared and just what she thought she could control.

The relationship between the succourer and her transvestite

husband also has hidden dangers for the transvestite. At best he is an adequate cartoon of a woman whilst his wife is an ever-present model of perfect femininity. He may feel himself so undermined in his efforts by her natural femininity which he cannot match that he seeks an independent existence on his own. On the other hand, the succouring wife fulfils an immense need as his producer, cast, audience, and "licence to act". In the transvestite terminology the succourer in the typical "R.G." (real girl) or in America "G.G." (genuine girl) who is a regular partici-pant in transvestite society affairs. The abbreviations character-istically illustrate the transvestite's desperate unwillingness to put into words his own lack of realness or genuineness.

Purely objective evidence for the importance of the symbiote mother is absent. Certainly there is no evidence that transvestites commonly have this sort of mother or that bisexual mothers commonly have transvestite sons. Stoller's claim that the symbiote mother leads her son specifically to transvestism rather than, say, homosexuality needs more explanation than he provides.

Very little can be said about the children of transvestites. Certainly many children are aware of their father's transvestism either because they have discovered it or because they have been brought up in the knowledge of it. No study has been published on the children of transvestites and of course the reports of transvestites themselves are biased. Equally there is little positive evidence that these children are in any way profoundly disturbed by the knowledge. A father's transvestism seems a rare matter in psychiatric case studies.

The following extract from a letter from a transvestite illustrates the usual attitude in children as expressed by transvestite fathers:

> We have effectively switched roles and I am virtually a full-time female now, except for two day spells during the school holidays in which I do the more butch pursuits with my boys. However, both have said that it doesn't matter to them whether we pursue these activities with me in trousers or a skirt.

Perhaps the sting here, if any, lies in the phrase "it doesn't matter". One transvestite reported that as his wife had died when his daughter was young he had been both father and mother to her. She fully accepted his dual role and seemed not to be at all distressed by it. When she left home for university she became involved with a group of undergraduate youths he felt were undesirable. When he attempted to intervene she angrily said, "You have been doing your thing for all these years, now I am going to do mine." At least his role would have seemed to have undermined his ultimate authority but of course similar occurrences are found in many orthodox households. There could just be the implication that the father's behaviour was something which "didn't matter".

Prince (1967), who is himself a transvestite and publishes a good deal of transvestite literature, has produced a book dealing specifically with the problems of "The Transvestite and His Wife" (Argyle Books), particularly relevant to counselling.

The next problem in management is of a different quality again. Assuming that all has been achieved in helping the transvestite to accept his problem attention can be turned to the task of adapting his behaviour so that it has the greatest chance of becoming socially acceptable. In other words, if he is to continue to cross-dress what can be done to lessen the social threat to himself and his family, and how can the risk of distress to others be minimised? The danger here lies in our ignorance of the relationship between transvestism and transsexualism. We do not know how far in aiding the transvestite to "pass" as a woman without giving offence we are promoting in him desires for sex reassignment. If gender theory is correct and transvestism and transsexualism can be differentiated according to the origin of the gender dysphoria, gender core identity or gender role, the danger is small. On the other hand, perhaps sex reassignment is rather meaninglessly restricted to psychiatrically diagnosed transsexualism.

Laub and Fisk (1974) make an immensely important point in a follow-up study of a number of males who had been through surgical sex reassignment. These authors are plastic surgeons with considerable experience in this field. They followed up subjects who had been diagnosed as transsexual, transvestite, and homosexual but had all been reassigned. One would have assumed that those diagnosed as transsexuals would have adjusted after reassignment better than either of the two other groups. This proved not to be the case and all three groups did equally well. The only important factor in predicting the success of sex reassignment was the success of a preoperative trial period in the opposite sex role. The psychiatric diagnosis appeared academic.

Clearly the first stage of assisting the transvestite to a satisfactory standard of behaviour has to do with the skills and habits involved in feminine deportment, speech, mannerisms, and so on. The transvestite is often unaware of the subtle and distinct differences of behaviour between males and females and he may well have some impatience with a slow detailed coaching of his behaviour. The package of social skills training, e.g. Argyle *et al.* (1974), is not so much one single technique in behaviour modification but an application of a wide range of learning-based methods appropriate to the adaptation of social behaviour. No case of the application of such a technique in a case of transvestism has been published but Yardley (1976) has described a case of preoperative transsexualism treated in this way with some success.

The first stage in this treatment was to video tape the transsexual with one or two other people of both sexes. The video tapes were then shown to a group of observers who were not informed of the problem but were asked to describe the patient's behaviour as they saw it. They selected out a number of target areas where the subject was apparently judged unfeminine. These were body movements, head movements, body tonus, posture, gestures, gaze, voice, control of interaction, manner of relating to others, appearance, facial expression, mouth expressions, courtship behaviour.

The next stage was to play back the tape and the judges' observations to the patient. The effect of doing this is often rather distressing to the transsexual and transvestite because he has firmly held beliefs about his behaviour and appearance which are starkly refuted by the video tape. Indeed video taping often surprises the therapist also! Without using such a method the patient is likely to deny the need for the help being offered. In Yardley's procedure the client was seen for twenty weekly 2 hour sessions. The basis of the training was simply instruction, modelling, and feedback. As an example in the area of interactions with other people she was trained to maintain more eye contact, to exhibit behaviour showing warmth, and less assertive behaviour. Role playing was also employed with the help of confederates, e.g. in work on courtship behaviour. Films were used as models also. Voice training seems to have been the most difficult area and employed conventional drama and speech-therapy techniques such as humming to improve the upper range of the voice. The following schedule of training focii is given by the author:

Weeks	1 to 2	Assessment and evaluation.
	3 to 5	Body and head positions.
	6 to 7	Facial expressions.
	8 to 9	Hand movements.
	10 to 20	Voice.
	15 to 17	Courtship behaviour.
	17 to 20	General social situations.

Clearly from Yardley's account the informal relationship between the therapist (female) and the subject was important and there was a good deal of *in vivo* interaction between them. It seems important that the therapist was able to form a relationship with her at a mature level and to experience the relationship as being with a woman rather than a man. Generally speaking it is more often than not easy to accept the majority of transsexual patients as being of the elected role, male or female. It is less easy with transvestites who are less consistent and sometimes unwilling to see themselves as others see them because they are more distressed by doing so.

Yardley's procedure was undoubtedly effective both in terms of before and after ratings and the simple fact that the patient eventually found work as a fashion model and an actress. However, some elements of social-skills training were not exploited. Much of the transvestite's success in passing is not so much a matter of behaviour as less objective factors like "confidence". The transvestite is far more prone to disclose himself by his anxious demeanour, his fear of eye contact, and his guilty behaviour, than he is by many of the minutiae which were an obstacle to Yardley's case. Techniques of relaxation training, coping talk (Meichenbaum, 1971), and more specifically constructed social-training hierarchies would be involved in more radical social skills training of transvestites.

Advice from the beautician might be regarded as part of social-skills training. Under this heading is included a range of guidance about dress and cosmetics much of which involves correcting the false beliefs held by the transvestite. Dressing a man as a woman invariably seems to make him appear a younger person than he really is. Very often the transvestite has difficulty in gauging his age group as a woman and on this depends a great deal in make-up and dress. Quite often the transvestite is preoccupied with styles of make-up which may symbolise femininity to him but at the same time do not make him appear feminine. Note, for example, the reference to the "Cupid's bow" lips in the case of D.N. in Chapter 5. Similarly transvestites tend to choose colours and styles out of keeping with the dress of the time and their age group. The problem is one of deciding how far the transvestite can adopt certain badges of femininity, like bright colours and high-heeled shoes, and how far he needs to be simply unobtrusive.

In effect the beautician has to view the task of creating something like a basic blank canvas and then imposing on it the features of femininity and in many ways the fewer of these features emphasised the better. She may well need to start at the level of simple body shape since many transvestites resort to extremes of padding and corsetry to produce figures they consider to be feminine. Not infrequently they simply succeed in drawing attention to themselves by the extremity of their efforts.

The task is a complex one in that if successfully carried out the beautician will create not a mask but an individual. It may be that the transvestite has only a shadow to guide him, he does not see himself as a real whole woman. He will choose clothes which he feels he admires, or will hide parts of him which he would prefer not to show, but he will rarely choose clothes which are simply comfortable, warm, and durable as the average woman might. He might apply his make-up painstakingly but only a model really does this, the average woman does her make-up instinctively, with no great striving for effect and usually with one eye on the clock. The transvestite may carry this over-preparation too far. It is not uncommon to find both transvestites and transsexuals dressing in expensive clothing which only a wealthy or fashion-conscious woman would wear and the overall impression is false, as if the individual was wearing someone else's clothes.

Up to this point little has been suggested which the transvestite himself could not and would not attain himself if reasonably advised, the further steps are more irrevocable and invoke all manner of personal obstacles for the therapist. There is simply inadequate evidence on which to base the essentially medical decisions about those forms of therapy which are going to promote permanent physical changes. The decisions must rest with the individual therapist.

Transvestites as well as transsexuals request hormone therapy. They both do so under the impression that hormones have the effects of a magic potion with many wonderful feminising effects. This is not the place to deal with medical aspects of hormone therapy but it is appropriate to clarify the many fallacies to which the transvestite might adhere. This is primarily because there is little point in embarking on a possibly serious and dangerous path of treatment in the pursuit of something unlikely to be achieved. Transvestites asking for hormones expect the following to occur:

1. *Development of breasts.* The initial effect of oestrogens on males is to produce a thickening of the "plate" of glandular tissue behind the pigmented area around the nipples. Then an increase of fat and water accumulates behind this plate to produce something like a female breast. The pigmentation

around the nipple and the nipple itself may not change a great deal and rarely will assume the size and colour of a female. Indeed in some men there will be virtually no breast development at all. Some men develop breasts which are transient and disappear once the hormones are withdrawn. In others the breast tissue seems fairly permanent.

In no sense is the breast ever a functioning organ since it is essentially only a deposit of fat. There seems to be a real limit in the size of the bust developed and it does not follow that increasing the dose of oestrogens increases the breast size although the patient will often believe that it will and insist on taking excessive amounts. It has been suggested that breast development might be inhibited if the oestrogen doseage is too high. Certainly some transsexuals show adequate breast development on far smaller amounts of oestrogens than would normally be prescribed.

2. *Body contour changes.* The expectation of miraculous changes includes thinking the whole body, even the bone structure, will change size quite considerably. Some insist that they have lost even a couple of inches in height but nothing of this kind has ever been infallibly confirmed. Fat is likely to be deposited around the hips and thighs and there may be an increase in subcutaneous fat which fills out the face and obscures prominent veins. The effect is to give a younger and certainly a more feminine appearance. Again it may not occur at all and depends on the individual case.

3. *Hair changes.* The belief is that the hair distribution will change, the beard will grow less, the scalp hair will grow softer and more luxurious, and bald patches disappear. Some testify to all these effects but what is obvious to the optimistic transvestite is usually invisible to the observer. There is no evidence that hair growth is affected to a degree which could be called feminising.

4. *Emotional changes.* The transvestite may experience emotional changes and temperamental effects which seem to him to be like feminine feelings. It seems well documented that some diminution of drive, assertiveness, and activity occurs. The

individual becomes more placid and quiescent, he may find it apparently an effort to keep up his role at work. This may be a secondary effect of the loss of sex drive rather than anything to do with femininity. Some emotional changes may occur in that he may begin to weep easily, sometimes for reasons he barely comprehends. He feels himself "being silly" and welcomes this as a feminine trait but it may well have more to do with his suggestibility than with his hormones.

5. *Voice changes.* Oestrogens will be expected to lighten the voice and raise its pitch but there is no evidence that they do—indeed it is unlikely. Voice changes can be effected by practice rather than by hormones.

6. *Skin changes.* The blood supply to the skin may be increased and this may improve the appearance. The expected smooth silky translucence does not often, if ever, occur.

7. *Sexual changes.* It is hard to say what sexual changes the transvestite hopes for. Most are aware of the sexual depressant effect and some welcome the inhibition of their sexuality quite apart from any ideas of feminisation, whilst others claim that feminine sexual interests develop. At any rate whatever the subjective experience of sexual changes, it is almost never an objection to hormone therapy as far as the transvestite is concerned although it must impair his marital sexual life considerably. This is in sharp contrast with most sexual deviants who often object to the sexual-depressant effects of hormone therapy.

Against these supposed benefits of hormones the transvestite rarely balances the disadvantages. He may well find that he cannot tolerate oestrogens because they may induce gastritis, nausea and vomiting, and dizziness. Other effects like nightmares might not be a direct result but nevertheless may prevent the individual from continuing. The serious possible side effects range from pituitary tumours, pulmonary embolism, to cancer of the breast. Whilst such dire consequences are not all that rare they are seldom if ever accepted as adequate reasons for "not trying". The hope is that the undesirable effects will happen to someone else.

A prescribing doctor will always take into consideration a number of definite contra-indications to the use of oestrogens and whatever the transvestite believes these would not be properly waived.

Generally the hormones used are the naturally occurring hormones, in particular, Premarin which is a preparation of various hormones extracted from the urine of pregnant mares. This is in tablet form. Other oestrogen preparations can be given as injections at monthly intervals or as an implant at longer intervals. Formerly a synthetic oestrogen, stilboestrol, was used but is now largely discontinued because it was felt to have more undesirable side effects than natural hormones.

Antiandrogens, e.g. cyproterone acetate (Androcur), which depress the production of androgens (male hormones) have recently come into use. They are expensive and there is nothing to suggest many special advantages. On the whole it seems that they may be less likely to produce the effect the transvestite wants although when they do it will be a result of the individual's own oestrogen secretions.

Electrolysis of facial hair is a service readily available outside medical clinics. A major cause of the detection of a transvestite is the readily apparent facial hair. Apart from the use of very heavy make-up the colour of a dark beard cannot be obscured and the texture of the skin is unfeminine. Because of this the transvestite's face, no matter how skilfully the make-up is applied, is readily recognised as a male.

As with the other processes, electrolysis is seen by the transvestite as a rather magical process turning a grizzled coarse face into a smooth clear complexion. In reality the wish is not fulfilled. Electrolysis simply denudes the face of its whiskers. The texture of the skin itself remains largely unaltered and often rather more "orange peel" than "peaches and cream".

There are various processes in electrolysis in professional use but by far the most common employs high frequency electric current. A fine platinum needle is slipped along the hair follicle and the current applied for a fraction of a second. The current cauterises the hair root destroying it permanently. In fact the

treatment usually progressively weakens the strong hair growth
of a male beard and each hair requires a number of treatments
before disappearing. Other methods such as the Depilex system
do not employ needles but are less commonly used and more
expensive.

A great deal of variation occurs in the length of treatment
necessary. Obviously the stronger and more profuse the beard
the longer the treatment will take. So too will stronger currents
be more rapidly effective but the higher the current the greater
the risk of scarring. An average male beard may take 200 to 250
hours of electrolysis. Most transvestites find that the experience
of electrolysis is not pleasant, some find it intolerable in the
intensity required for the removal of a male beard. The
experience is much that of a series of stinging electric shocks
followed by some local swelling and reddening of the skin
which may last for several days. Sometimes the treatment causes
a rash of small red scabs again taking a few days to disappear.
Some limitation is placed on the speed of treatment by the
tolerance of the skin. It may not be possible to carry out more
than 1 or 2 hours electrolysis each week. This means that the
complete treatment of a transvestite could be up to 5 years.

The legal aspects of a certificate which in some sense offers
support to the transvestite has already been discussed. It cannot
represent any social immunity and simply acts as evidence that
a responsible body recognised that the particular transvestite
is unlikely to wilfully cause social disorder or commit offensive
acts. Such a certificate could be used to assure people who might
question the transvestite of his intentions.

The convictions which have to underlie the provision of such
a document are the obvious ones involving a judgement that the
transvestite will be acceptably behaved. He should not distress
others by in any way drawing attention to himself as a
transvestite for any reason. Unfortunately it follows that many
transvestites could not "qualify" because of their physical
inabilities to pass as a woman in any circumstances. It would be
necessary to judge whether or not the simple appearance of the
person is likely to be offensive and this may be dependent on

the help which can be given in other ways. This is not at all simple since more often than not the transvestite is the least fitted to judge his appearance. He will produce endless flattering photographs selected from an even vaster array some of which might really show his true appearance. Equally it is not easy to make a judgement without some degree of trial. Sometimes men who make almost indescribable travesties of women prove entirely successful. It could be that they appear to be women of such unfortunate appearance that most people would find it heartless to risk accusing them. On the other hand, the transvestite who is just "passable" is more open to scrutiny and challenge. Certainly some very obese, swarthy, deep-voiced, or excessively tall transvestites are able to pass with incredible ease. It is likely that the imponderables such as confidence, composure, and openness are overwhelmingly important for no transvestite is more likely to be detected than the shifty-eyed, tense, furtive person, with a face half obscured, scurrying along avoiding everybody's gaze.

The certificate needs to be conditional and if the transvestite cannot prove socially acceptable it can only be withdrawn, which amounts to saying that it would need to be a renewable document to be credible.

It is quite clear that this discussion of the management of transvestism has overlapped that of the transsexual. No apologies for this are indicated since the boundary is hazy and many of the needs are shared. It does not, however, seem appropriate to consider here the question of surgical procedures either in removing sex organs or the more superficial alterations of facial features, etc. Nevertheless the work of Laub and Fisk (1974) has been mentioned which indicates that the outcome for certain transvestites of reassignment with surgery may be desirable. The obstacle to this thinking is the assumption that it is a process to be avoided at all costs and only to be accepted if there is some inevitable psychological need or an insatiable demand. Few writers have felt able to regard the question of sex reassignment without strong emotion but Armstrong (1966), one of the earliest medical workers in the area, points out that "reassignment

or change of sex is not necessarily an extreme psychological
hazard and psychologically injurious". Evidence such as that of
Walinder (1967 and 1975) suggests that the success rate for sex
reassignment is high. Walinder says "the treatment programme
appears to be fully justified both medically and ethically". In
Walinder's careful examination of the contraindications for
reassignment surgery it is interesting that not one point is related
to the psychiatric diagnosis of transsexualism. He feels, as Laub
and Fisk clearly did, that the most important requirement is that
the individual has a reasonable chance of successfully
impersonating a female. There may therefore be a case for saying
that some persons diagnosed as transvestite rather than transsexual would be more content in the female role even though
the gender-core identity was male.

No writers have paid a great deal of attention to the problem
of rejected patients. Patients can be found who tour from
department to department seeking help, making demands, issuing
threats of suicide and sometimes carrying them out. The question
is what is to happen to the patient whose trial period is a failure,
he cannot simply be discarded on the assumption that he will go
away taking his problem with him? Indeed this whole question
is unexplored. It is inconceivable that a trial period with attendant
training, hormone therapy and the like will not reinforce
transvestite fantasies in many cases. Therefore, the decision to
take these steps cannot be made lightly by any means.

Decisions of the kind involved in the management of
transvestism are difficult because they pose the question "Who
should decide?". As Bancroft (1974) points out, in the U.K. all
effective decisions in the area of sexual deviancy are made in a
medical or paramedical setting. It is important, socially, to face
the fact that whilst this might be convenient it may also be
inappropriate.

Stoller says that it is the resolution of the social problem which
primarily motivates the transvestite to come for help and not a
seeking for therapy in any conventional sense. At the very worst
we may coerce the transvestite into sex-reassignment surgery
because it is the most effective medical solution to the social

problem. Many transvestites and transsexuals express hostility to the system which demands that the only access to help is through the medical man, who is judged, more often than not, to have inadequate knowledge, and patently neither adequate training nor real interest. This is a situation which in time may change if techniques in therapy develop, specialisms appear within medicine, and transvestites become differently motivated. This position is not foreseeable and for a credible helping service it seems that broader skills than medical and paramedical ones must be involved in the decision-making.

Bancroft sees attempts at "treatment" of "patients" with sexual disorders as meaning that the client is the "physician's", but it does not imply that he is "ill". Conversely one might ask why if he is not ill should he be a patient in treatment and in some way in the possession of a physician? The question has to be raised if the physician indeed has such wide and unique skills as to justify this restriction of the client. Perhaps even more important is the question whether it is not a neglect of the physician's real skills to concern himself so much with this type of problem and its social implications. Trethowan (1977) puts this argument very clearly:

> ... there seems to be an ever-growing number of those who consult their doctors on account of personal problems who, although clearly and often understandably distressed, cannot really be considered as ill—at least in any truly medical sense. If this is correct, it may be fair to suggest that their distress may not primarily be the concern of doctors who already have more than enough to do in coping with patients about the medical nature of whose illnesses there can be little doubt. For those who are relatively indigent the social services may prove to be the answer; for others the voluntary organisations—though there should be better built in mechanisms for medical and psychiatric consultations than at present exist.

An aspect of the problem never taken into account is the reluctance in the mind of the patient to prejudice his relationship with his medical advisor. To raise a problem to do with sexual deviance is likely to do just that and in that sense a consultation becomes possibly prejudicial to health care available from the doctor. This situation is neither just to doctor nor patient.

Conventional medical channels also present some problems in anonymity. One might accept that transvestism is a personal matter without consequences for anyone other than the client and his family. Nevertheless society does not think so apparently and it is incongruous that there are no sources of anonymous help outside the voluntary organisations. Society seems to demand protection but does little to further and facilitate help for those from whom it wishes to be protected.

In transvestism a number of decisions need to be taken. Some of these are social in that they have to do with the acceptance by society of the problem. Some are medical in that physical methods of treatment are involved. Some are psychiatric in that pathological processes of depression and emotional disorder may be concerned. Some are psychological in the need for psychotherapy, behaviour modification and counselling. The list becomes long because the problems are also moral, legal, occupational, and so on. Clearly the task is a truly multi-disciplinary one which could involve not only medical and paramedical services but also such help as could be given by a clergyman, a lawyer, an administrator, and others.

Trethowan suggests the locus of such a service might be in the social services. This is logical but local authority social services do not seem to be equipping themselves as either adequately accessible or sufficiently multi-disciplinary in orientation. Open access for clients to be able to seek consultation in anonymity without commitment and formality is essential if a material part of problems like transvestism is to be helped. This is clear from the much higher numbers of persons seeking help through self-help agencies than through formal channels. The highest number of transvestites studied in a research project in medical channels is not greater than about thirty, yet in one study (Kemmett, personal communication, 1977) 600 cases have been assembled through a self-help group. Exactly the same can be said of American researches. Trethowan also suggests that voluntary organisations might also form a focus for this type of consultative service provided that more effective professional consultation can be established. A number of such counselling bodies already exist, like "Friend" and the charitable trusts such as the Albany Trust and the Beaumont Trust, which if adequately supported might exercise a most valuable first counselling function.

However, there is no clear solution at present which possesses the correct blend of public status, professional competence, and medical resource. The most desirable course at present is to encourage liaison between the voluntary bodies, medical and paramedical services.

It is almost 20 years since Edward Glover (1960) wrote about homosexuality:

> . . . the answer to this problem, if it be a problem, is in the development of greater tolerance amongst sections of the community which at present tend to make a scapegoat of homosexuality. In this sense the treatment of homosexuality as a whole should be directed as much at the "diseased" prejudices of society as at the "diseased" propensities of the individual homosexual.

The intervening years have made a little progress along the lines of Glover's prescription and his view of the needs for tolerance are as appropriate to transvestism as to homosexuality. It is, however, vital to appreciate that the progress has not been nearly so great as often assumed and there is a long, long way to go.

CHAPTER 10

Research and Summing-up

To label this final chapter "Conclusions" would be presumptuous. The present purpose of this book has been to draw together data, theory, and opinions about an area of a-typical human behaviour which is poorly researched. There is little upon which many people would fully agree. At almost no point can it be said that reports and research yield unequivocal results on even the most limited front. In few cases does the use of the term "transvestite" have any great consistency. Perhaps this is reflected in the number of terms which have been employed in this area.

Table 14 gives many of these terms and classifications which writers have devised leaving aside words like "femmiphile" (Prince and Bentler, 1972), "femmepersonater" or "transgenderist" which belong to the transvestite societies. Surely not many aspects of the behaviour of minority groups have stimulated such difficulty in naming and classifying amongst so little research.

Transvestism, literally, is clearly the wearing of the clothes pertaining to the opposite sex. In this sense fashion, particularly the current female fashion for wearing trousers, hacking jacket, waistcoat, shirt, tie and man's cap; or male fashion for wearing make-up, are unequivocally transvestite. Because they are "fashion" does not make them less transvestite nor does regarding them as "fashion" explain the motivation behind such fashion. The fashion of women wearing male attire must surely be an offshoot of the women's liberation movement which is frankly associated with gender role dissatisfaction—perhaps justifiably and rightly so. Perhaps what constitutes "fashion" is simply the

TABLE 13. *Some attempts at the classification of cross-dressing*

Ball (1967)	Symptomatic	Secondary to other states,
	Simple	No psychiatric disorder, homosexuality, sex-change wish and confined to cross-dressing
Battig (1952)	Transsexual	
	Homosexual	
	Bi-sexual	
	Heterosexual	
	Auto-sexual	
	also:	
	Apparent	Psychoreactive in origin
	Genuine	Constitutional desire to change sex
Benjamin (1953)	Psychogenic	Not wanting sex change but wanting society to change attitudes
	Intermediate	Inclined to homosexuality
	Somatopsychic	Profound belief in being female
Bruce (1967)	(Primary motivations)	
	Urge to self-adornment	
	Need for virtue	
	Identification with social woman	
	Relief from masculine aggression	
	Relief from social expectancy	
Dukor (1951)	Heterosexual	
	Autosexual	
	Homosexual	
Ellis (1928)	Type 1	Mainly confined to clothing
	Type 2	Feeling to belong to opposite sex
Gutheil (1954)	("Psychopathological factors")	
	Latent homosexual	
	Sado-masochistic	
	Narcissistic	
	Scoptophilic	
	Exhibitionist	
	Fetishistic	
Hirschfeld (1910)	Complete	Wishing to change sex
	Partial	Cross-dressing only
	Constant	
	Periodical	
	In name	Adopting name of opposite sex
	Narcissistic	
	Homosexual	
	Bi-sexual	
	Metatropic	Inverted love object
	Automonosexual	Auto-erotic
Hamburger (1953)	Symptomatic	Accompanying other deviation
	Psychic hermaphrodism	Feeling of being a female personality in a male body
Kinsey *et al* (1948)	Permanent	Identifying with opposite sex at all times
	Partial	Identifying with opposite sex on occasions
Krafft-Ebing and Moll (1924)	Homosexual	
	Heterosexual	
	Obsessive	Not a psychosexual disorder
	Pseudo-transvestism	Cross-dressing for an ulterior motive
Pettow (1922)	Type 1	Men adopting women's clothes
	Type 2	Women adopting men's clothes
	Type 3	Adults adopting the clothing of children
Stoller (1971)	Fetishistic	
	Transsexual	
	Effeminate homosexual	
	Overt, borderline, or latent psychotic	
	Mixed	
	Biologically induced	
	Casual	

number of people adopting this style of behaviour. "Punk rock" is rather proscribed and involves a degree of "indecency", e.g. a girl is prosecuted for wearing a badge on which is written an offensive word. It seems likely that this state of affairs will only remain until there is a substantial enough public following. Indeed, a commercially promoted "punk rock" group can spit and use the same offensive words to a crowd and incite them to unrest and violence without prosecution even for "behaviour likely to cause a breach of the peace".

Transvestism in the broad sense also fades into a vast area involving curious modes of dress which somehow have not been questioned. We recall Stoller's description of the phallic woman with her haughty expression and predatory air, dominating and authoritarian. Her hair is tightly drawn back, she is dressed in severe black and white with her long phallic shiny leather boots, whip, and spurs. She does not only appear in pornographic literature, but she can also be found at almost every meet of the local hunt. Uniforms be they the swastika banded, gun-carrying, jack-booted Nazi fanatic, or the Army cadet, have some significance to the individual beyond tradition and the simple badges of group membership. This signficance is quite as likely to be sexual or genderal as that of transvestism. In a more frankly sexual way people dress in many unusual styles. People who are sexually aroused by dressing as executioners, menial servants, corpses lying in coffins, in the simulated harness tail and mane of a horse, or wearing the chains and manacles of a prisoner, are by no means uncommon. Specific garments of fetishistic importance include constrictive garments especially those fabricated in rubber, like skin-diving suits, or leather as the specially made underwear freely advertised and worn by both sexes. Everyday wear such as dirty and faded jeans, mackintoshes, or even wet clothing proves sexually provocative for some people.

The amount of research into the behaviour of persons who dress in such ways is miniscule. Two reasons for this seem likely. Firstly, such behaviour is very private. Who knows what motivates the huntswoman on her hunter to conform to her stereotype; who can explain why a murderer has elected to make the trappings of militarism his hobby. The people themselves are unlikely to tell us even if they really know. Secondly, we must recognise the difficulty which society has, and which is incorporated in all of us to some degree, in acknowledging that in many of us there is more than a streak of non-conformity which if exposed might seem starkly bizarre. If we cannot admit to this then perhaps we do not know ourselves, let alone know others in any depth.

Historically, sexual non-conformity is first ruthlessly repressed. It is seen as wickedness either of wilful or demoniac origin and it leads to death or severe forms of punishment. To well within this century transvestism could well lead to birching. It then passes from being wickedness to sickness. It is medically treated, but still socially excluded and condemned. Finally, it may achieve social tolerance, with or without understanding and acceptance. Transvestism lies, at the time of this book, in an uneasy state still sometimes a disproportionately punished act of wickedness, with a little social tolerance and uncertain medical care of limited acceptability.

In all this ignorance the underlying question to be found in these pages is whether or not we can usefully refine a concept of transvestism distinct from fetishism, transsexuality and homosexuality, etc. This question itself may lead us into the familiar error of treating such concepts as exclusive categories. That is to say that transvestism might be mistakenly assumed never to be found in association with any elements of homosexuality for instance. It may seem as if the transvestite must by definition be immune from some of the characteristics of the other categories. Nor can we reasonably regard the categories as distinct as if at some point all fetishism is extinguished and transvestism (as solely gender motivated) commences. It is far more realistic to regard these concepts as areas around the stereotype representing regions of adjustment of some stability or significance. In a purely behavioural sense fetishism, heterosexual transvestism, transsexualism, and homosexuality are distinct, apparently independent and recognisable patterns. The difficulty arises when we attempt to interpret or explain these behavioural patterns. It is at this stage that somewhat imponderable concepts such as "latent homosexuality" begin to suffuse the debate. Unless we can be reasonably clear and publicly meaningful in the concepts we use, our explanations are likely to be esoteric and mystic leading only to further confusion.

Categorisations, even as behavioural complexes, are only useful if they have stability and predictive utility. They have stability if they persist without material change long enough for the individual to feel "this is what I am". A large number of males (almost 40% according to Kinsey) pass through rare, brief homosexual erotic experiences, maybe largely determined by chance. The behaviour and the experience may be homosexual, but to the individual it is so fleeting that he does not perceive himself even at the time as "homosexual". This is probably equally so of fetishes if not also of cross-gender behaviour. Experiences of this kind approach meaningless chance occurrences which say little about the individual and are virtually incapable of direct study.

Predictive utility in a category may mean only that it is a state which will continue unchanged for the present, or that it tells something of the past and future development of the individual, or that it is ground to expect specific consequences, of say, therapy. Questions of the stability and predictive validity of the heterosexual transvestite pattern are crucial. Components of long-term drift and short-term variation are involved. In the long term we may be seeing stages in a progressive change from erotically involved fetishism to gender motivated transsexualism. Clinically, the impression of this continuity may be derived from an all too evident resolution in transvestites and transsexuals to obliterate their origins. The transvestite wishes to discard and exorcise all trace of his sexually motivated fetishistic origins. The transsexual insists on his woman status and resents his transvestite antecedents bitterly. The writer discovered a vivid example of this rejection of the past in seeking permission to use some case material from a transvestite. The following is an extract from the reply (paraphrased for annonymity): "I have now lived *(sic)* for eighteen months. I feel I have made a new life and references to 'femme name', '391' and 'transvestite' distress me. I prefer no further correspondence."

The question of the identification of separate groups amongst cross-dressing patients was examined by the writer. A questionnaire was constructed using thirty-eight of the views commonly expressed at interview by the various types of cross-dressing patient (Appendix). This questionnaire was given to twenty-five cross-dressers and the item intercorrelations subjected to factor analysis. The first three factors were suggestive although of course, the limited availability of subjects makes the group small, especially for such a technique of analysis. The factors describe groups as follows:

Factor 1. This clearly represents a transsexual picture. The subjects tend to be single. They reject the suggestion that re-assignment surgery is unnecessary and believe they have a mentality that is completely that of a woman. The idea of being a female is consistent and not felt to be a fantasy. The individual never feels to be a male. When he is living as a male, it seems to be a pretence. His problems are different to those of "other transvestites".

Factor 2. This group express a belief in their right to choose their own sex roles. They feel they have feminine sides which are much nicer persons than their male sides. The female side has to be expressed at times and readily emerges in cross-dressing. There is no desire to be "cured" so as to be like other males. This group is not drawn from people of any particular marital status.

This seems to describe fairly closely the attitudes of the transvestite group as has been considered here.

Factor 3. Members of this group tend to have marital difficulties. They express the wish that they were not cross-dressers and regard transsexualism as an illness. When dressed in female clothing they experience no personality variation and just feel as though they were themselves dressed up.

This third group could be consistent with a purely fetishistic cross-dressing group. Certainly it seems to be one without cross-gender features.

Thus it seems that this evidence, albeit only suggestive, is consistent with the picture of the three groups of fetishists, transvestites, and transsexuals amongst cross-dressing males.

If the classification is meaningful questions follow about the developmental path of the transvestite. These are especially interesting because they involve not only questions of the type "why did this person become transvestite?". Or perhaps the question should be framed in terms of Bancroft's concept of gender identity as being in a state of homeostatic balance. In which case we ask what factors and circumstances are likely to displace the gender identity further or are there features about transvestism itself which may promote even further gender identity displacement towards transsexualism? That is to say, does transvestism set up its own reward systems and prove self-reinforcing?

Buckner (1970), who seems to have been an associate of Prince and Bentler (1972) in their early part of their study (although curiously the fact is not acknowledged), has described what he sees as the developmental basis of transvestism. Factually, he takes 262 replies to a questionnaire issued to readers of *Transvestia* (perhaps part of the Prince and Bentler survey) and, largely dependent on interview with seven transvestites, he discusses what he calls "the transvestic career path". Essentially, this can be structured as follows:

Basis   Biological condition with low sex and social drive and lack of aggression.

Stage 1   Age 5 to 14 years.
(a)   Association of feminine garment with masturbation.
(b)   Fantastic socialisation. Child acts out roles he cannot be expected to adopt in later life, e.g. cross-sex roles.
(c)   Child notices traits in himself like mother or sister and reinforces this by wearing their clothes.
(d)   Feminisation is encouraged by mother.
Stage 2
(a)   Perception of heterosexual difficulties despite normal

sociosexual roles.
(b)   Fear of inadequacy because:
   (i)   may be a perfectionist,
  (ii)   exaggerated notion of masculine demands,
 (iii)   constitution too weak to accept masculine role,
 (iv)   exaggerated fear of failure in male role,
  (v)   a failure which he interprets as inadequate masculinity,
 (vi)   feelings of being an inadequate sexual performer.

Stage 3
(a)   Blockage of homosexual outlet because:
   (i)   socially unacceptable,
  (ii)   lack of opportunity for learning homosexual behaviour.
(b)   Recognition that he is a double failure unable to 'make' it as heterosexual or homosexual and reverts to fetishism.

Stage 4
(a)   Elaboration of masturbation and fantasies into a feminine self.
(b)   Assumption of transvestite practices from discovering what is appropriate to a transvestite, e.g. a female name.
(c)   "Legitimations" found in magazines make him more comfortable.
(d)   Drive to completion or perfection.

Stage 5   Age 18 to 20 years. Fixing the gratification pattern based on:
(a)   the feminine alter ego providing a "synthetic dyad" within. He can play out social patterns, e.g. making gifts to his alter ego, and sexual acts by masturbating;
(b)   escape from real-life problems.

Buckner makes very little of the findings of his survey to justify these factors. Indeed there is a certain amount of evidence which already exists to render some parts of Buckner's scheme very suspect. For example, findings of objective personality studies and of surveys like Prince and Bentler's do not support the rather fundamental concept of a "biological condition with low sex and social drive and lack of aggression". However, Buckner's work is a source of broad hypotheses of a type which could give rise to profitable research.

The very task of measuring masculinity/femininity, no matter how it is defined, has not been solved by any means. It is an odd challenging fact that most personality tests seem either to ignore or to compensate for gender differences. Yet one might have thought that a strong gender-related factor should exist.

Cattell *et al.* (1970) find objective differences between males and females (British, American, and Japanese). Men are more dominant, suspicious, and have higher ego strength. Women are more outgoing, tender minded, and more prone to guilt and tension. However, in the 16PF test Cattell deals with these sex differences in black and white fashion by deriving separate norms for men and women. This means that the involvement of a substantial masculinity/femininity factor is precluded. Curiously, despite the fact that Cattell reports clear differences in factor patterns between the sexes he does not detect a gender factor even at second- or third-order level. Guildford and Guildford (1936), in a test of rather similar type and factor analytical design, found three factors. The third of these was call M (for masculinity). It seems to have been rather similar to Cattell's factor E and near to ascendance—submission. It rather suggests social attitudes to masculinity and Allport (1937) regarded it as unconvincing. Allport cynically commented that factor analytic studies had such difficulty in identifying their factors that they tended to take the easy way out and give them abstract symbols and synthetic names rather than show they measured "substantial elements" like masculinity.

Chapter 2 discussed a number of researches bearing on the differing personality characteristics of males and females and, of course, there are many others. Some are largely empirical lists and others more objective. Rosenkrantz *et al.* (1968) considered sex-role stereotypes or consensual beliefs about the differing characteristics of men and women. They also attempted to examine how the sex-role stereotype differed from the sex-role self-concept.

From groups of male and female students they obtained a lengthy list of items differentiating men and women. Those which were most consistently rated and best differentiated the sexes were chosen. All the subjects rated themselves on those qualities. The authors rightly say that the results obtained are likely to be dependent on the "set" created in the minds of the subjects. It is not surprising, though, if a person asked to say what is typical of his or her sex does not also say that he or she possesses that trait. Thus the self-concepts and the sex stereotype were very similar. Some investigation was also made of whether male traits are more socially desirable or not. It was found that they were. It seems, though, that "socially desirable" might mean "effective in the existing social order", in one context, and "morally and aesthetically good" in another. Thus the male features of, say, aggressiveness, dominance, and unemotionality may be more or less desirable than female gentleness, tact, and awareness of feelings, according to the circumstances.

There were twenty-nine male traits and twelve female ones in Rosenkrantz's list but there were considerable differences from Cattell's findings. Both agree on male dominance but not on the latter's finding that males are suspicious and of high ego strength. For women both agree on tender-mindedness but differ about them being outgoing and prone to guilt and tension. In fact overall little in Cattell's results support the Rosenkrantz list. Neither does the list include bi-polar differences. Females are talkative, quiet, and neat of habits but males are not conversely untalkative, noisy, and untidy. Nor for that matter are males dominant and females submissive.

The orientation of personality tests seems to be away from dealing with sex differences whilst work with stereotypes seems to assume the simple fixed stereotype irrespective of a wide variety of conditions and expectations. It seems that a wide range of stereotypes might exist in different social conditions and personality tests show how people function within such imposed roles. Perhaps our deeply held belief in the difference between male and female personalities is itself a social phenomenon, a myth which has far less substance than we think.

Use was made in an earlier chapter of the results from the Terman–Miles Attitude Interest Test. Much the longest and most complex test of gender it consist of a mixture of a wide variety of questions. It simply gives rise to an overall score of masculinity which seems to discriminate between males and females, hetero-sexuals, transvestites and other males. Bancroft's (1972) comment on the test is that it could be no more than an assessment of sex-typed interests. In some respects this in itself would not be bad and could be valuable. It would be far less useful as a test if it simply recorded the obvious without contributing to our knowledge. Masculinity could be measured by an inventory of such items as hair length, capacity to sing a tune two octaves above middle C, and a knowledge of the rules of boxing! A test like this certainly would differentiate males and females but tell us almost nothing we did not already know. The sub-tests of the Terman–Miles Test do not seem to be closely related to more reliable personality factors but at the same time the test has justified more careful research than it has received. It is very much dated in its standard form of course. On the credit side it is a test which is not readily perceived as a test measuring things to do with gender and neither would it be at all easy to fake. Whether the individual who adopts a false feminine attitude throughout the test, rather than simply devise feminine answers to particular items, would "feminise" his score is unknown.

The masculinity–femininity scale of the Minnesota Multiphasic Personality Inventory seems to have little of value. It is highly affected by intelligence and class, and again tells us nothing about the issues involved in gender differences. Slater's Selective Vocabulary Test simply demonstrates that men know more about one thing and women know more about another. It gives no clue why this should be.

The Grygier Dynamic Personality Inventory has curious origins in that it was based on the dissatisfactions of two psychoanalysts, Krout and Tabin (1954), with conventional personality questionnaires. Basing their new test on psycho-analytic concepts they devised a test which was "validated by negation". That is to say, they argued that if the test was reliable, in test-retest terms, but not apparently related to any other personality measure of a conventional kind, then it must be a valid test of something new. This argument is hard to refute and in its turn invalidates many of the researches criticising the D.P.I. essentially on the grounds that it does not correlate with tests the independence of which originally justified the Krout–Tabin test! Unfortunately the argument is so much like many psychoanalytic arguments and outside that system does not have a great deal of meaning. Interestingly, though, factor analytic studies have shown one or more important factors related to gender in the test. Kline (1968) and Stringer (1970). In this respect the D.P.I. is specially interesting if only in testing out the consistency of the psychoanalytic formulations of transvestism.

Repertory grid methods have been applied to gender problems, e.g. Bancroft (1970) and Davison *et al.* (1971). The technique could investigate, for instance, two major questions. Firstly, how does the transvestite see himself as feminine differing from a genetic female? Secondly, what changes in personality are seen by the transvestite as marking his movement towards a cross-gender identity.

The assumption may be made by the transvestite that his feelings and the role he is seeking are the true feelings and role of a female. To the observer this is rarely if ever so, a fact that annoys transvestites and infuriates transsexuals! The distinction is not easy to define but very important. It is especially relevant to the problem of the extent to which transvestism is simply an evasion of male roles. Buckner's "career path" clearly indicates elements like his Stage 2 which are solely to do with avoidance of the male role. The outcome of evasive transvestism need only be a caricature of femininity. Stage 1 forces should lead to the much more precisely acquired characteristics of femininity because environmental and inter-personal pressures are specifically imposing a feminine role. Moreover, the imposed role is not simply that fantasised by the transvestite but impressed and modelled for him by the females about him.

The general impression of transvestite, and often transsexual femininity, is heavily tinged with a fantasy of doll-like simpering prettiness of the "movie star" but stripped of the sexuality and many hard realities of life, and women are not really like that. The development of "femininity" in the transvestite has been little debated but the assumption seems to be made in the writings of transsexuals that the condition is fairly static.

Jan Morris writes of the way her fimininity dates back to very early years and the inference is that it is only the change in the environment which alters the course of the individual's life. Della Aleksander, on the other hand, indicates a developing femininity independent of the environment but is unusual in doing so. Clinically observation very much supports the feeling that whatever the patient reports, his feminine fantasies are very much a developing and sometimes maturing thing. Some illustrations of the use of repertory grid in individual cases can be presented to illustrate the developmental paths of three people.

These examples are drawn from routine clinical studies, they are not presented as necessarily typical as much as to indicate how the grid technique can be employed. The principle of the grid technique was outlined in Chapter 2. The three subjects all scored highly on one of the three factors derived from the questionnaire in the appendix. In this case amongst the elements (some of which are omitted here for clarity) some are age linked like "me at age 15", and relate to ages 15, 25, 35, 45, and the subject's present age. Also "the person I would most like to be" was included. A detailed analysis for each grid is too complex to be appropriate but some general features can be gleaned from the first two components.

Case A.A. is a transsexual aged 26 years. He is a man with considerable physical difficulties as a transsexual being well over 6 feet tall and balding. Unusually he is a rather retiring person with very little contact with other transsexuals nor does he seem to have read books or articles about transsexualism. He is an intelligent man with a public-school education and an apparently successful professional artist. The description of factor 1 previously given describes his case closely.

His grid, Fig. 13, shows that he sees considerable changes in

CASE A.A.

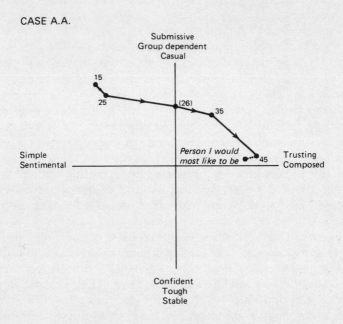

FIG. 13. Case A.A.

himself over the last 11 years and almost as great a change in the next 19 years. He feels that he is going to attain the characteristics of the person he really wants to be. As a 15-year-old his construct system describes him as a simple and sentimental person, rather group dependent and submissive. He has lost some of his naivety but not gained a lot in confidence. He anticipates, probably in the context of sex-reassignment, to gather a considerable amount of confidence, toughness, and stability to become an essentially composed and reliant sort of person. Generally this clear path of development seems to characterise the grids of transsexuals, rather in contrast to the belief in an undeveloping state of femininity. Also the personality changes might at first sight seem to be opposed to increasing femininity, e.g. in the increase of "dominance", but this is where we become aware of our lack of knowledge of the nature of femininity. Grids of female transsexuals showing changes in an almost opposed direction could be presented.

CASE B.B.

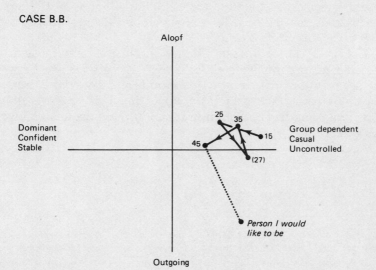

FIG. 14. Case B.B.

At the opposite extreme, Fig. 14, is the grid of case B.B. He is a married man with one child but his wife has recently discovered his cross-dressing and cannot accept it. He is a policeman, doing well in his job and likely to be promoted shortly. He fears that his cross-dressing will be discovered and ruin his marriage and career.

This case scores highly in factor 3 which we have suggested looks most likely to be associated with fetishistic cross-dressing. Because his wife is upset by his cross-dressing he can only do it in the privacy of his bedroom. He dresses largely in his wife's clothing which she has reluctantly given him, he does not have his own "wardrobe". The clothing he wears has a rather special type. He would prefer black patent leather high-heeled shoes, black nylons and undies. He rarely dresses completely as a woman and as he is a tall powerfully built man there is no question of his passing as a woman when dressed in his wife's clothes. He also has a copious moustache and sideburns which would make his appearance grotesque but they do not "impair" his cross-dressing. When he dresses up he usually masturbates after a short period of time.

The grid plot contrasts sharply with the previous one in showing no progressive course. Indeed the differences between the age points seems to have no meaning and may be determined only by chance. The person he would most like to be is simply more outgoing but he does not apparently expect any change in this direction.

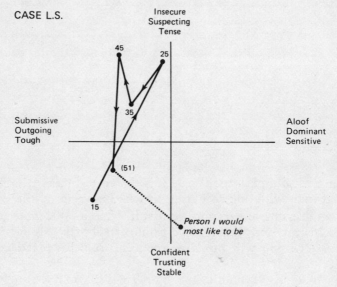

FIG. 15. Case L.S.

The third grid, Fig. 15, is that produced by Case L.S. whose autobiography was presented previously. He gave a high score on factor 2 and, of course, he was recognised as typically transvestite. His developmental path is complex but suggests considerable changes during his adult life. He is older than either A.A. or B.B. and the path in the grid relates to changes which are past. These changes seem interpretable responses to his life pattern. The first crisis was in his twenties when he had troubles at university and had psychoanalysis. Following that he married and the changes between 25 and 35 are perhaps associated with his more stable masculine role as a husband and father. Unfortunately his marriage broke down before his mid-forties and whilst that experience could have been disruptive, he has regained some stability since he has returned to his batchelor state. In fact he returns to roughly the same point in his construct system he held at age 15. This point is nearer to what he would like to be than any point between adolescence and the present time. The major changes have been along a dimension of tension and insecurity.

It has to be added that grids of this kind do not tell us what has actually occurred but only what the subject feels has occurred or will occur.

Bancroft's (1974) admirable summary of the research and clinical objectives in the general field of sexual deviancy defines three possible patient preferences in therapy. Roughly these are the desire to enjoy a heterosexual relationship with or without removal of the deviant interests; reduction in the sexual interest itself; and reduction in the problems of deviant adaptation, e.g. maintaining a homosexual relationship. It seems that the transvestite, and even more so the transsexual, can often make a fourth demand. This is the preference for an enhancement of his transvestite behaviour as well as immunity from what he sees as society's inability to adapt to him. It is not entirely an unjustified point of view in the sense that social reactions to the transvestite are out of all proportion to the harm he causes—if any. He is not irrational in pointing to society's enthusiasm for drag acts and an apparently hypocritical abhorrence of less obtrusive transvestism.

It might then be valid to direct research towards social responses to transvestism. To the person in the role of therapist or helper in this field of sexual minority problems an understanding of social pressures is important and they are by no means rational. It is just as important as it is currently lacking. Why should political groups take up different attitudes on such issues? What are the fears that the transvestite actually generates? One has the feeling that at some levels "the law and order" issue is more to do with the ephemera of pornographic magazines, homosexuals in high places, and ill-conducted strip clubs, than it is to do with blackmail, fraud, and drunken drivers.

Perhaps there are two tasks to be undertaken, those concerned with the problems of the client and those concerned with the problems of society. Too little attention has probably been paid to the latter problem. It is characteristic of the homosexual pressure groups that they have assailed heterosexual groups which have failed to accept them. They have failed to appreciate that they arouse irrational anxieties and concerns, which may be derived from a sincere concern to be "understanding". The churches have begun to discuss the position of the homosexual in the congregation and with concern ask what can be done to accept him as part of the religious community. The answer is neither as simple as the homosexual asserts, that he is excluded from prejudice, nor so simple as to be solved by seminars or statements of policy. It seems to be to do with a whole mass of fears, misunderstandings and anxieties which are equally painful to both parties. Similar problems for the transvestite have barely reached this stage but may well do so before very long.

Within the whole field of sexual deviancy little is known of the clients who pass from view. Kinsey's data suggests that many men who have lived exclusively homosexual lives for a period cease to do so. It is likely that this is also true of transvestites. Even some operated transsexuals revert to a male role. This conflicts with an implicit belief that such groups of people do not spontaneously relinquish their a-typical pattern of life. We know nothing of the patients who are rejected. It seems unlikely that the transvestite or transsexual who is rejected from sex reassignment consideration goes contentedly away. He may go to the self-help groups but again there is no evidence that this is so.

To find data on such cases would be exceedingly difficult because of the need for intrusion in a very sensitive area. It is barely ethical to as much as risk the re-awakening of fantasies in a person who may have relinquished them. It would incur all manner of dangers to the personal life of the ex-client. Yet this sort of information is vital because with such limited "normalising" skills, rejection could be preferable to therapy. Perhaps here the role of clinics in a non-medical setting offers some promise of more prolonged contact but we have noted the reluctance of the transvestite to look backwards.

So it seems that in transvestism we have a fairly uncharted area of human behaviour. It is a condition which appears to be by no means rare but because it is essentially secretive is usually practiced or perhaps suffered in privacy. There is nothing to indicate that transvestism in itself can be properly regarded as illness or neurosis if by these terms we mean some broad impairment of the individual's life pattern. On the contrary it looks as if the weight of present evidence is towards transvestism being associated with achieving and able individuals rather than the reverse.

The case has been made out for transvestism as a gender dysphoria or a discomfort in the masculine role. That is to say the transvestite's dis-ease is better regarded as social and inter-personal than biologically sexual. The heterosexual behaviour of the transvestite would seem to be barely impaired if at all. Writers have an almost general agreement on the distinction between homosexuality and transvestism. This does not mean that a transvestite may not be a homosexual just as any person may be but it seems that rather fewer than expected are.

It is a condition which may involve no other person and almost never concerns people outside the transvestite's own family and friends. He is not, in his transvestism, a person who often seeks or demands notice but rather looks for an unremarkable acceptance in his cross-gender role. The practice has rewards and pleasures for the individual and he usuallycannot understand his causing distress to others particularly if he is supported by his wife. In this context he is very poorly motivated for therapy of any kind, preferring to claim the right to be what he wants to be if it does not harm others.

There is no unequivocal evidence to suggest any form of therapy to be effective in resolving the gender dysphoria. Some techniques in behaviour therapy have suggested that a sexual deviance might be corrected and in this area the transvestite would be as motivated as any individual with a sexual problem. The rectification of a fetish would be unlikely to materially change the nature of the gender dysphoria which appears in transvestism.

No satisfactory services are available for the helping and treatment of sexual problems. There are good reasons for regarding them as falling outside the mandate of the Health Services unless clear-cut "illness" is involved. It seems most likely that services based on charitable and voluntary organisations are best suited to organise and co-ordinate facilities. To carry out such a function government support for these services and the formalising of medical and paramedical support services is essential. It is also merited in the sense that the present inexpert medical and social resources consumed by this type of problem are considerable. To provide adequate care in a medical context will demand the development of a new breed of specialist in psychosexual medicine and an open-access orientation foreign to the existing pattern of the health and social services in Britain.

The transvestite's problems and unhappiness are to be found mostly in his conflict with society by whom he feels victimised and misunderstood. Whilst no law prohibits his behaviour he is liable to prosecution by laws which permit only trivial punishments but stimulate catastrophic social destruction of his family and his career. The search for understanding and social enlightenment is of vast importance in the humanitarian approach to the transvestite.

A transvestite can have the last word:

Midinette

A renaissance of
Duality.
A figure of neutrality.
An ambivalent creature,
Who keeps a strange alliance, as
With Mars.
Your environment has made you,
Created you, besotted you.
AND now it wants to spit on you;
Sad figurine of a Picasso.

Shirley Aston

Appendix (see p. 228)

(see p. 228)

QUESTIONNAIRE

Put a tick in the right hand column against those statements you regard as TRUE. (There is no need to mark statements which are not true.)

1. I am married
2. I am widowed
3. I am single
4. I am divorced
5. I am married but separated
6. I was divorced but have remarried
7. I am a parent
8. Most transsexuals are homosexual
9. In feminine clothes I am just myself dressed up
10. A transsexual operation would not help me at all
11. A sex-change operation would only help by making my transvestism legal
12. Cross-dressing sometimes makes me feel very unhappy
13. I take or have taken female hormones
14. My mind is completely that of a woman
15. I wish I was not transvestite or transsexual
16. Transvestism is just another form of sex
17. It is the feeling of femininity which matters more than the dress
18. I think I am less sexually aroused by women than most males are
19. Transvestites are "kinky"
20. I used to feel I wanted an operation to be rid of male sex organs
21. My feelings change, sometimes I would really prefer to be a man
22. Going whole time is an attractive idea but I know I won't actually do it
23. Anyone has a right to choose his sex role
24. I sometimes think of myself as a sort of lesbian
25. The feminine side of myself has to be expressed at times
26. I want to be cured and be like any other man
27. When I dress it takes quite a long time before I feel I really am feminine
28. I would like to take hormones if I could
29. Transvestism is an illness
30. Transsexualism is an illness
31. When I am dressed I am a different personality
32. My feminine self is much nicer as a person than my male self
33. I know that the idea of being a woman is only a fantasy
34. I sometimes think that I need to take hormones to make my body more feminine
35. Someday I must cease to pretend to be a man
36. My problems are not much different to those of any other transvestite
37. Life would have been easier for me if I had remained single
38. I would like a sex change operation but only if it was easy and safe

244

Bibliography

Aberle, D. F. and Naegle, K. D. (1952) Middle-class fathers' occupational role and attitude toward children. *Am. J. Orthopsychiat.* 22, 366-378.

Allport, G. W. (1937) *Personality.* Constable, London.

Anchersen, P. (1956) Problems of transvestism. *Acta psychiat. Scand. Suppl.* 106, 249.

Andry, R. G. (1957) Paternal and maternal child relationships. *Brit. J. Delinq.* 8, 34-48.

Argyle, M., Trower, P. E. and Bryant, B. (1974) Explorations in the treatment of personality disorders and neurosis by social skills training. *Brit. J. med. Psychol.* 63-72.

Armstrong, C. N. (1955) Diversities of sex. *Brit. med. J,* 1, 1173-1177.

Armstrong, C. N. (1958) Transvestites. In *Symposium on Nuclear Sex,* Eds. Smith D. R. and Davidson, W. A. Heinemann, London.

Armstrong, C. N. (1966) Treatment of wrongly assigned sex. *Brit. med. J.* 2, 1255.

Armstrong , C.N. and Marshall, A. J. (1964) *Intersexuality.* Academic Press, London.

Ball, J. R. B. (1960) Transsexualism. Unpub. M.D. thesis, University of Newcastle, England.

Ball, J. R. B. (1967) Transsexualism and transvestism. *Aus. & N.Z. J. Psychiat.* 1, 4, 188-195.

Bancroft, J. (1970) A comparitive study of two forms of behaviour therapy in the modification of homosexual interest. Unpub. M.D. thesis, Univ. Cambridge.

Bancroft J. (1972) The relationship between gender and sexual behaviour. In *Gender Differences,* Eds. Ounsted, C. and Taylor, D. C. Churchill Livingstone, London.

Bancroft, J. (1970) A comparative study of two forms of behaviour therapy in the

Bandura, A., Ross, D. and Ross, S. A. (1963) A comparative test of the status envy, social power, and secondary reinforcement theories of identificatory learning. *J. abnorm. Soc. Psychol.* 67, 527-534.

Barahal, H. S. (1953) Female transvestism and homosexuality. *Psychiat. Quart.* 27, 390.

Barker, J.C. (1965) Behaviour therapy for transvestism. A comparison of pharmacological and electrical aversion techniques. *Brit J. Psychiat.* 111, 268.

Barker, J. C. (1966) Transsexualism and transvestism. *J. A. M. A.* 198, 488.

Barker, J. C., Thorpe, J. G., Blakemore, C. B., Lavin, N. I., and Conway, C. G. (1961) Behaviour therapy in a case of transvestism. *Lancet,* 1, 510.

Barlow, D. H., Reynolds, E. J. and Agras, W. S. (1973) Gender identity change in a transsexual. *Arch. gen. Psychiat.* 28, 569-576.

Barr, M. L. and Bertram, E. G. (1949) A morphological distinction between neurones of the male and female and the behaviour of the nucleolar satellite during accelerated nucleoprotein synthesis. *Nature,* 163, 676.

Barr, M. L. and Hobbs, G. E. (1954) Chromosomal sex in transvestites. *Lancet,* 1, 1109.

Barry, H., Bacon, M. K. and Child, E. L. (1957) A cross-cultural survey of some sex differences in socialisation. *J. abnorm. soc. Psychol.* 55, 327-332.

Bateson, G. (1936) *Ceremony of Naven.* Cambridge Univ. Press.

Battig, F. (1952) *Beitrag zur Frage des Transvestitismus.* Dissertation. Buchdruckerei Fluntern, Zurich.

Beigel, H. G. and Feldman, R. (1963) The male transvestite's motivation in fiction, research and reality. In *Advances in Sex Research,* Ed. Beigel, H. G. Harper Row, New York.

Benjamin, H. (1953) Transvestism & transsexualism. *Int. J. Sexol.* 7, 12-14.

Benjamin, H. (1954) Transexualism and transvestism as psychosomatic and somato-psychic syndromes. *Am. J. Psychother.* 8, 219-230.

Benjamin, H. (1964) Nature and management of transsexualism. With a report on 31 operated cases. *West. J. Surg.* 72, 105.

Bennett, E. M. and Chohen, L. R. (1959) Men and women: personality patterns and contrasts. *Genet. Psychol. Monogr.* 59, 101-155.

Bentler, P. M. and Prince, C. (1970a) Psychiatric symptomatology in transvestites. *J. clin. Psychol.* 26, 4343-4435.

Bentler, P. M., Sherman, R. W. and Prince, C. (1970b) Personality characteristics of male transvestites. *J. clin. Psychol.* 26, 3, 287-291.

Blakemore, C. B., Thorpe, J. G., Barker, J. C., Conway, C. G. and Lavin, N. I. (1963) The application of faradic aversion in a case of transvestism. *Behav. Res. Ther.* 1, 29.

Boulougouris, J. C. and Marks, I.M. (1969) Implosion (flooding)—a new treatment for phobias. *Brit. med. J.* 2, 721-723.

Bowman, K. K. and Engle, B. (1957) Medicolegal aspects of transvestism. *Am. J. Psychiat.* 113, 7, 583-588.

Brierley, H. (1965) An aversion therapy using Faradic shock applied to cases of sexual deviation. Paper read to Manchester Regional Psychiatric Ass.

Brierley, H. (1974) the heterosexual transvestite: a gender anomaly. Paper read to 1974 Annual Conference of Brit. Psychol. Soc. *Bull. Brit. Psychol. Soc.* 27, 95, 156-157.

Brierley, H. (1975) Gender as a component of sexual disorders. Paper read to 1975 conference to Brit. Psychol. Soc. *Bull. Brit. Psychol. Soc.* 28, 224-225.

Bronfenbrenner, U. (1960) Some familial antecedents of responsibility and leadership in adolescents. In *Studies in Leadership,* Eds. Petrullo, L. and Bass, B. M. Holt, New York.

Bruce, V. (1967) The expression of femininity in the male. *J. Sex. Res.* 3, 2, 129-139.

Buckner, H. T. (1970) The transvestic career path. *Psychiatry,* 33, 381-389.

Burich, N. (1976) A heterosexual transvestite club: psychiatric aspects. *N. Aust. N.Z. J. Psychiat.* 10, 4, 331-335.

Burich, N. (1977) A case of familial heterosexual transvestism. *Acta psychiat. scand.* 55, 3, 199-201.

Burich, N. and McConaghy, N. (1976) Transvestite fiction. *J. nerv. ment. Dis.* 163, 6, 420-427.

Cattell, R. B., Eber, H. W., and Tasuoka, M. M. (1970) *Handbook for the Sixteen Personality Factor Questionnaire.* I. P. A. T., Illinois.

Cautela, J. R. (1966) Treatment of compulsive behaviour by covert sensitisation. *Psychol Rev.* 16, 33-41.

Cawley, R. (1976) The teaching of psychotherapy. Paper read to Conference of University Teachers of Psychiatry, London.

Clark, D. F. (1965) A note on avoidance conditioning techniques in sexual disorder. *Behav. Res. Ther.* 3, 203-206.

Conn, J. H. (1940) Children's reactions to the discovery of genital differences. *Am. J. Orthopsychiat.* 10, 747-755.

Darke, R. A. (1948) Heredity as an etiological factor in homosexuality. *J. nerv. ment. Dis.* 107, 251-268.

Davenport, W. (1965) Sexual patterns and their regulation in a society of the Southwest Pacific. In *Sex and Behaviour,* Ed. Beach, F. A. Wiley.

Davison, K., Brierley, H. and Smith, C. (1971) A male monozygotic twinship discordant for homosexuality. *Brit. J. Psychiat.* 118, 675-682.

Deutsch, D. (1954) A case of transsexualism. *Am. J. Psychother.* 8, 239-242.

Devereux, E. C., Bronfenbrenner, U. and Suci, G. J. (1963) Patterns of parent behaviour in the United States of America and the Federal Republic of Germany. *Int. Soc. Sci. J.* 14, 2-20.

Devereaux, G. (1937) Institutionalised homosexuality of Mohave Indians. *Human Biology,* 9.

Devore, I. and Jay, P. (1963) Mother–infant relations in baboons and langurs. In *Maternal Behaviour in Mammals,* Ed. Rheingold. Wiley, New York.

Diamond, M. (1965) A critical evaluation of the ontogeny of human sexual behaviour. *Q. Rev. Bio.* 40, 147-175.

Dukor, B. (1951) Probleme um den Transvestitismus. *Schweiz. med. Wehnschr.* 81, 516-519.

Edelstein, E. L. (1960) Psychodynamics of a transvestite. *Am. J. Psychother.* 14, 121-131.

Ehrhardt, A. A., Evers, K and Money, J. (1968) Influence of androgen and some aspects of sexually dimorphic behaviour in women with late-treated adrenogenital syndrome. *Johns Hopkins med. J.* 123, 115-122.

Ehrhardt, A. A. and Money J. (1967) Progestin-induced hermaphroditism: I. Q. and psychosexual identity in a study of ten girls. *J. sex. Res.* 3, 83-100.

Ellis, H. (1928) *Studies in the Psychology of Sex,* Vol. 7. Davis, London.

Epstein, A. W. (1961) Relation of fetishism and transvestism to brain and particularly temporal lobe dysfunction. *J. nerv. ment. Dis.* 133, 247.

Erickson, E. H. (1951) Sex differences in the play configurations of pre-adolescents. *Am. J. Orthopsychiat.* 21, 667-692.

Eyres, A. (1961) Transvestism (employment of somatic therapy with subsequent improvement). *Dis. nerv. syst.* 21, 52.

Eysenck, H. J. (1960) *Behaviour Therapy and the Neuroses,* Ed. Pergamon Press, Oxford.

Eysenck, H. J. (1963) Behaviour therapy, extinction and relapse in neurosis. *Brit. J. Psychiat.* 109, 12-18.

Falloon, I. R. H., Lindley, P., McDonald, R., and Marks, I. M. (1977) Social skills training of out patient groups. *Brit. J. Psychiat.* 131, 599-609.

Farnsworth, P. R. (1960) The effects of role taking on artistic achievement. *J. Aesthetics and Criticism,* 18, 345-349.

Feldman, M. P. and MacCulloch, M. J. (1965) The application of anticipatory avoidance learning to the treatment of homosexuality. *Behav. Res. Ther.* 2, 165-183.

Feldman, M. P. MacCulloch, M. J. and MacCulloch, M. C. (1968) The aversion therapy treatment of a heterogenous group of five cases of sexual deviation. *Acta psychiat. scand.* 44, 113-124.

Feldman, M. P. and MacCulloch, M. J. (1971) *Homosexual Behaviour: Therapy and Assessment.* Pergamon Press, Oxford.

Fenichel, O. (1930) The psychology of transvestism. *Int. J. Psychoanal.* **11**, 211.

Fookes, B. H. (1969) Some experiences in the use of aversion therapy in male homosexuals, exhibitionism and fetishism-transvestism. *Brit. J. Psychiat.* **115**, 339-341.

Foote, R. M. (1944) Diethylstilbestrol in the management of psychopathological states in males. *J. nerv. ment. Dis.* **99**, 928-935.

Freud, S. (1905) Three essays on the theory of sexuality. The sexual abberrations. In *Complete Psychological Works of Sigmund Freud.* Hogarth Press, London.

Freud, S. (1933) *New Introductory Lectures on Psychoanalysis.* Hogarth Press, London.

Gaillardet, F. (1972) *Memoirs of the Chevalier d'Eon,* trans. White, A. Corgi, London.

Gatewood, M. C. and Weiss, A.P. (1930) Race and sex differences in newborn infants. *J. genet. Psychol.* **38**, 31-49.

Glover, E. (1960) *The Roots of Crime.* Imago, London.

Glynn, J. D. and Harper, P. (1961) Behaviour therapy in transvestism. *Lancet,* **1**, 619.

Gold, S. and Neufeld, I. L. (1965) A learning approach to the treatment of homosexuality. *Behav. Res. Ther.* **2**, 201-204.

Gordon, J. E. and Smith, E. (1965) Children's aggression, parental attitudes, and the effects of an affiliation-arousing story. *J. Pers. Soc. Psychol.* **1**, 654-659.

Gray, S. W. and Klaus, R. (1956) The assessment of parental identification. *Genet. Psychol. Monogr.* **54**, 87-114.

Grinder, R. E. and Judith, C. S. (1965) Sex differences in adolescents' perception of parental resource control. *J. genet. Psychol.* **106**, 337-344.

Guildford, J. P. and Guilford, R. B. (1936) Personality factors S, E, and M and their measurement. *J. Psychol.* **2**, 109-127.

Gutheil, E. (1954) The psychological background of transsexualism and transvestism. *Am. J. Psychother.* **8**, 231-239.

Hall, C. A. (1964) A modest confirmation of Freud's theory of a distinction between the superego of men and women. *J. abnorm. soc. Psychol.* **69**, 440-442.

Hall, C. A. and Domhoff, B. (1963) Ambiguous sex difference in dreams. *J. abnorm. soc. Psychol.* **66**, 278-280.

Hamburger, C. (1953) Desire for change of sex. *Acta Endocr.* **14**, 361-375.

Hamburger, C., Sturup, G.K. and Dahl-Iversen, E. (1953) Transvestism: Hormonal, psychiatric, and surgical treatment. *J. A. M. A.* **152**, 391-394.

Hamilton, M. (1973) Psychology in society: ends or end? Presidental address to Brit. Psychol. Soc. Liverpool. Transcript in *Bull. Brit. Psychol. Soc.* **26** 185-189.

Hampson, J. L. (1964) Deviant sexual behaviour. Homosexuality, transvestism. In *Human Reproduction and Sexual Behaviour,* Ed. Lloyd, C. W. Lea & Febiger, Philadelphia.

Hampson, J. L. and Hampson, J. G. (1961) The ontogenesis of sexual behaviour in man. In *Sex and the Internal Secretions,* Ed. Young, W. C. Williams & Wilkins, Baltimore.

Hartley, R. E. (1959) Sex-role pressures and the socialisation of the man's role. *Psychol. Reps.* **5**, 457-468.

Hartley, R. E. (1966) A developmental view of female sex-role identification. In *Role Theory,* Eds. Biddle, B. J. and Thomas, E. J. Wiley.

Hartley, R. E. and Klein, A. (1959) Sex-role concepts among elementary school age girls. *Marr. fam. Living,* **21**, 59-64.

Hartup, W. W. and Moore, S. G. (1963) Avoidance of inappropriate sex-typing by young children. *J. consult. Psychol.* **27**, 467-473.

Bibliography 249

Henderson, D. and Batchelor, I. R. C. (1962) *Henderson & Gillespie's Textbook of Psychiatry.* O. U. P., London.
Henry, A.F. (1957) Sibling Structure and perception of the disciplinary roles of parents. *Sociometry,* 20, 67-74.
Henry, J. (1964) *Jungle People.* Vintage Books.
Hetherington, E. M. (1965) A developmental study of the effects of sex of the dominant parent on sex-role preference, identification, and imitation in children. *J. Pers. soc. Psychol.* 2, 188-194.
Hirschfeld, M. (1910) *Die Transvestiten.*
Homme, L. (1965) Perspective in psychology. 24. Control of coverants, the operants of the mind. *Psychol. Rec.* 15, 501-511.
Hooker, E. (1965) An empirical study of some relations between sexual patterns and gender identity in male homosexuals. In *Sex Research: New Developments,* Ed. Money, J. Holt, New York.
Hooker, J., Brodsky, M., and Manassero, J. A. (1964) Sex differences in verbal interaction as a function of severity of pathology. *J. clin. Psychol.* 20, 1, 94.
Hoopes, J. E., Knoor, N. J., and Wolf, S. R. (1968) Transsexualism: considerations regarding sexual reassignment. *J. nerv. ment. Dis.* 147, 5, 510-516.
Hunter, B., Logue, V., and McMenemy, W. H. (1963) Temporal lobe epilepsy supervening on a longstanding transvestism and fetishism. *Epilepsia,* 4, 60.
Jacobson, B. (1974) The sex changers. *World Medicine,* 9, 10, 15-27.
Johnson, M. M. (1963) Sex role learning in the nuclear family. *Child Develpm.* 34, 319-333.
Jones, K. (1960) The effect of stilboestrol in two cases of male transvestism. *J. ment. Sci.* 106, 1080.
Journal of Homosexuality (1977) Cross dressing illegal in Chicago. Legal Section. *J. Homosexuality,* 3, 1, 97-98.
Kaberry, P. (1952) *Women of the Grassfields.* H. M. S. O.
Kagan, J., and Lemkin, J. (1960) The child's differential perception of power attributes. *J. abnorm. soc. Psychol.* 61, 440-447.
Kallman, F. J. (1952) A comparative twin study of the genetic aspects of male homosexuality. *J. nerv. ment. Dis.* 115, 283-298.
Karlen, A. (1971) *Sexuality and Homosexuality.* McDonald, London.
Karpman, B. J. (1947) Dream life in a case of transvestism. *J. nerv. ment. Dis.* 106, 292.
Kelly, G. A. (1955) *The Psychology of Personal Constructs.* Norton, New York.
Kinsey, A. C., Pomeroy, W. B. and Martin, C. E. (1948) *Sexual Behaviour in the Human Male.* Saunders, Philadelphia.
Kline, P. (1968) The validity of the Dynamic Personality Inventory. *Brit. J. med. Psychol.* 41, 307-313.
Kline, P. (1972) *Fact and Fantasy in Freudian Theory.* Methuen.
Koch, L. (1956) Sissiness and tomboyishness in relation to sibling characteristics. *J. Genet. Psychol.* 88, 231-244.
Kohlberg, L. (1967) A cognitive developmental analysis of children's sex role concepts and attitudes. In *The Development of Sex Differences,* Ed. Maccoby, F. E. Tavistock, London.
Krafft-Ebing, R. (1924) *Psychopathia Sexualis,* Ed. Moll.
Krout, M. H. and Tabin, J. K. (1954) Measuring personality in developmental terms. *Genet. Psychol. Monogr.* 50, 289-335.
Lagrone, C. W. (1963) Sex and personality differences in relation to fantasy. *J. Consult. Psychol.* 27, 270-272.

Lang, T. (1940) Studies on the genetic determination of homosexuality. *J. nerv. ment. Dis.* 92, 55-64.

Laub, D. R. and Fisk, N. (1974) A rehabilitation program for gender dysphoria syndrome by surgical sex change. *Plast. Reconstr. Surg.* 53, 388-403.

Laubscher, B. J. F. (1937) *Sex Customs and Psychopathology,* Routledge, London.

Lavin, N. J., Thorpe, J. G., Barker, J. C., Blackemore, C. B. and Conway, C. G. (1961) Behaviour therapy in a case of transvestism. *J. nerv. ment. Dis.* 133, 346.

Levin, H. and Sears, R. P. (1956) Identification with parents as a determinant of doll play aggression. *Child Develpm.* 27, 135-153.

Liebman, S. (1944) Homosexuality, transvestism and psychosis—study of a case treated with electroshock. *J. nerv. ment. Dis.* 99, 945.

Linton, R. (1936) *The Study of Man.* Appleton, New York.

Lipsitt, L. P. and Levy, N. (1959) Electroactual threshold in the human neonate. *Child Develpm.* 30, 547-554.

Lukianowicz, N. (1959) Survey of various aspects of transvestism in the light of our present knowledge. *J. nerv. ment. Dis.* 128, 36-64.

McClelland, D. (1953) *The Achievement Motive.* Appleton-Century Crofts, New York.

McGuire, R. J. and Vallance, M. (1964) Aversion therapy by electric shock. *Brit. med.* 151-153.

McGuire, R. J., Carlisle, J. M., and Young, B. G. (1965) Sexual deviations as conditioned behaviour. *Behav. Res. Ther.* 2, 185-190.

Marks, I. M. and Gelder, M. G. (1967) Transvestism and fetishism: clinical and psychological changes during faradic aversion. *Brit. J. Psychiat.* 113, 771-729.

Marks, I., Gelder, M. and Bancroft, J. (1970) Sexual deviants two years after electric aversion. *Brit. J. Psychiat.* 117, 173-185.

Martensen-Larsen, O. (1957) The family constellation and homosexualism. *Acta genet. Statist. med.* 7, 445-446.

Mayer-Gross, W., Slater, E. and Roth, M. (1954) *Clinical Psychiatry,* 1st ed. Cassel, London.

Mayer-Gross, W., Slater, E. and Roth, M. (1960) *Clinical Psychiatry,* 2nd ed. Cassel, London.

Mead, M. (1950) *Male and Female.* Penguin.

Meichenbaum, D. H. (1971) *Cognitive Factors in Behaviour Modification.* Univ. of Waterloo, Waterloo.

Meltzer, H. (1943) Sex differences in children's attitudes to parents. *J. genet. Psychol.* 62, 311-326.

Meyer, V. and Chesser, E. S. (1970) *Behaviour Therapy in Clinical Psychiatry.* Penguin, Harmondsworth.

Mitchell, W., Falconer, M. A., and Hill, D. (1954) Epilepsy with fetishism relieved by temporal lobectomy. *Lancet,* ii, 626.

Money, J. (1955) Hermaphroditism, gender and precocity in hyperadreno-corticism: psychologic findings. *Bull. Johns Hopkins, Hosp.* 96, 253-264.

Money, J. (1970) Sexual dimorphism and homosexual gender identity. *Psychol. Bull.* 74, 425-440.

Money, J. (1974) Two names, two wardrobes, two personalities. *J. Homosexuality,* 1, 1, 56-70.

Money, J. and Hampson, J. G. (1955) Idiopathic sexual precocity in the male. *Psychsomat. Med.* 17, 1-15.

Money, J., Hampson, J. G. and Hampson, J. L. (1955a) Hermaphroditism. Recommendations concerning assignment of sex and psychologic management.

Bull. Johns Hopkins Hosp. 98, 43-57.

Money, J., Hampson, J. G. and Hampson, J. L. (1955b) An examination of some basic sexual concepts. The evidence of hermaphroditism. *Bull. Johns Hopkins Hosp.* 97, 301-357.

Money, J., Hampson, J. G. and Hampson, J. L. (1957) Imprinting and the establishment of the gender role. *A. M. A. Arch. Neurol. Psychiat.* 77, 333-336.

Morgenstern, F. S., Pearce, J. P. and Rees, L. W. (1965) Predicting the outcome of behaviour therapy by psychological tests. *Behav. Res. Ther.* 3, 253-258.

Moss, H. A. (1970) Sex age and the state as determinants of mother–infant interaction. In *Readings in Child Socialisation,* Ed. Danziger, K. Pergamon Press, Oxford.

Murdock, G. P. (1937) Comparative data on the division of labour by sex. *Social Forces,* 15, 4, 551-553.

Mussen, P. and Rutherford, D. E. (1963) Parent–child relations and parental personality in relation to young children's sex role preferences. *Child Develpm.* 34, 589-607.

Newman, L. E. and Stoller, R. J. (1974) Non transsexual men who seek sex reassignment. *Am. J. Psychiat.* 131, 4, 437-441.

Nye, F. I. and Hoffman, L. W. (Eds.) (1963) *The Employed Mother in America.* Rand McNally.

Oakley, A. (1972) *Sex, Gender and Society.* Temple Smith, London.

Osgood, C. E., Suci, G. J. and Tannenbaum, P. H. (1957) *The Measurement of Meaning.* Univ. Illinois Press, Urbana.

Ostow, M. (1953) Transvestism (correspondence). *J. A. M. A.* 152, 1553.

Oswald, I. (1962) Induction of illusory and hallucinatory voices with considerations of behaviour therapy. *J. ment. Sci.* 108, 196.

Parkes, N. (1969) Approved School absconding. Unpub. thesis, Univ. Newcastle-upon-Tyne.

Patterson, G. R., Littman, R. A. and Hinsey, W. C. (1964) Parental effectiveness as reinforcers in the laboratory and its relation to child rearing practices and child adjustment in the classroom. *J. Pers.* 32, 180-199.

Peabody, G. A., Rowe, A. T. and Wall, T. H. (1953) Fetishism and transvestism. *J. nerv. ment. Dis.* 118, 339.

Pearce, J. F. (1963) Aspects of transvestism. Unpub. M. D. thesis, Univ. London.

Pennington, V. M. (1960) Treatment in transvestism. *Am. J. Psychiat.* 117, 250.

Pettow, Z. (1922) Der Kranhafte Vetkliedungstrieo Butrage Zur Erforschung der Transvesie. *J. Baum.* Pfullingen, Wurtenburg.

Philpott, W. H. (1966) Behavioural change by response interference and response facilitation. Paper presented to Behaviour Therapy Seminar, St. Johns, Newfoundland, (personal communication).

Prince, C. V. (1954) Homosexuality, transvestism and transsexualism. *Am. J. Psychother.* 2, 80-86.

Prince, C. V. (1967) *Transvestite and His Wife,* Argyle Books.

Prince, V. and Bentler, P. M. (1972) Survey of 504 cases of transvestism. *Psychological Reports,* 31, 903-917.

Rabban, M. (1950) Sex role identification—young children in two diverse social groups. *Genet. Psychol. Monogr.* 42, 81-185.

Rabin, A. I. (1958) Some psychosexual differences between kibbutz and non-kibbutz Israeli boys. *J. Proj. Techniques,* 22, 328-332.

Rachman, S. J. and Teasdale, J. (1969) Aversion therapy: and appraisal. In *Behaviour Therapy: Appraisal and Status,* Ed. Franks, C. M. McGraw Hill, London.

Radzinowicz, L. (1957) *Sexual Offences.* McMillan, London.

Ramsey, G. V. (1943) The sexual development of boys. *Am. J. Psychol.* 56, 217.
Randell, J. B. (1959) Transvestism and transsexualism. *Brit. med. J.* 2, 1448.
Randell, J. B. (1975) Transvestism and transsexualism. *Brit. J. Psychiat. Spec.* No. 9, 201-205.
Raymond, M. J. (1956) Case of fetishism treated by aversion therapy. *Brit. med. J.* ii, 854.
Rosen, I. (Ed.) (1964) *The Pathology and Treatment of Sexual Deviation.* O. U. P., London.
Rosenkrantz, P., Vogel, S. Bee, H., Broverman, I., and Broverman, D. M. (1968) Sex-role stereotypes and self-concepts in college students. *J. consult. clin. Psychol.* 32, 287-294.
Roth, M. (1975) Personal communication.
Roth, M. and Ball, J. R. B. (1964) Psychiatric aspects of intersexuality. In *Intersexuality,* Eds. Armstrong, C. N. and Marshall, A. J. Academic Press, London.
Sears, R. R., Maccoby, E. E. and Levin, H. (1957) *Patterns of Child Rearing.* Row Peterson, Illinois.
Seward, G. E. (1946) *Sex and the Social Order.* McGraw Hill, New York.
Sexton, P. (1970) *Feminised Male: Classrooms, White Collars, and the Decline of Manliness.* Random.
Shirlaw, L. M. (1961) Behaviour therapy in transvestism. *Lancet,* 1, 619-620.
Slater, E. (1958) The sibs and children of homosexuals. In *Symposium on Nuclear Sex,* Eds. Smith, D. R. and Davidson, W. A. Heinemann, London.
Slater, E. (1962) Birth order and maternal age of homosexuals. *Lancet,* 1, 69-71.
Sonnenberg, M. (1955) Girls jumping rope. *Psychoanalysis,* 3, 3, 57-62.
Sontag, L. W. (1947) Physiological factors and personality in children. *Child Develpm.* 18, 185-189.
Stekel, W. (1923) *Der Fetishismus.* Berlin.
Stoller, R. J. (1966) Treatment of transvestism and transsexualism. *Curr. Psych. Ther.* 92-103.
Stoller, R. J. (1967) Transvestites' women. *Am. J. Psychiat.* 124, 333-339.
Stoller, R. J. (1968) *Sex and Gender.* Hogarth Press, London.
Stoller, R. J. (1970) Pornography and perversion. *Arch. gen. Psychiat.* 22, 490-500.
Stoller, R. J. (1971) The term Transvestism. *Arch. gen. Psychiat.* 24, 3, 230-237.
Stoller, R. J., Garfinkel, H. and Rosen, A. C. (1960) Passing and the maintenance of sexual identification in an intersexed patient. *Arch. gen. Psychiat.* 2, 379.
Stringer, P. (1970) A note on the factorial structure of the Dynamic Personality Inventory. *Brit. J. med. Psychol.* 43, 95-103.
Tasch, R. J. (1952) The role of the father in the family. *J. Exp. Ed.* 20, 319-361.
Taylor, A. J. and McLachlan, D. G. (1962) Clinical and psychological observation of transvestism. *N.Z. med. J.* 61, 496-506.
Taylor, A. J. and McLachlan, D. C. (1963a) M. M. P. I. profile of six transvestites. *J. clin. Psychol.* 19, 33.
Taylor, A. J. and McLachlan, D. C. (1963b) Further observation and comments on transvestism. *N.Z. med. J.* 62, 527-529.
Taylor, A. J. and McLachlan, D. C. (1964) Transvestism and psychosexual identification. *N.Z. med. J.* 63, 369-371.
Terman, L. M. and Miles, C. C. (1963) *Sex and Personality.* McGraw Hill, New York.
Thompson, G. N. (1949) Electroshock and other therapeutic considerations in sexual psychopathy. *J. nerv. ment. Dis.* 109, 531-539.

Trethowan, W. H. (1977) A psychiatrist's view of lay psychotherapy. *Brit. J. med. PsychoL* 50, 33-37.

Walinder, J. (1967) *Transsexualism: A Study of 43 Cases.* Scand. Univ. Books, Goteburg.

Walinder, J. (1975) *A social-psychiatric follow-up Study of 24 Sex-reassigned transsexuals.* Scand. Univ. Books, Goteburg.

Ward, N. G. (1975) Successful lithium treatment of transvestism associated with manic depression. *J. nerv. ment. Dis.* 161, 3. 204-206.

Watson, J. B. and Raynor, R. (1920) Conditioned emotional reactions. *J. exp. PsychoL* 3, 1-14.

Weller, G. M. and Bell, R. Q. (1965) Basal Skin conductance and neonate state. *Child Develpm.* 36, 647-657.

West, D. J. (1974) Thoughts on sex law reform. In *Crime, Criminology and Public Policy,* Ed. Hood, R. Heinemann, London.

Wilmott, M. (1975) Cognitive characteristics and sexual orientation-observations based on 3 highly selected groups. Unpub. M.Sc. thesis, Univ. Newcastle-upon-Tyne.

Worden, F. G. and Marsh, J. T. (1955) Psychological factors in men seeking sex transformation, *J. A. M. A.* 157, 1292.

Wortis, H., Braine, M., Cutler, R. and Freedman, A. (1964) Deviant behaviour in 2½ yr old premature children. *Child Develpm.* 35, 871-879.

Yardley, K. M. (1976) Training in feminine skills in a male transsexual. *Brit. J. med. PsychoL* 42, 4, 329-339.

Index